AT HOME IN nantucket

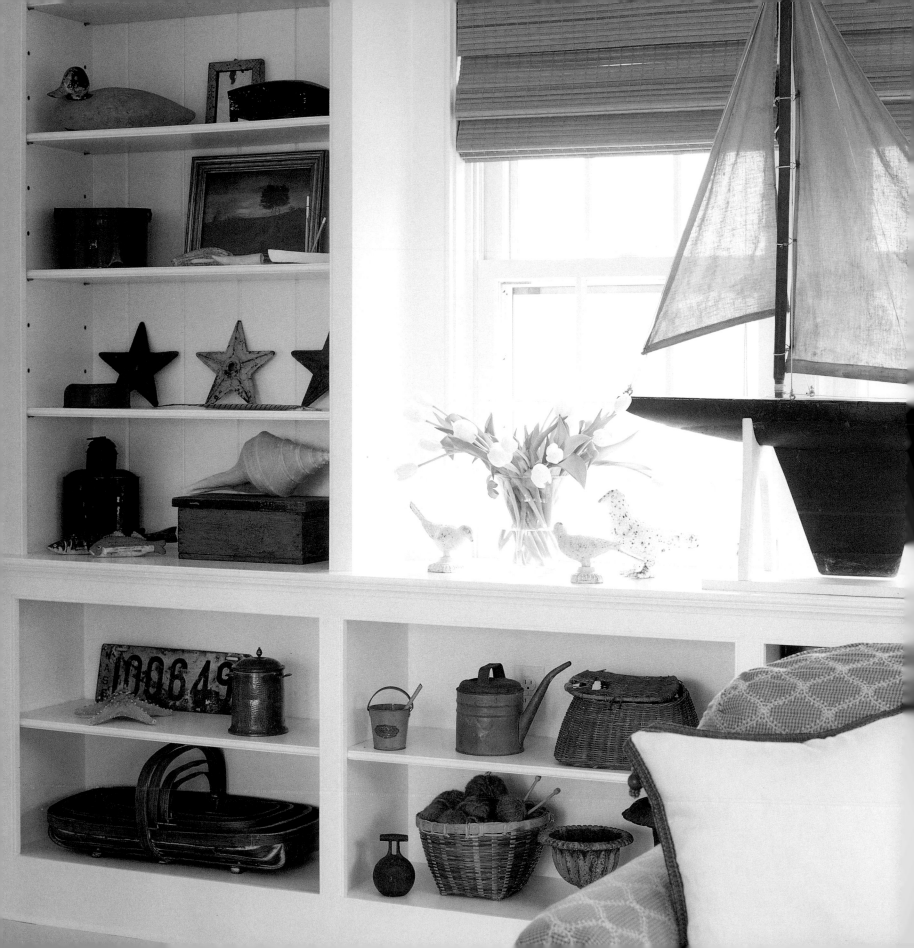

AT HOME IN nantucket

by Lisa McGee

photographs by Paul Whicheloe

CHRONICLE BOOKS

SAN FRANCISCO

Library of Congress Cataloging-in-Publication Data available.

ISBN: 0-8118-4080-8

Manufactured in China.

Designed by Teikna Design Inc.: Claudia Neri and Brian Kroeker

Distributed in Canada by Raincoast Books
9050 Shaughnessy Street
Vancouver, British Columbia V6P 6E5

10 9 8 7 6 5 4 3 2 1

Chronicle Books LLC
85 Second Street
San Francisco, California 94105

www.chroniclebooks.com

Frontispiece: A corner of the Franco's living room provides ideal space for the painted boxes and small paintings the couple loves to collect.

dedication/acknowledgments

Dedicated to my maternal grandmother Marion Joan Walton.
For her inspirational strength and courage.
(July 12, 1911 — April 22, 1998)

Many thanks to my devoted husband, James, whose love, support, and patience of a saint guided me through the project, and to my daughter, Sophia, who adapted so well to my busy work schedule and fills every day with delight and wonder.

Without the dedicated work of photographer Paul Whicheloe, the homes in this book would never have come to life so beautifully. He worked long hours and produced amazing results despite our aggressive shooting schedule. It was such a pleasure working with him.

Thanks to my parents, Alexander and Jilly Walsh, I was introduced to Nantucket for the first time in 1976. They helped instill in me a great love and appreciation of this special island. I thank them especially for their many days of enthusiastic babysitting, enabling me to write and travel back and forth to the island.

I also extend many thanks to everyone who helped me in his or her individual way with this wonderful project: Maria Amore, Jack Bangs, Anne Becker, Dan and Nancy Bills, Susan and Bill Boardman, Bess Clarke, Geo. P. Davis, Leslie Davisson, Cam and Gardiner Dutton, Jeffrey and Shari Dutton, Richard and Kim Franco, Rob Geary, Michael Getter, John Gilliland, Stefanie Hall, Jay Harman, E. J. and Robin Harvey, Kathleen and Robert Hay, Jaime Hurley, Rebecca Jusko, Illya Kagan, Michael La Scola, Reggie Levine, Kendra Lockley, Terri March, Gary McBournie, Diane McLaughlin, Anne Mensini, Peggy and George Mitchell, Michael Molinar, Carol Mulling, Andy Oates, Elizabeth Oldham, Kevin Paulsen, Elizabeth and John Raith, Daisy and Steve Rapp, Susan Simon, Van and Ann Smith, Nisha Sondhe, Nina Stewart, Pat Taafe, Pat Tyler, Connie Umberger, Eugenie Vorhees, Elizabeth and Todd Winship, Nancy Whitcomb, Ken and Deborah Whitlaw, and Guy Yale.

Finally, I'd like to thank my editor at Chronicle Books, Mikyla Bruder, for giving me the opportunity to produce my first book and guiding me through it with great patience and understanding. It has been a wonderful experience that has taught me a tremendous amount about my own capabilities. I look forward to many more in the future.

contents

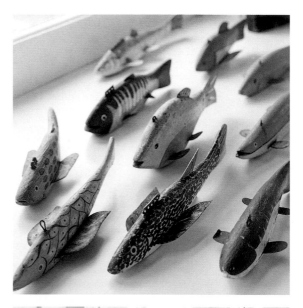

introduction   8

chapter one: spring   11

harbor view   13

simple retreat   21

italian refuge   33

a collector's cottage   43

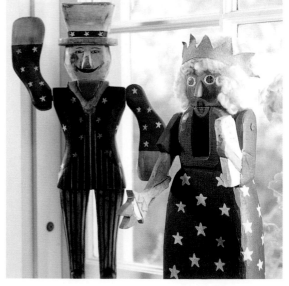

chapter two: summer   51

nantucket hacienda   53

a patriotic barn   65

sanctuary in white   75

stylish simplicity   85

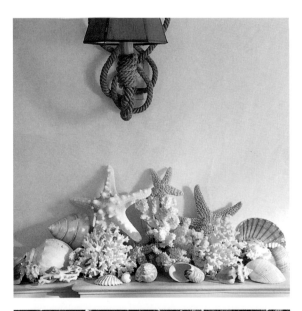

chapter three: autumn   99

european treasure   101

painted cottage   115

a pair of collectors   127

tradition restored   139

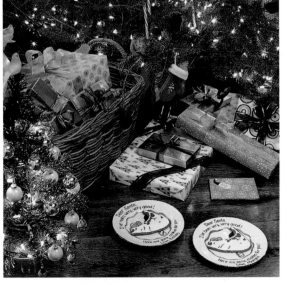

chapter four: winter   153

creativity abounds   155

family haven   167

minimalist barn   177

private museum   183

visitor's guide   195

contributors   198

index   202

introduction

Nantucket Island has a range of homes as varied and distinctive as the people who live and visit here. The grand homes along cobbled Main Street stand as testament to the prosperous whaling days of the mid-nineteenth century. Along the beaches, shacks offer basic amenities for casual summer living. Other residences have been upgraded and filled with the latest luxuries to make summer living as convenient as during the rest of the year. The permanent homes run the gamut from a collector's hideaway to a carpenter's creation to minimalist spaces in a converted carriage house and timber-frame barn. The homes are vastly different, and some might seem as well suited to other parts of the country as they are to Nantucket, but tying them all together is the love each homeowner feels for this special "faraway" island.

Although Nantucket is affected by the seasons, as an island it can experience such changes quite differently from the mainland. Sometimes the weather "skips" the island altogether; other times it hits Nantucket harder. As in many places, spring is a time for rejuvenation and renewal after the long winter months. The island comes alive with a wide array of flowering bulbs and the green of new grass. Summer is the island's busiest season. The springtime tranquility disappears, and Nantucket is soon swarming with visitors and summer residents. Bicyclists fill the bike paths, and the marinas are crowded with boats. Just when the heat and throngs get to be too much, autumn arrives, and the island clears out significantly. It's easier to find parking on Main Street or even book a meal at a favorite restaurant in town. Things quiet down even more after Thanksgiving,

although up through Christmas, people include the island in their holiday plans. Once the New Year has arrived, the dead of winter sets in. Depending on the year, the snow could be piled up along the sidewalks, and upon occasion the ocean has frozen all the way to the mainland, even as recently as the winter of 2003. The people who live on Nantucket year-round know the seasons intimately and have adapted their homes to echo them all. Some houses are simple and white inside, evoking beachside living. Others are layered with texture and color, like the landscape itself. And still others change with the seasons like a set on a stage.

At Home in Nantucket celebrates the diversity of the island, featuring sixteen homes that range from renovated barns to cozy cottages to elegant period abodes. Each of the four chapters, one for each season, relates the stories behind the homes and the people who live in them. Recipes sprinkled throughout offer a chance to bring a little bit of the island into your kitchen. At the back of the book, the visitor's guide offers basic information about getting to Nantucket, where to stay, and what to do.

Nantucket is an island rich with inspiration. Inspiring people, inspiring arts and dining, inspiring landscapes, and inspiring homes. Step inside a minuscule cottage filled from floor to ceiling with a very personal art collection; relax in a light-filled house overlooking the ocean; find comfort in a family's warm "gathering room." Bring a piece of this captivating island home with you to share with family and friends. Perhaps they'll tag along on your next visit.

Opposite: A passion for collecting is evident in this Nantucket home.

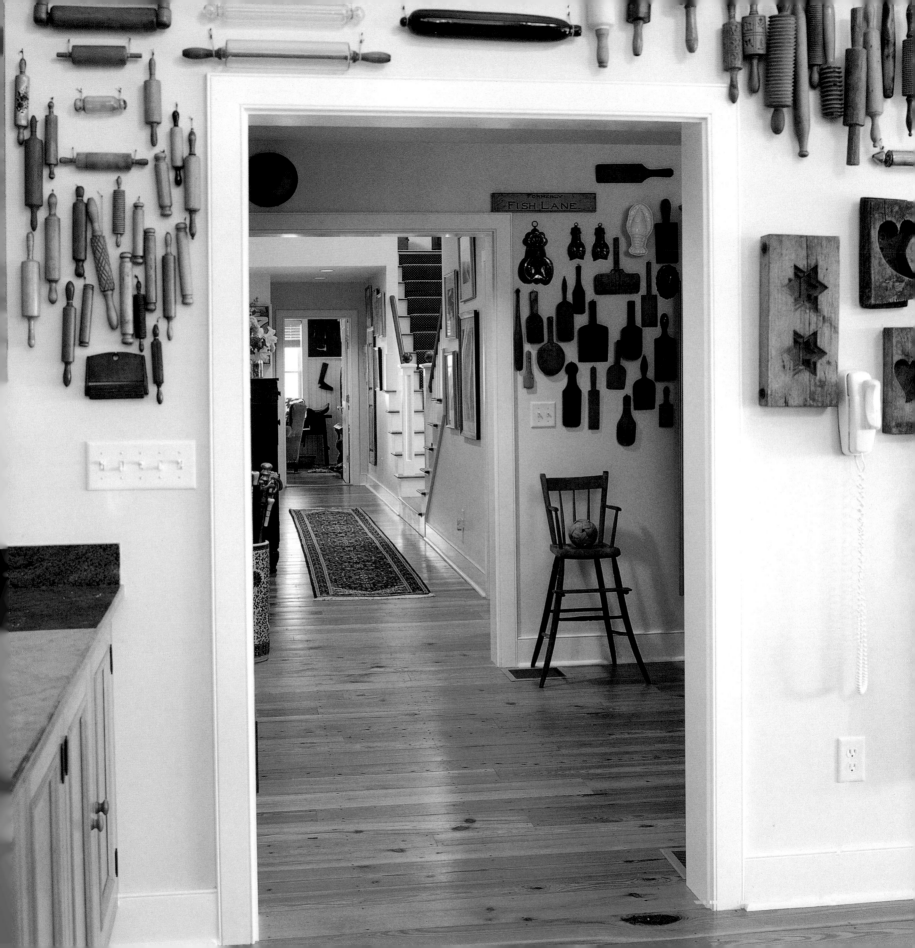

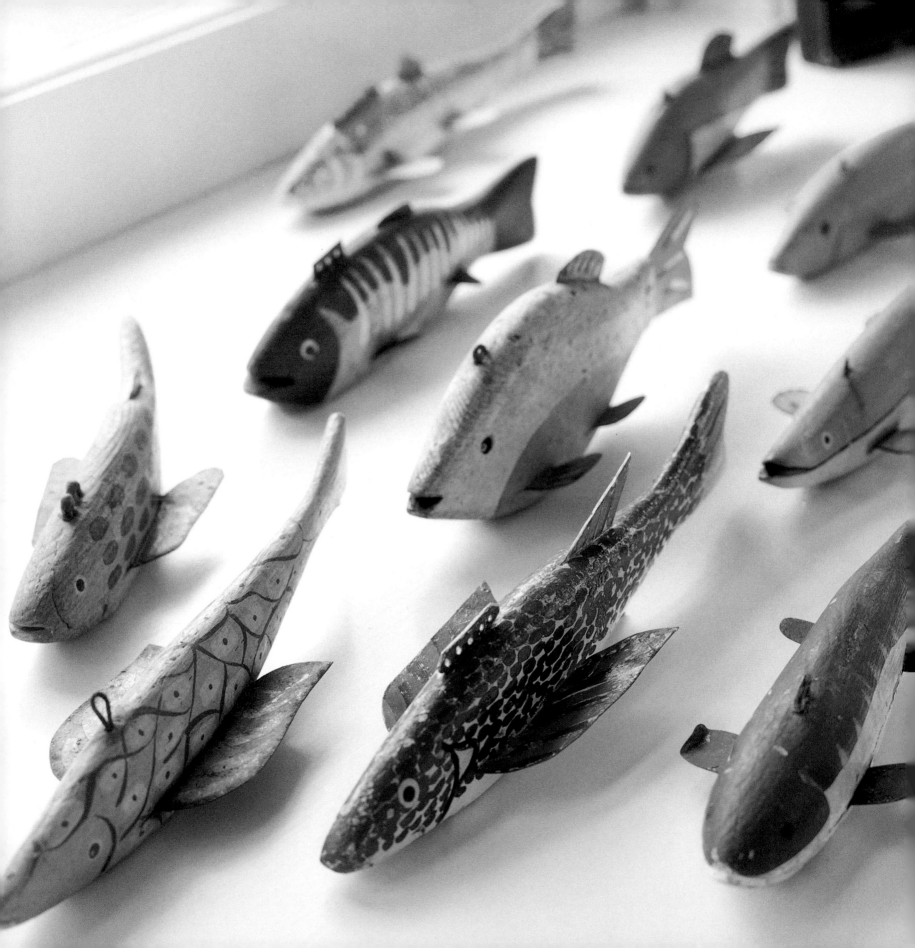

chapter one:
spring

After the long winter, spring brings a welcome change to life on the island. Windows begin to open, decks are spruced up in anticipation of outdoor living, and color returns to the bleak landscape. The blooming of thousands of sunny daffodils signals the returning warmth. To celebrate, the island hosts its annual Daffodil Weekend in April. Antique cars drive up Main Street decked out in the cheerful flowers, and afterward the participants and onlookers enjoy a festive tailgate picnic.

From their sun-warmed deck, Van and Ann Smith watch the harbor fill with windsurfers, fishing boats, and a rainbow of colored sails. The Smiths' home has the lighthearted, casual feel of a traditional boathouse; it's the perfect place to toast the onset of spring.

As the days wear on, sunshine becomes more dependable, and Richard and Kim Franco's cheerful summer home in Siasconset is the ideal place for an outdoor gathering. Outdoor living is the watchword here, and simple, clean decor provides the perfect backdrop for an Easter brunch. On Main Street, Anne Mencini's Victorian house has the spacious feel of an old Italian villa, infused with the bold spirit of the country she loves.

Nestled in the historic district, Diana McLaughlin's cottage offers a cozy retreat. Filled with her collections of fine leather-bound books, porcelain Staffordshire dogs, and other items gathered during her international travels, this welcoming hideaway harbors many fascinating stories.

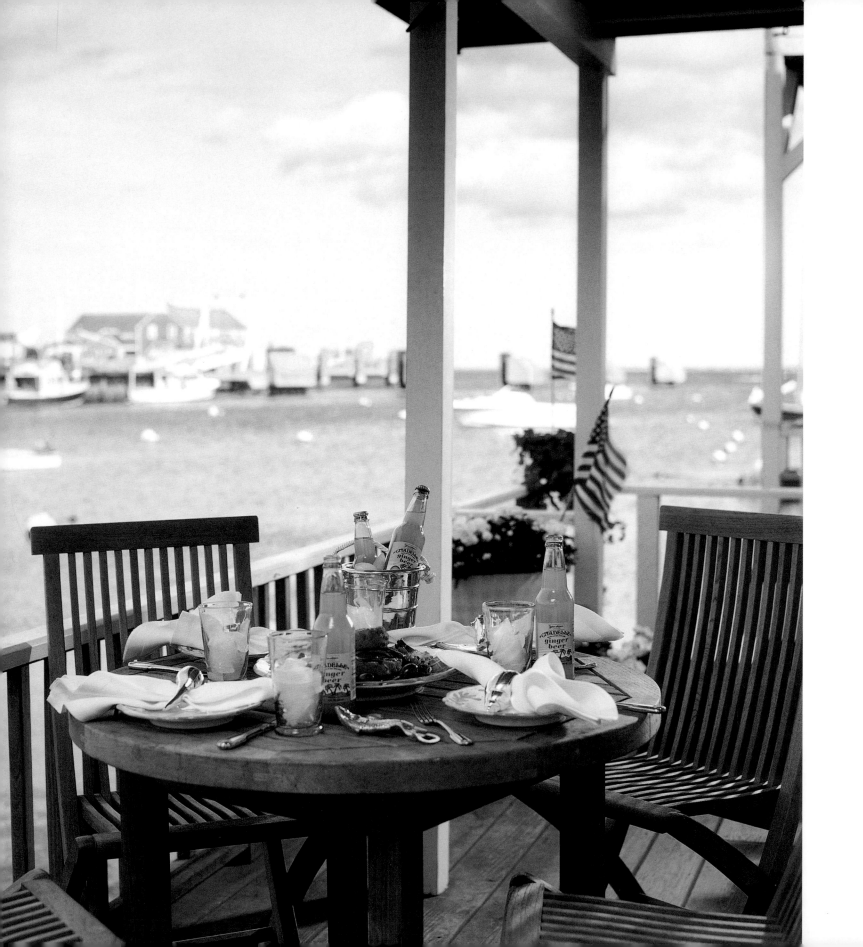

A great example of a quintessential vacation home is that of Van and Ann Smith. Sitting literally on the water and overlooking the harbor and ferry dock, Van and Ann couldn't have picked a better location. Although they are in the heart of downtown, on a historic wharf, they are isolated just enough from the crowds to enjoy themselves to the fullest.

Built in 1922 as a summerhouse, it was made to look like the existing boathouses along the wharf. When the Smiths bought the place in 1998, it was structurally very sound. A year later they decided to update it and embarked on some renovating.

The downstairs, which basically consists of one big room and a small bathroom/laundry room, was given mainly cosmetic work. Floors were sanded, fresh paint was applied to the walls, and old electrical features were given a new lease on life. At the harbor side of the main room, rolling doors, each with a porthole, open onto the idyllic deck outside. The room accommodates a substantial seating area, two dining areas, and a kitchen—and from basically anywhere in the room, you can look out onto the harbor.

"It was important to us to maintain the character of the house as a simple, very informal, unpretentious, almost rustic dwelling," says Ann. "We wanted exposed wall studs on the first floor but also wanted to add a few conveniences such as a little electric heat and upgraded plumbing."

Upstairs a larger bedroom was formed from two former bunk rooms. An existing bathroom was renovated and another added. With a master suite and two delightful guest rooms, there is plenty of space for family and friends to come and stay. The rooms have been decorated in a fun, casual palette of summery colors. In one of the guest rooms, twin beds each have a similar handmade quilt and the headboards and bed skirts are made out of the same red-and-white-checked fabric. The other guest room is slightly larger and holds a queen-size bed outfitted in blue,

Page 10: A school of wooden fishing lures from the 1920s swims on a shelf in the Franco's living room. *Opposite:* A simple lunch of crab cakes and salad has been laid out on the harbor side deck.

Right: Keeping with the rustic feel, the wall studs remain exposed and a rope banister leads upstairs.

Opposite: The main seating area faces the fireplace and large wooden doors with portholes roll back and open onto the deck.

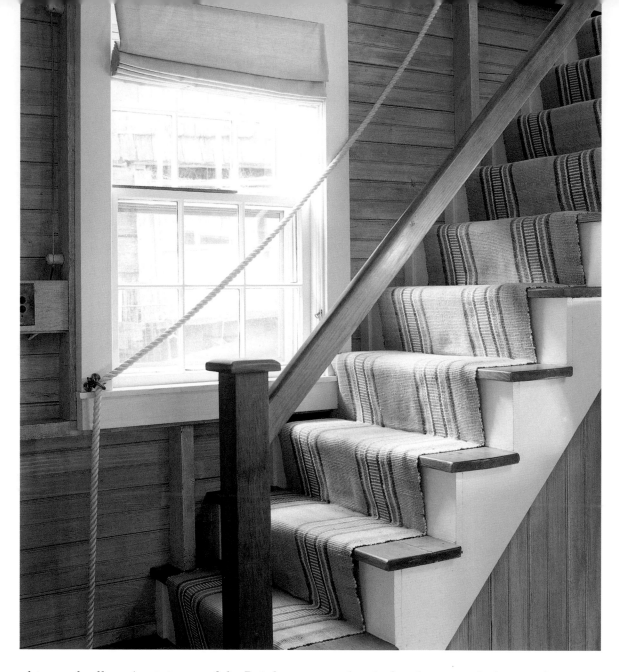

white, and yellow. A miniature of the Rainbow Fleet, the island's famous catboat fleet, sails along a support beam between the bedroom and the hall. Bare painted floors add to the casual feel. There is very little artwork throughout the house, but model boats and other references to the surrounding sea have been placed here and there.

When spring comes to an end, just before the summer season starts, Van and Ann return to what is for them an ideal spot. Ann says, "The location is perfect for us. Our family is water orientated. We are very happy that this cottage has given us the opportunity to introduce our children and grandchildren to the island in a way that is special and unique, incorporating some of the historic fabric of the island. We keep a little runabout tied to the deck in the summer and we can take the grandchildren to the beach at Coatue in a few minutes."

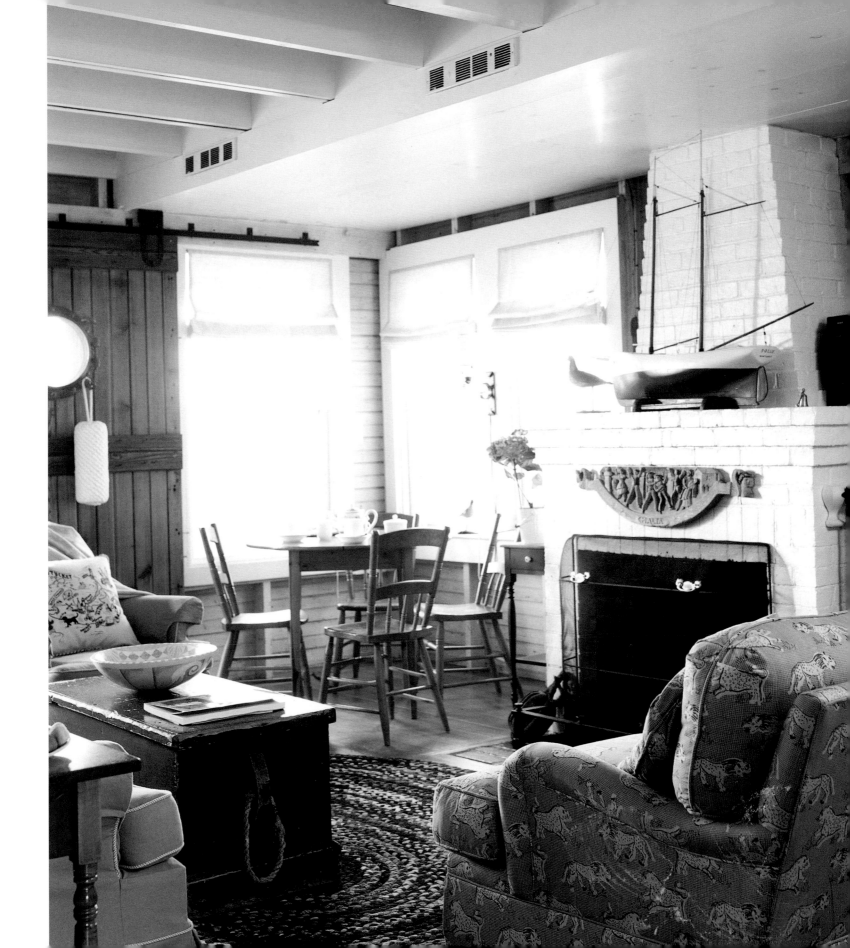

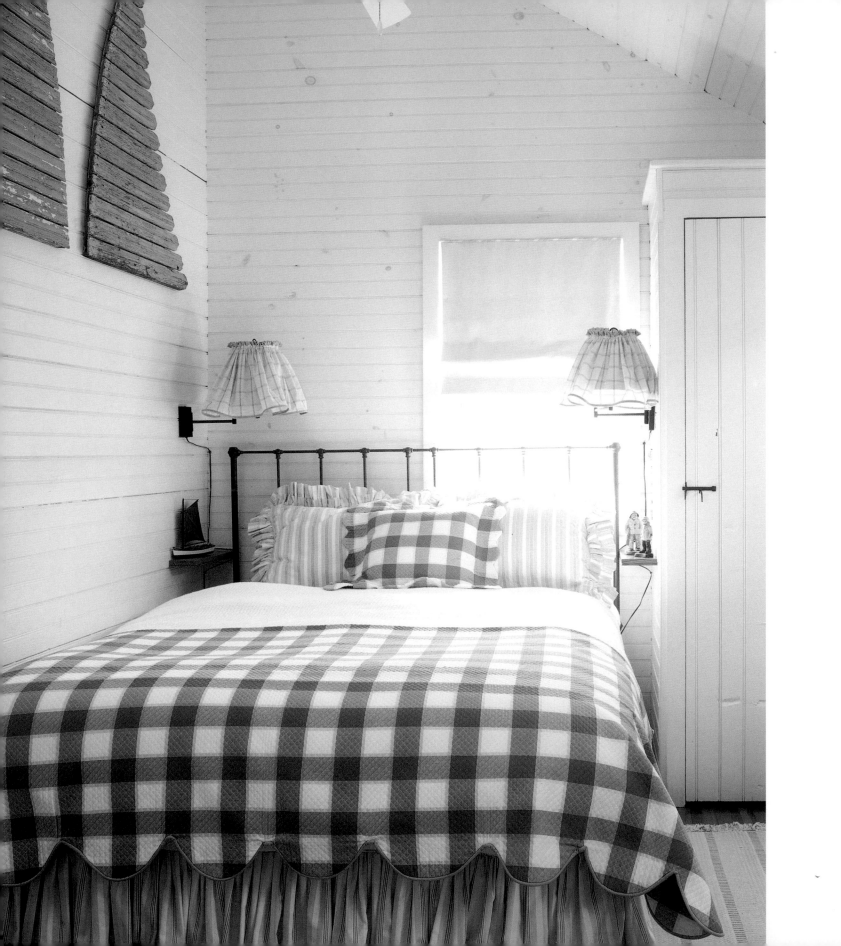

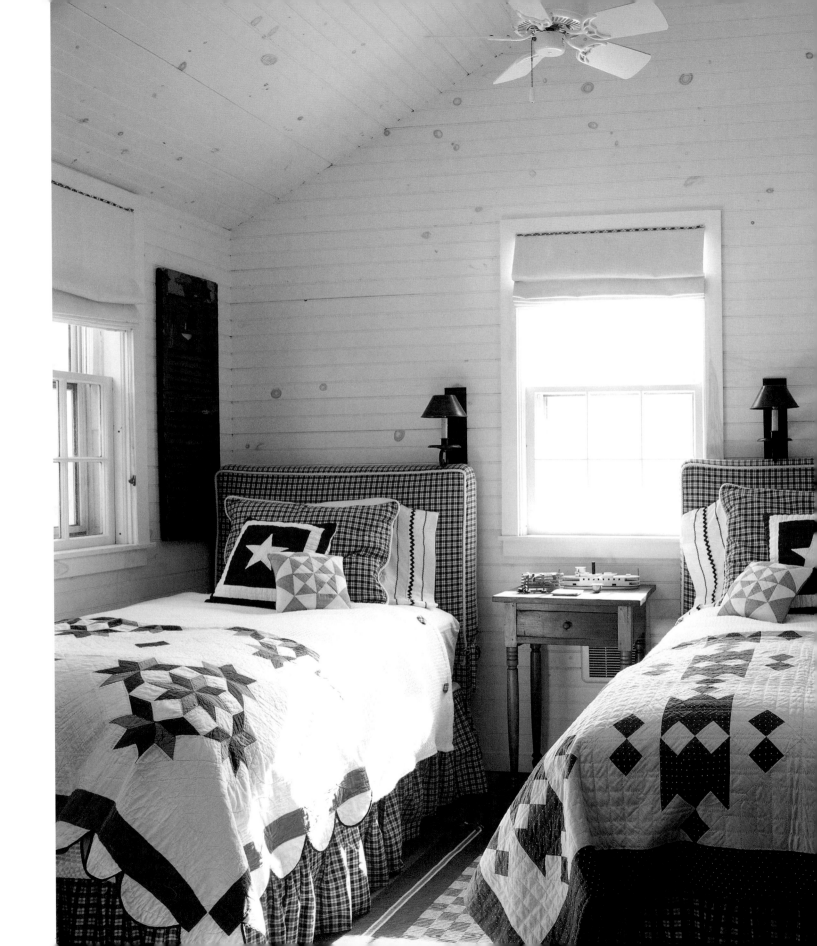

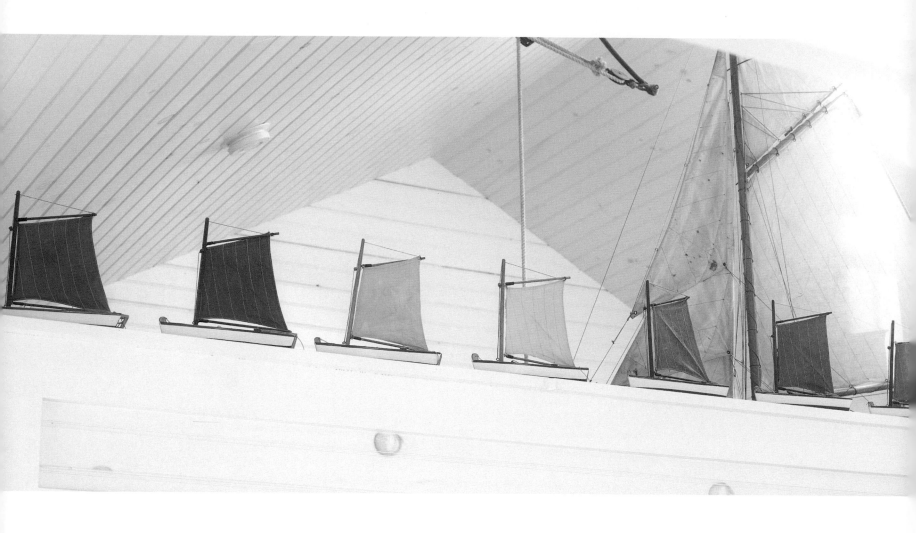

THE RAINBOW FLEET

Memorial Day weekend kicks off the busy season on the island, and it's no more evident anywhere than in the harbor. The wide-beamed, gaff-rigged catboats with colorful sails are set out for the water. Collectively known as the Rainbow Fleet, these boats have been a Nantucket institution since the early twentieth century. (Although they can't be rented, you may be lucky enough to know someone who owns one on the island and would be willing to take you for a spin around the harbor.) The fishing boats also return, packed with eager recreational fishermen, and windsurfers zip around the harbor. Going sailing or fishing is, of course, part of what makes Nantucket such a desirable vacation spot. Numerous companies offer fishing charters and sailboat and sailboard rentals. Contact the Nantucket Visitor's Service at (508) 228-0925 for a listing.

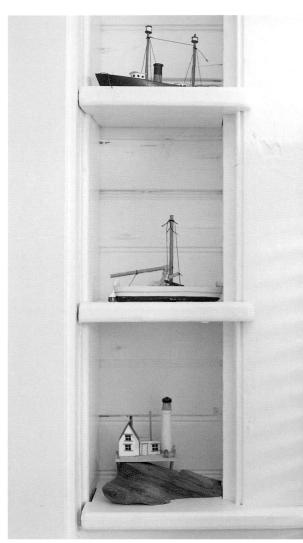

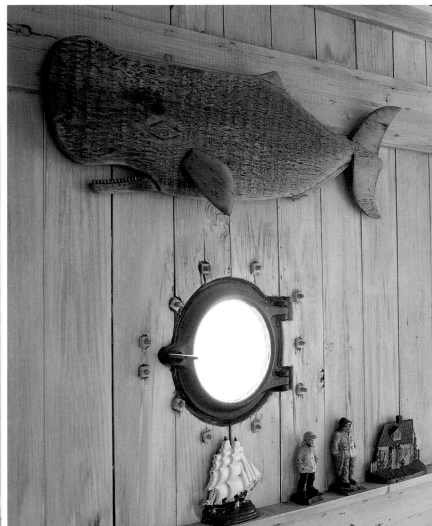

Previous spread, left: A guest room is given a clean look with whitewashed walls and bedding in yellow and blue.
Previous spread, right: Another guest room has a patriotic feel with twin beds outfitted in red, white, and blue.
Opposite: A miniature Rainbow Fleet sails along the partition between the guest room and hallway.
This page: In the guest bathroom, miniature models fill shelves (above) and a map of Nantucket (right) covers the floor. A porthole looks into the kitchen from the entryway (top right).

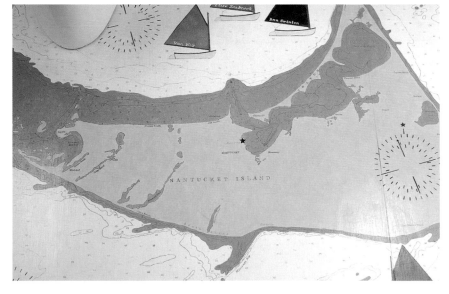

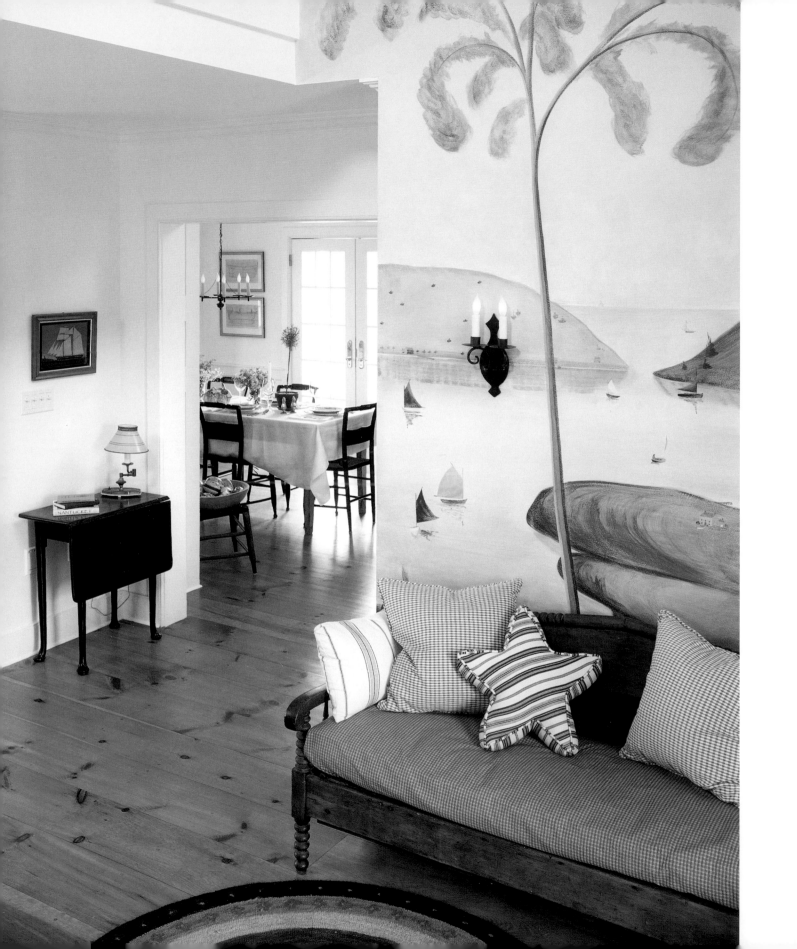

simple retreat

On the easternmost point of the island, approximately seven miles from the main town, is a small community called Siasconset. The name comes from Nantucket's Native Americans, the Wampanoag tribe, and it mean "place of the great bones." Perhaps large fish, or even whales, washed up on the sandy shores long ago, leaving behind their giant skeletons.

It began as a fishing village in the seventeenth century, but gradually the fishing shacks turned into proper homes, as people discovered the benefits of living away from the town of Nantucket. In the 1830s and '40s, when whaling captains were not out at sea, they escaped the hubbub of town in this quiet community. For a brief time Nantucket had a railroad, and when it reached Siasconset in 1899 there was a building boom. Many of those houses still stand. It is here, on this quiet end of the island, that Richard and Kim Franco decided to make their summer home.

The Francos, who live in Florida, have been summering on Nantucket for years. Siasconset made sense to them because it offered a refreshing change from the busy town, and the couple welcomed the chance to let their children explore on their own. "The children love their independence," says Kim. "They walk and bicycle all over." At the height of summer it is easy to walk to the nearby general store or the beach, or stroll along the narrow lanes, enjoying the rose-covered cottages.

The main house and its guest wing form an L shape. A porch runs along the front of the house and the wing, allowing for plenty of outdoor seating. Inside the front door is a colorful mural painted by local artist Audrey Sterk. With its whimsical feathery trees along a make-believe shoreline, the mural covers an entire wall and leads upstairs to the second floor.

"The Francos didn't want things too perfect," says their interior designer, Anne Becker. "Coming up with the unexpected was important to them, and I loved that approach." From the front hall, bare floorboards lead into the kitchen area, which is quite minimalist: A rectangular

Opposite: In the entryway, a colorful mural by Audrey Sterk fills the wall behind a nineteenth-century setee.

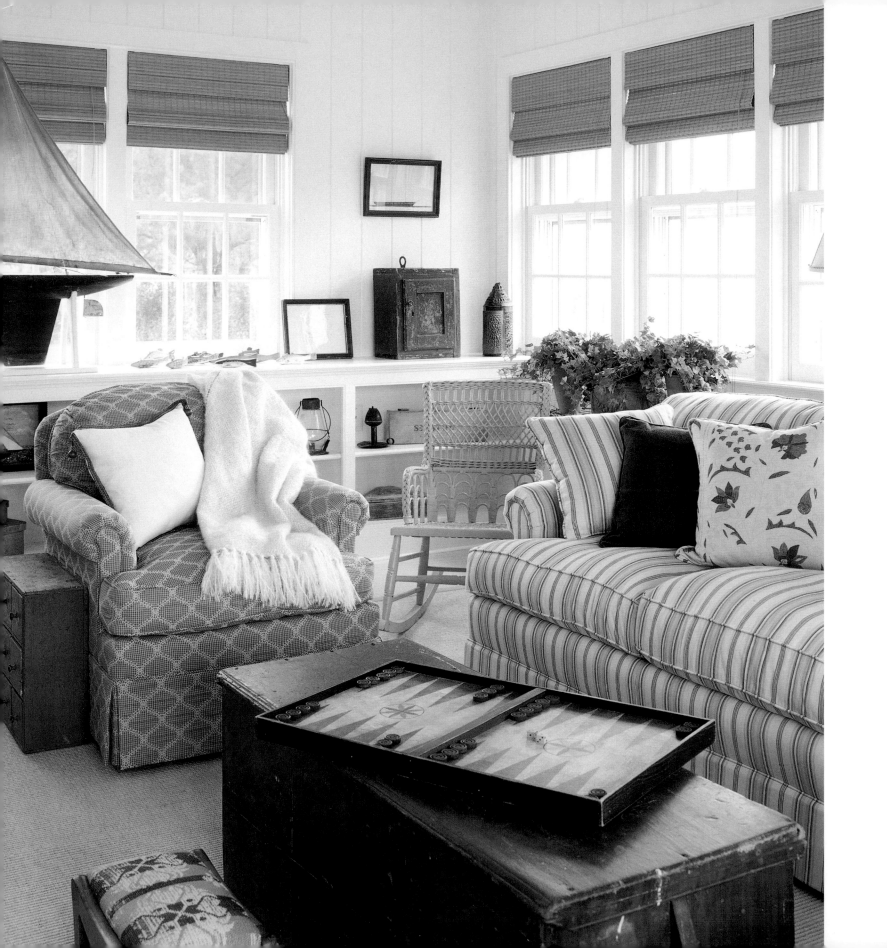

Opposite: The sunny living room is a favorite room for reading and playing games.
Right: An unusual book-press lamp adorns the hall table beside the front stairs.

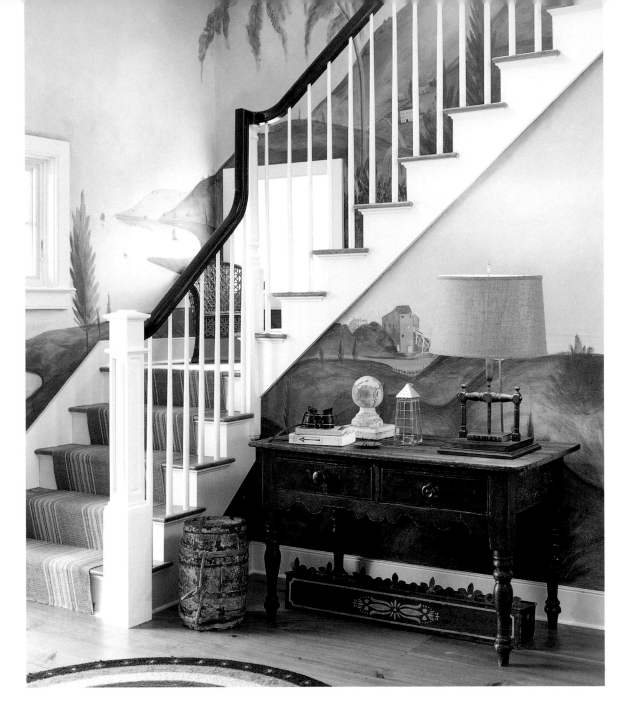

farm table serves as the dining room table. To soften the windows, Anne paired wooden blinds with long green drapes. The kitchen has a substantial island, ideal for entertaining, but there is little out on the counters to detract from the overall simplicity.

A long hallway leads from the kitchen to the guest wing, which houses two bedrooms, two bathrooms, and a seating area. Somewhat separated from the main house, it offers ample privacy even if the house is full. The bedrooms evoke a "sophisticated country" look, which is just what the Francos wanted. Anne Becker notes, "They have a real appreciation for quality, form, and color. We wanted the whole effect of the house to be charming but not too predictable."

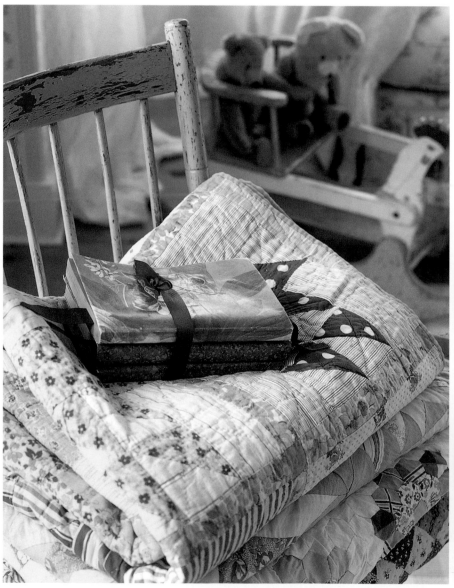

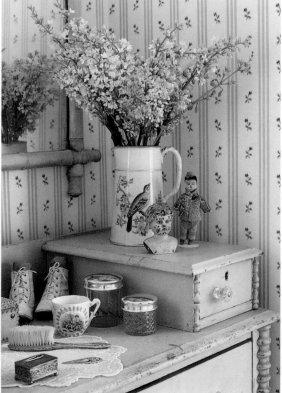

Left: Kim's collection of antique quilts is stacked on a chair in the guest room for visitors to enjoy.
Below: The bureau is given added charm with simple collectibles and a porcelain pitcher of lilacs.
Opposite: The downstairs guest room is made light and airy by high ceilings and simple sheer curtains.

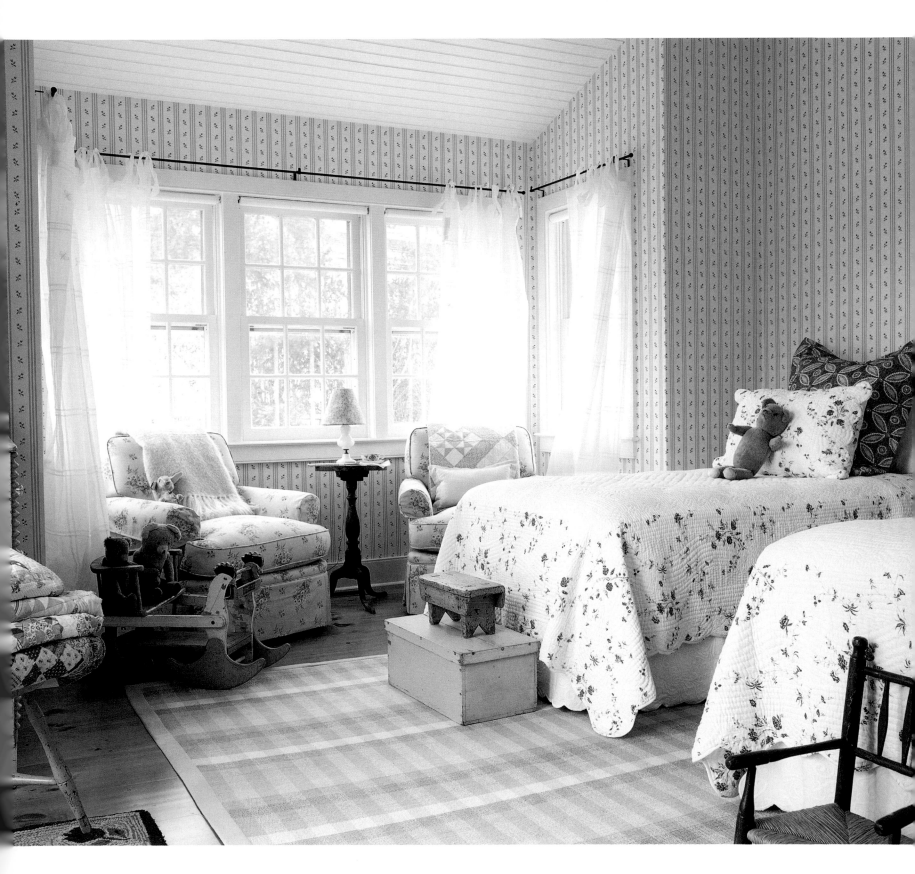

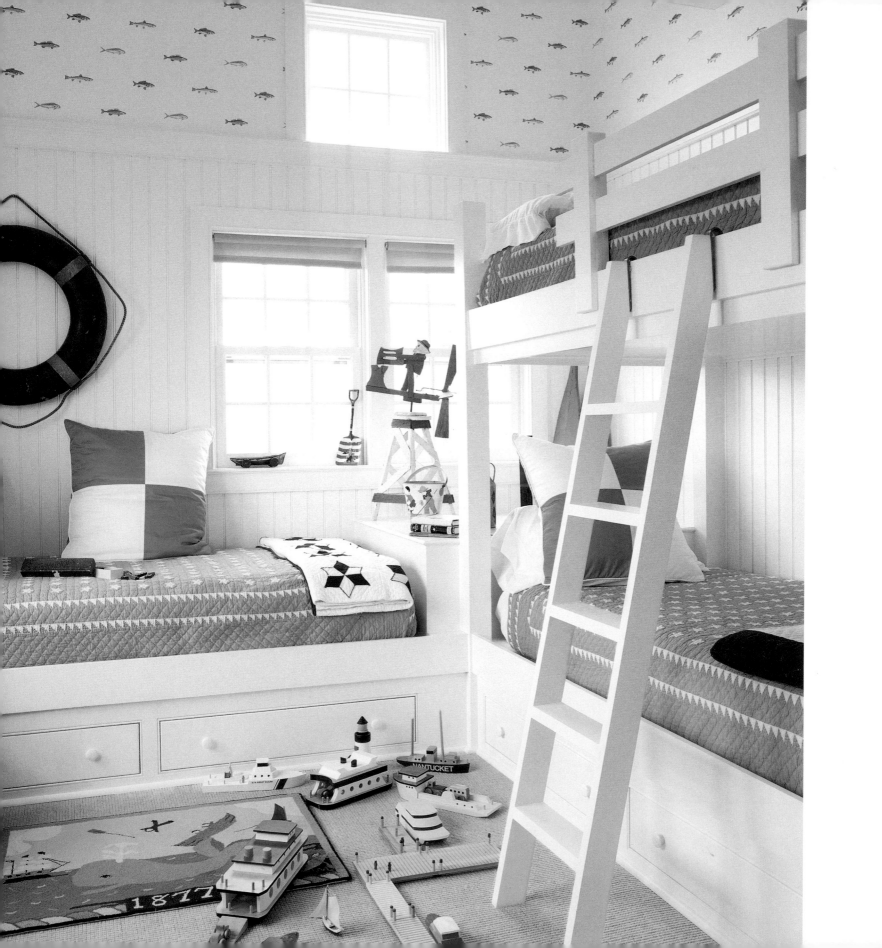

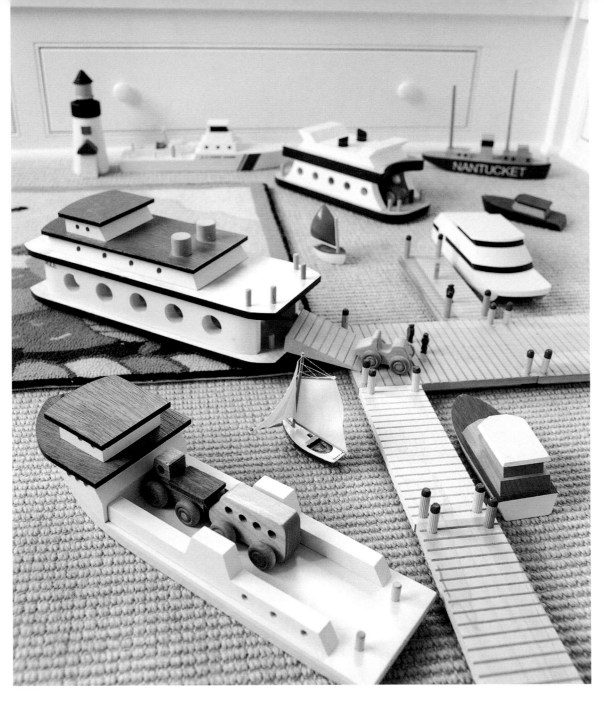

Opposite: This perfect boys' bunk room has a playful nautical theme along with colorful accent pieces.

Above: Toy wooden boats, part of the *Harbor* series, come from The Toy Boat, a store in downtown Nantucket.

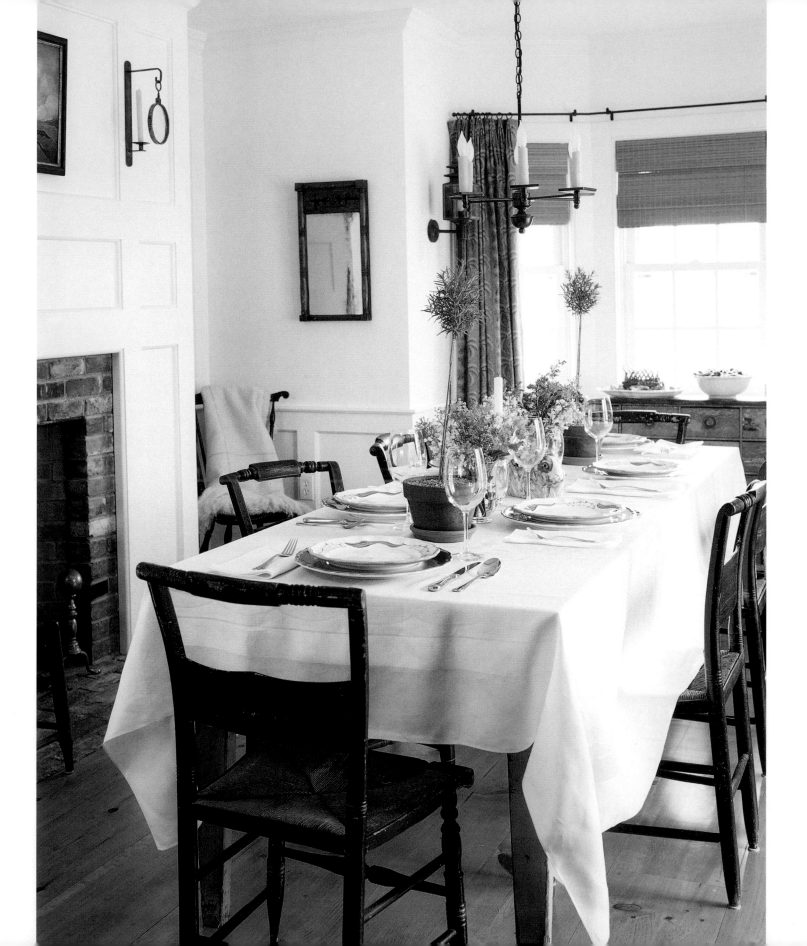

Easter Recipes

Easter on Nantucket coincides conveniently with the blooming of millions of daffodils. Both bring significance to the island by signaling a rebirth from the harsh winter months. Chef Michael La Scola, from American Seasons restaurant in downtown Nantucket, created these delicious Easter dishes. "Around the time of Easter there is a new freshness to the ingredients available," he says. "Gone are the heavy dishes of fall and winter. Spring is the optimum time for lamb, for obvious reasons; the potatoes are sweeter and the new vegetables fantastic. But when cooking in the spring, especially here on Nantucket, you remember that the weather can get cold at any second, so I tend to blend the new spring items with a little winter. By using Kalamata olives and truffles, I add a touch of earthy richness to the sweeter dishes I cook."

Kalamata Black Olive and Vermont Goat Cheese Potato Pave

Make 1 day ahead of time.

2 cups Kalamata olives, pitted and chopped

8 ounces goat cheese

3 large cloves garlic

1 cup finely chopped fresh herbs (oregano, thyme, and rosemary)

8 large russet potatoes

1 pound butter

Salt and freshly ground pepper to taste

1. Mix olives, goat cheese, garlic, and herbs together.

2. Preheat oven to 350 degrees F.

3. Peel and slice potatoes, preferably using a mandoline. Place slices in a large bowl.

4. Melt butter in a small saucepan (do not allow to come to a boil). Pour over potatoes and season with salt and pepper.

5. Line an 8-by-12-inch pan with greased parchment paper. Arrange one-fourth of the potatoes so that they slightly overlap to cover the bottom of the pan.

6. Spread one-third of the goat cheese mixture over the potatoes.

7. Arrange another one-fourth of the potatoes across the pan on top of the cheese layer.

8. Repeat with another one-third of the cheese mixture, then another layer of potatoes, then the rest of the cheese mixture, then the last of the potatoes. Cover the top layer of potatoes with greased parchment paper.

9. Bake approximately 1 hour, or until soft enough to yield to a knife. Remove from oven, allow to cool, and place in refrigerator overnight.

10. The next day, remove the pave from pan and place on a cutting board. Preheat oven to 450 degrees F.

11. Remove the parchment paper, then cut in 3-by-4-inch squares, then cut the squares in half again as triangles.

12. Bake on greased baking sheets until golden brown, about 20 minutes. Serve immediately.

Serves 10

Opposite: The Easter table has been set with hand-painted Italian plates and silver chargers. Small vases of flowers and rosemary topiaries add a subtle floral touch.

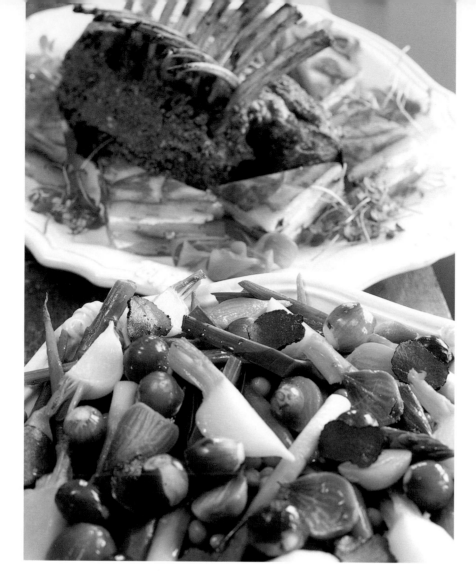

1 bunch baby leeks

2 bunches baby carrots

1 bunch candy-striped or
red beets

1 bunch golden beets

1 pound shelled English
spring peas

1 cup red pearl onions, peeled

2 bunches baby white turnips

2 bunches asparagus

3 tablespoons butter

1 teaspoon black truffle oil

1 clove garlic, minced

1 cup chicken stock

1 bunch fresh basil,
finely chopped

Salt and freshly ground pepper
to taste

2 tablespoons canned black
truffle, sliced

Melange of Truffled Petite Spring Vegetables

1. Clean and trim the vegetables, cutting off most of the greenery. Cut larger
    pieces in half. Blanch in salted boiling water, then cool quickly in ice water.

2. In a large sauté pan over medium heat, melt butter. Add truffle oil and garlic
    and sauté lightly. Drain the vegetables and pat dry. Add to sauté pan, making
    sure all are lightly coated with pan mixture.

3. Add chicken stock and basil. Season with salt and pepper. Allow the vegetables
    to warm through on medium heat. Do not cover.

4. Transfer to a warmed serving dish, garnish with truffle slices, and serve
    immediately.

Serves 8–10

Pesto-Crusted Rack of Lamb

1 full large rack of lamb
(about 6 pounds with the
bone in)

Salt and freshly ground pepper
to taste

3 tablespoons olive oil

3 large carrots

2 medium onions

1/2 stalk celery

1 1/2 cups pesto sauce
(recipe follows)

1. Preheat oven to 375 degrees F.

2. Trim excess fat from lamb, clean bones, and season meat with salt and pepper. Heat olive oil in a sauté pan over high heat until the oil bubbles, about 1 minute.

3. Place lamb, meat-side down, in the pan and sear until golden, about 2 to 4 minutes each side. Remove from pan and set aside.

4. Clean and roughly chop carrots, onions, and celery. Place the vegetables in a roasting pan and set lamb on top, bone-side down. Coat the meat with a thick layer of pesto.

5. Roast for 15 minutes for rare, or 6 to 8 minutes more for medium, depending on preference. Remove from oven and rest the meat for 10 minutes. Slice into chops and serve.

Serves 8–10

Pesto Sauce

1/2 pound chopped basil

1/2 pound chopped baby
spinach

6 large cloves garlic, minced

1/4 cup extra-virgin olive oil

1/4 cup pine nuts

1/2 cup grated Parmesan cheese

1 teaspoon sugar

Salt and freshly ground pepper
to taste

1. Place all ingredients in a food processor and blend until fairly smooth.

Makes 1 cup

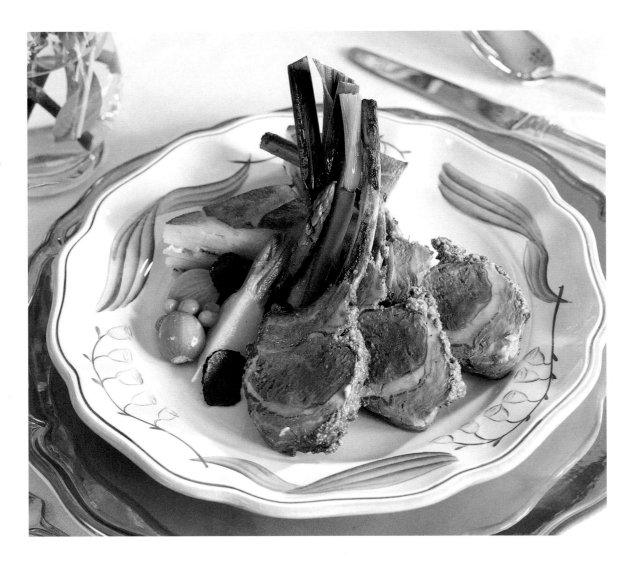

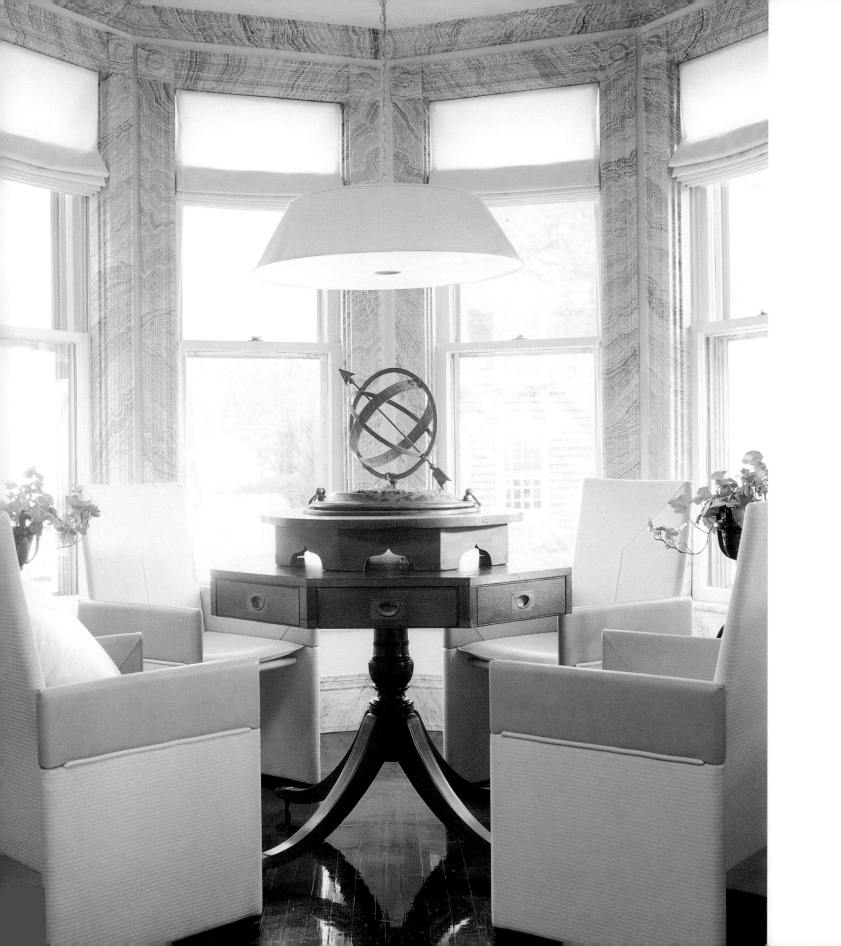

italian refuge

At the top of cobbled Main Street, which runs through the center of Nantucket town, Anne Mencini has carved out her own little piece of Italy. Her lifelong love affair with the country began at the age of seventeen, when a graduation gift took her across the Atlantic on the SS Constitution and she first sailed into the Bay of Naples. Several years later, she returned for a year abroad at the University of Florence. When she settled in Nantucket, she wanted her home to reflect the country she could never forget. The house she chose, an Italianate Victorian, was built in 1890 and had the right proportions to accommodate the large furniture she had brought back from Italy.

Upon entering the house, you feel as if you have walked into an old Italian villa. The foyer has a grand carpeted staircase, a substantial Italian antique armoire at one end, and a large majolica olive oil jar with a mustard yellow glaze holding walking sticks that belonged to Anne's grandparents and great-grandparents. On top of a console, an arched plaster relief depicting a mother and child leans against the wall.

Off to the right, facing Main Street, is an elegant dining room. The thin floorboards have been painted with a geometric pattern and covered with a pale wash; along the edges of the room runs a black border with a classic Greek key design. A long central table made of walnut—Anne had it copied from an old Italian lyre-legged refrectory table—has matching walnut chairs. The massive credenza was copied from another refrectory piece, also in walnut.

The house of the famous Swedish physician and writer Axel Munthe inspired the kitchen, which is situated at the back of the house. When Anne visited Munthe's home, Villa San Michele, on the island of Capri, it made such an impression on her, with its light and airy feel, that she just had to re-create some of it in her own home.

She hung copper pans over the counter, and infused blue and white throughout the space by using a large table with a traditional Italian ceramic top and keeping the walls white to fill the room with light.

The spacious living room lies across the entry hall from the dining room and kitchen. "The living room provides me with instant grounding—both in the Tennessee roots I was born with and the Italian roots I acquired," Anne says. The space has been divided into several seating areas. At the front of the room, a game table and chairs

Opposite: A focal point of the living room is the game table, where an armillary sphere, an old astronomical instrument, draws attention to the beautiful windows.

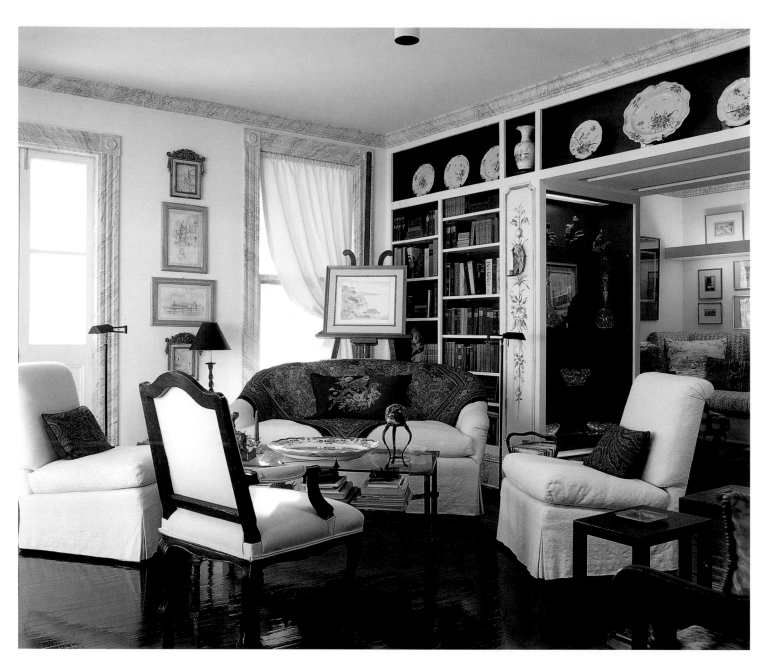

Above: On an easel behind one of several areas in the living room stands a sketch of the Bay of Lerici in Italy.
Opposite: The main living room leads back into two small reading nooks situated on either side of the fireplace.

have been set up in a bay window. Against one wall sits a large bench with Venetian lanterns on either side of it. Across from that, a small sofa and a trio of comfortable chairs form another seating area. From there the space leads back into a more intimate area, with two cozy reading nooks where the walls are filled with family photographs taken in Tennessee and plenty of

bookcases to hold the books passed down from generation to generation. Throughout the room, vignettes of Italian treasures have been set out on small side tables or up on a shelf.

Anne's annual trips to Italy, and the treasures she has accumulated at home, have helped her create a distinctive haven evocative of the places she loves best.

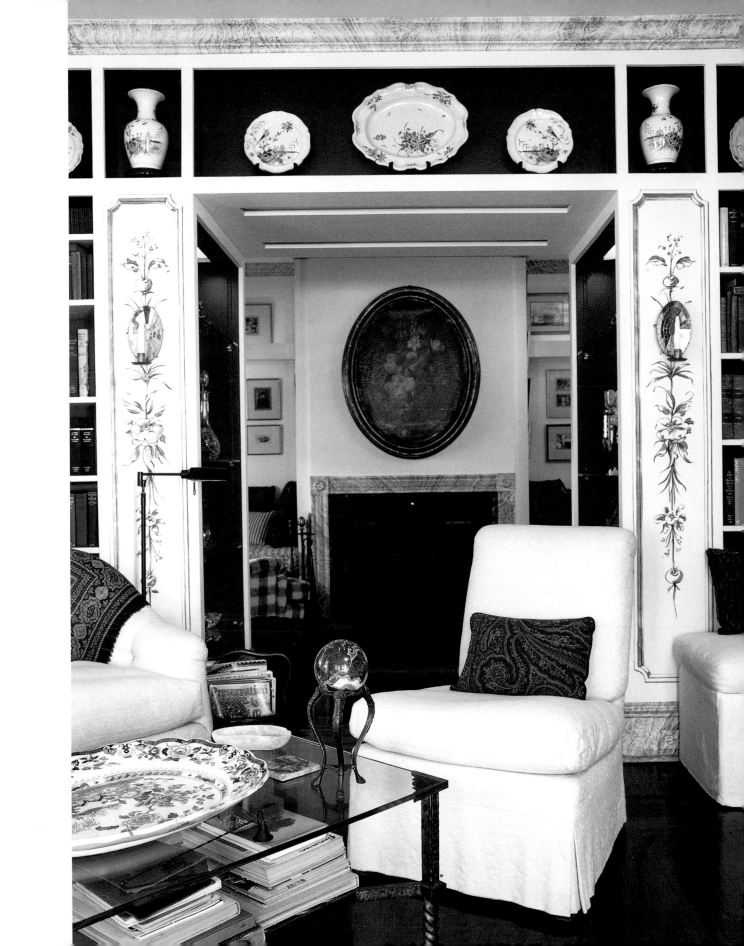

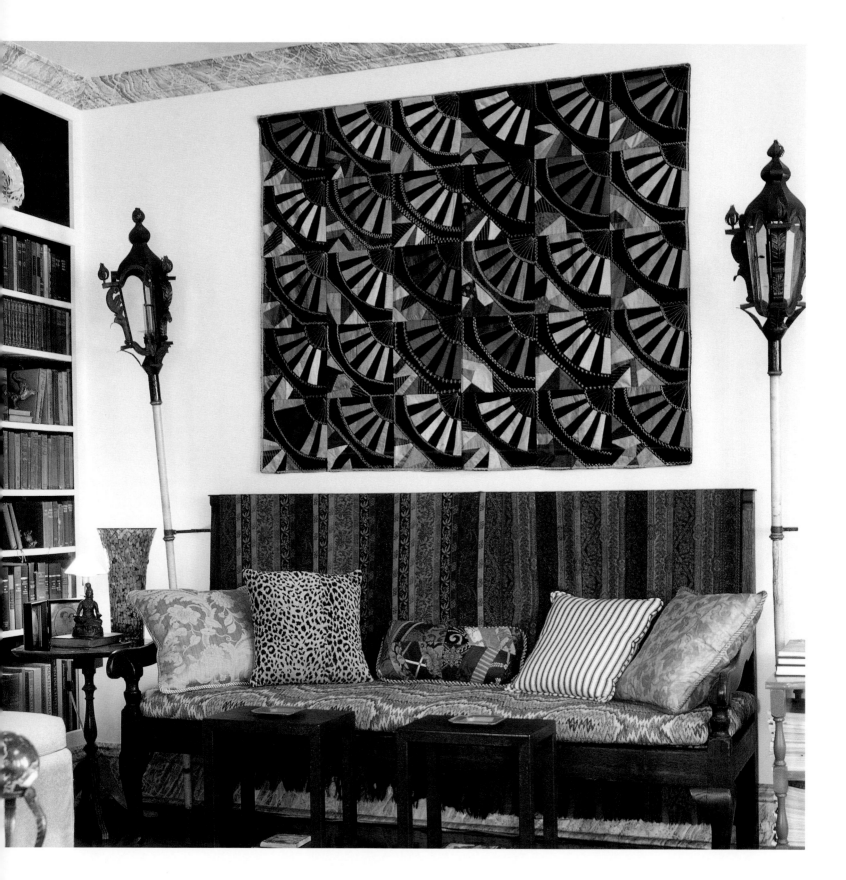

AT HOME IN NANTUCKET

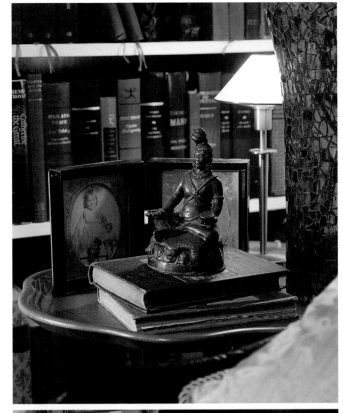

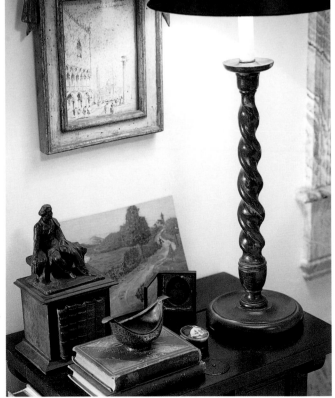

Opposite: Two Venetian *torchères* stand on either side of a heavy bench. Above the bench hangs an American quilt with a fan motif from the Victorian era.

Right, top: Ann has created many delightful still lifes throughout her home. Here, a small statue of a Nepalese holy man was brought back from Kathmandu. *Right, bottom:* A still life on a side table includes a statue of Alfred de Musset sitting on top of a leather-bound collection of his poems.

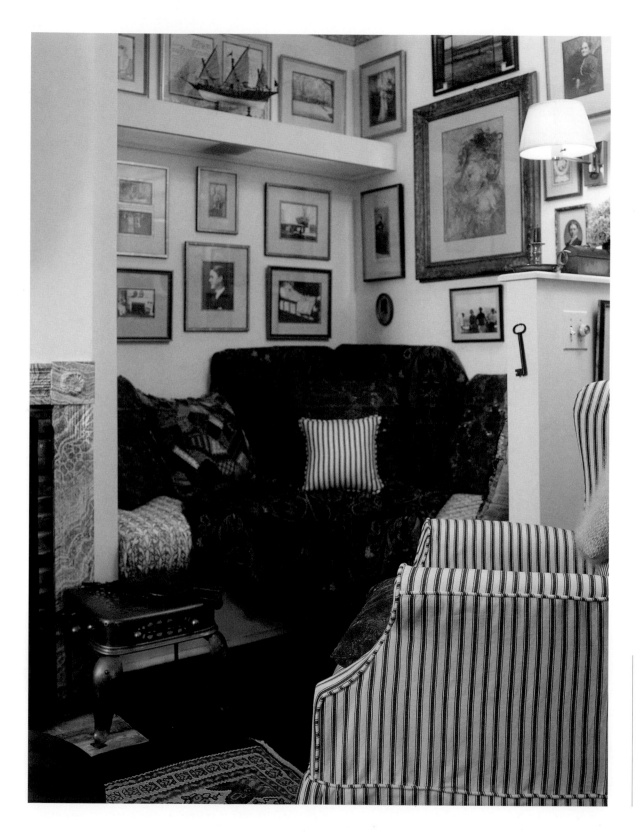

Left: To the right of the fire-
place, a collection of old
family photographs hangs
above the reading area.
Opposite: The banquette
in the reading nook is
decorated with a playful
mix of fabrics, including
ticking, toile, and a pillow
made from an antique rug.

AT HOME IN NANTUCKET

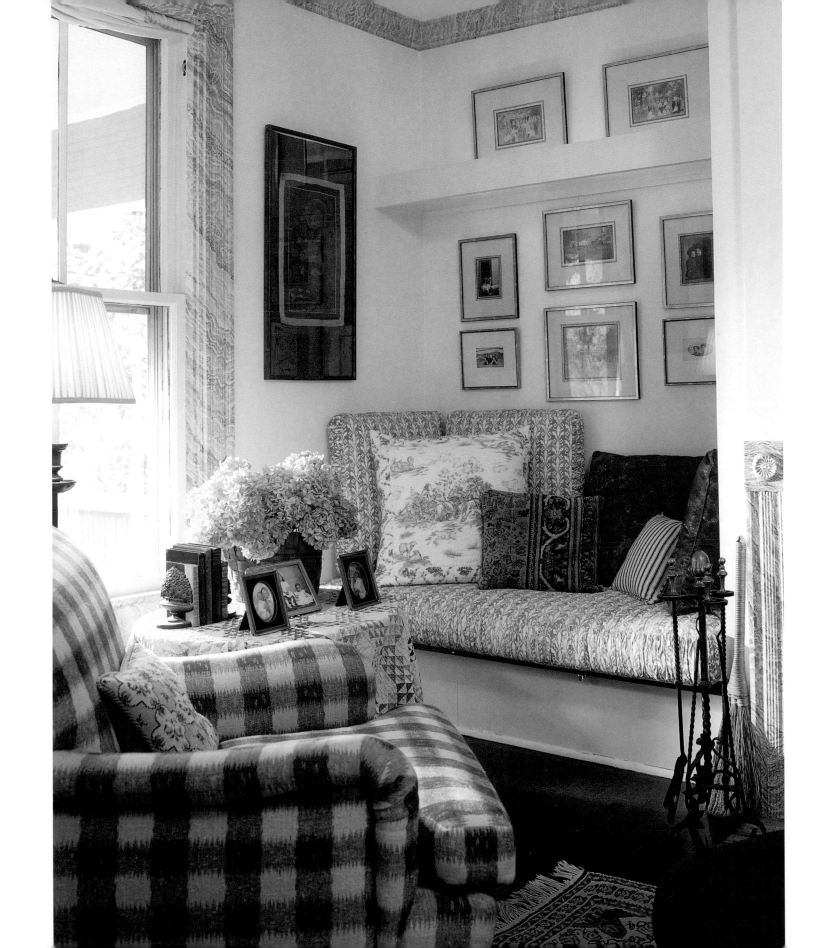

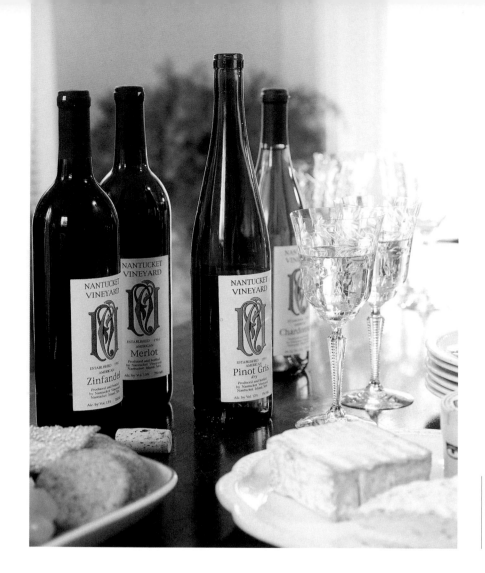

Left: A selection of wines from local winery Nantucket Vineyard is ready for an impromptu tasting.
Opposite: The dining room is the stage for a Nantucket wine tasting. Anne had the lyre-legged dining table and chairs made in Florence.

THE NANTUCKET WINE FESTIVAL

Around the second week of May, Nantucket hosts its annual Wine Festival. The festival began 1996, and its exploration of food and wine, emphasizing Nantucket's historic celebration of all things gastronomic, has grown in popularity each year. More than a hundred wineries of national and international acclaim send representatives to Nantucket for a week of public tastings in fine homes and meals in world-class restaurants. To find out more about festival activities such as the Grand Tasting, Winemaker Symposium, or Charity Gala, call (508) 228-1128 or go online at www.nantucketwinefestival.com.

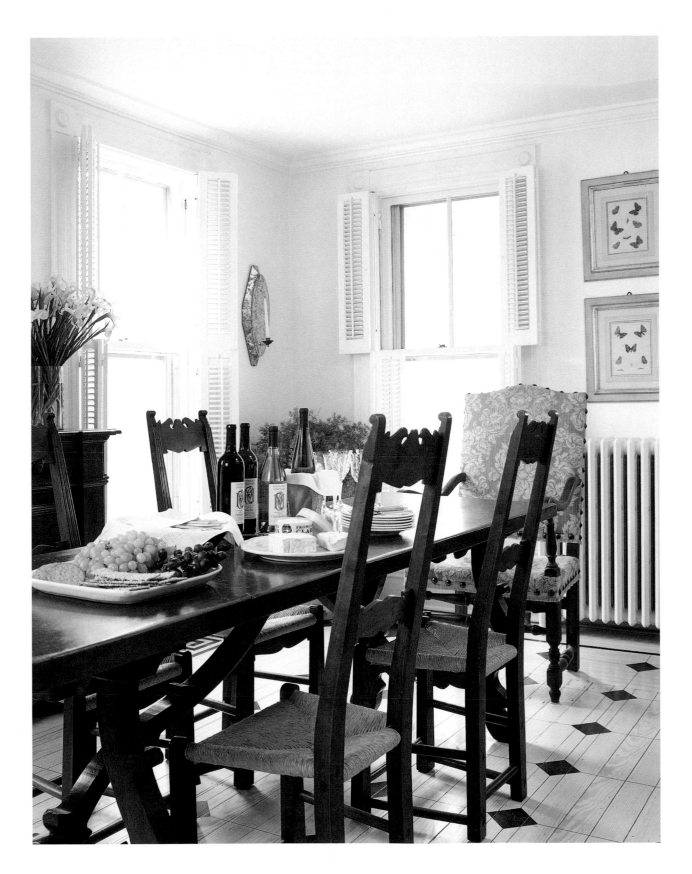

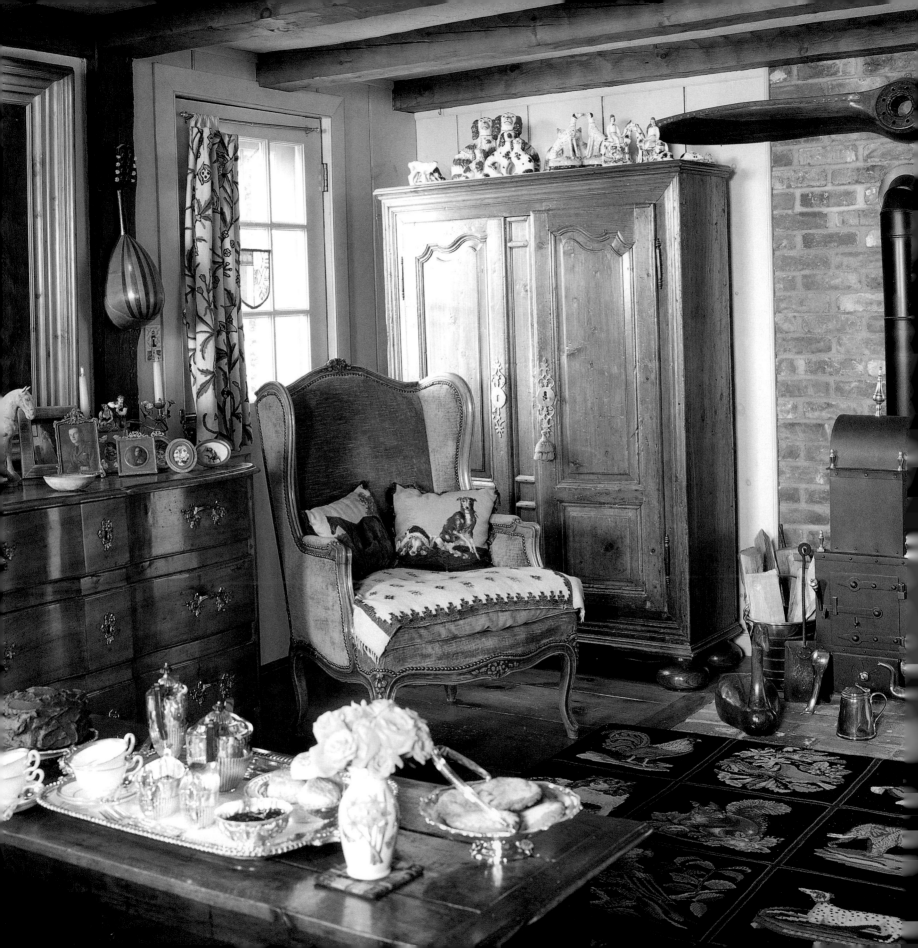

a collector's cottage

Down a quiet lane in the historic district of the town of Nantucket is the modest cottage belonging to Diana McLaughlin. Its gray-shingled exterior blends in with the surrounding houses, but inside it is a collector's haven. Born in Canada, Diana is an international traveler and an avid and knowledgeable collector with a soft spot for lead soldiers and figurines that bring back wonderful memories of her childhood in Toronto.

The front door opens into a minute foyer with a staircase leading to the second floor. Each step is carpeted with a hand-hooked stair mat that Diana made herself, each one depicting a different airplane, in homage to her son Christopher's long career as a pilot.

From the foyer, through a door to the left is the dark, inviting living room. Sitting between two windows that face out the front of the house is a large desk. Above it, a mirrored window frame gives the room added dimension. To the right of the desk is one of several glass cabinets in which Diana displays her remarkable collection of lead soldiers. This cabinet in particular houses some of the French Mignot soldiers—one of the premier producers of lead toy soldiers during the time of the French Revolution—that she found for Christopher in Paris. Dark timbers run across the ceiling of the room, reminiscent of old English houses. For rich texture, Diana used Indian-made wool crewel fabric to cover the sofa and a wing chair. Along another wall, a large, heavy bookcase is filled with a collection of rare books dating back to the eighteenth century. Their beautiful red leather bindings, perfectly aligned along the shelves, are in impeccable condition. In one corner, a French country cupboard made of fruitwood dates back to 1800. Assembled on top is a collection of Staffordshire dogs. Hanging on the wall close to the cupboard is a mandolin. "I just loved its shape and the colors in the wood," Diana says. At the other end of the room, opposite the desk, sits a *poêle au chocolat*, a unique stove from Strasbourg used for heating chocolate. Above the stove hangs a wooden propeller from a 1930s-era Gypsy Moth airplane.

Across the foyer from the living room is the

Opposite: At one end of this elegant living room Staffordshire dogs sit on top of a French cupboard made of fruitwood.

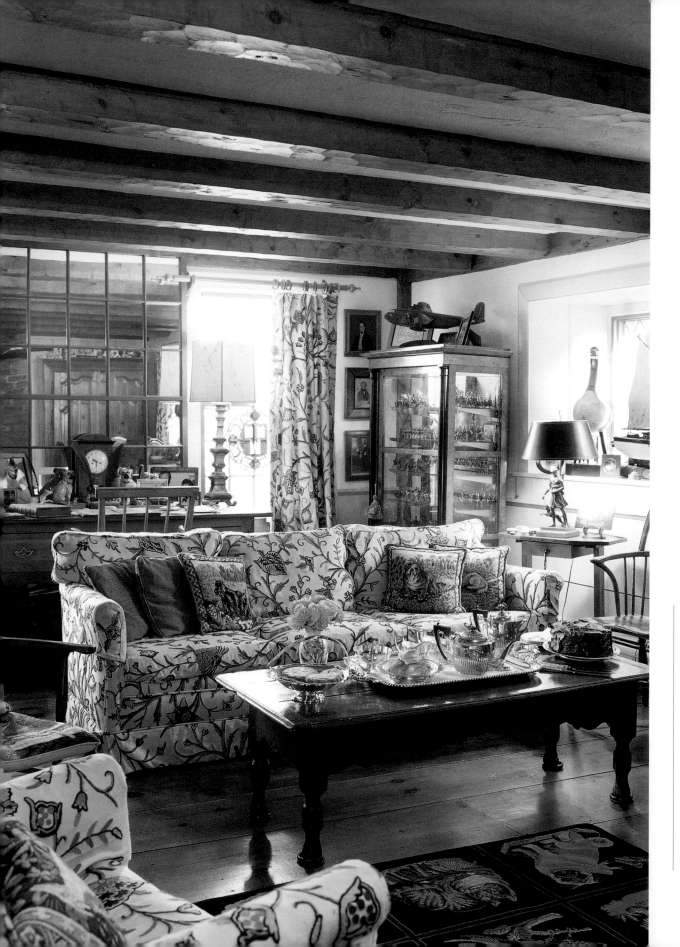

Left: The glass cabinet at the end of the living room houses an impressive collection of lead soldiers.
Opposite, top: A prize decoy (sitting), made by W. Roy Mills in 1935, is accompanied by a model of the ship *Toronto*.
Opposite, bottom left: A Spanish cupboard houses a delightful collection of English Staffordshire sheep.
Opposite, bottom right: The desk set made from old books.

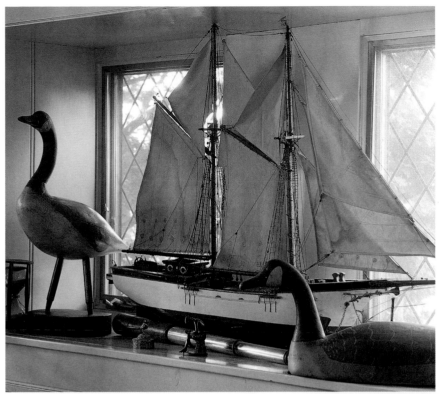

dining room. In the center of the room sits a pine table surrounded by four angel-back chairs. Two glass cabinets, one filled with more lead soldiers, the other with lead circus and farm animals, stand along adjacent walls. Atop both sit model airplanes, mostly windup toys dating from the early nineteenth century. A massive armoire with unusual rat-tail hinges, made of highly prized French Canadian pine, fills a third wall. Diana's love of collecting is evident when she starts describing specific pieces. She remembers where each one came from, who gave it to her, or the name of the shop where she found it. "Certain things you get such an excitement out of finding," she says. And although she has scaled her collecting back a bit, she still often comes across some coveted piece that she just has to add to her extensive collection.

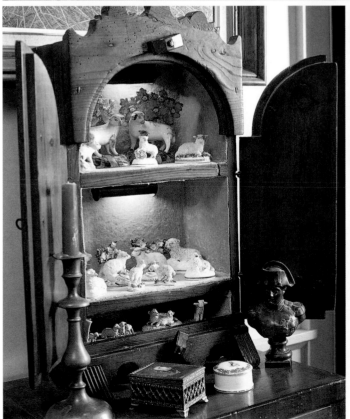

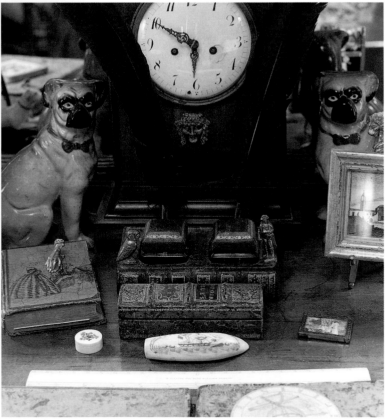

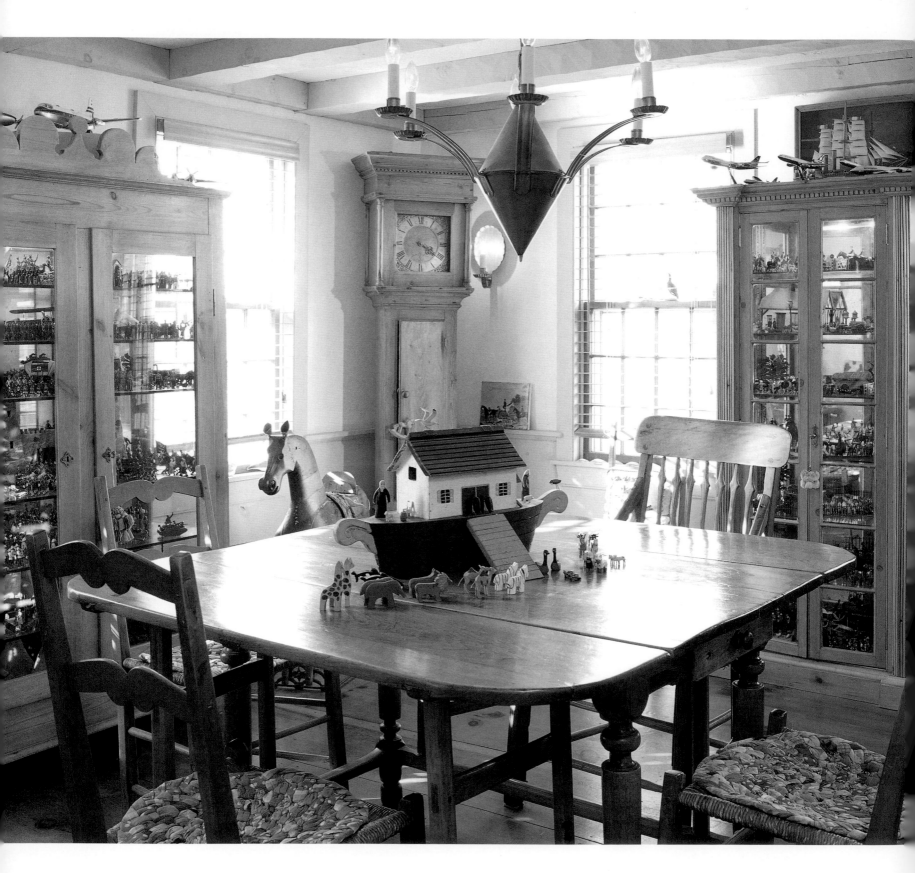

AT HOME IN NANTUCKET

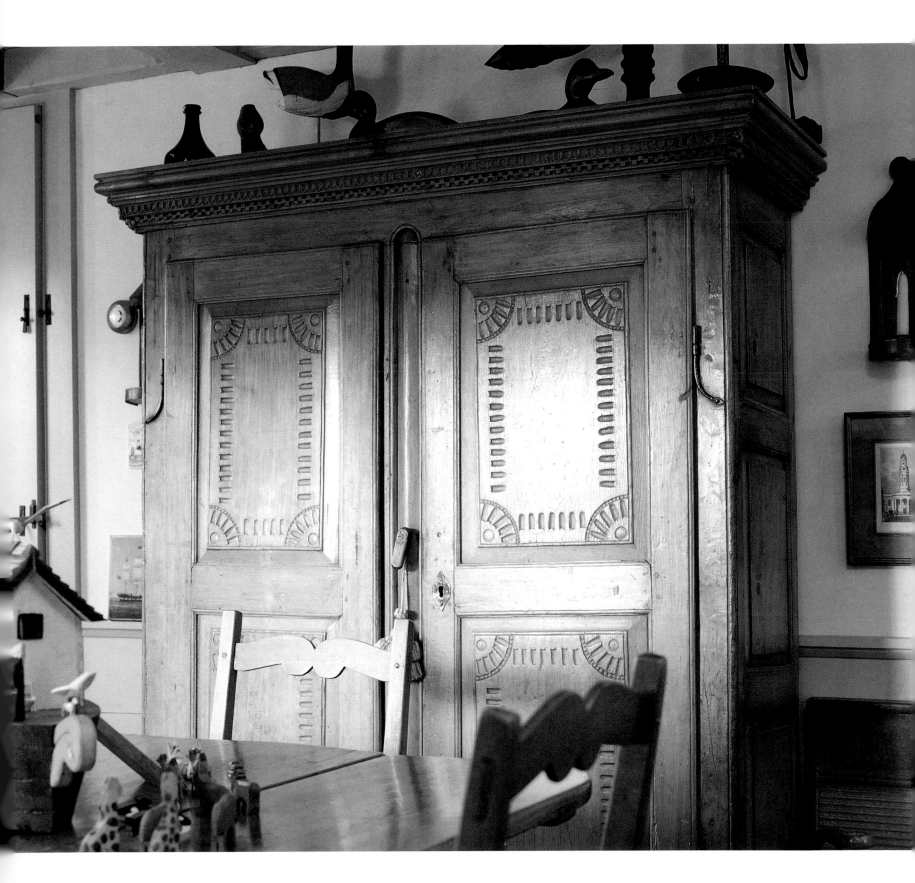

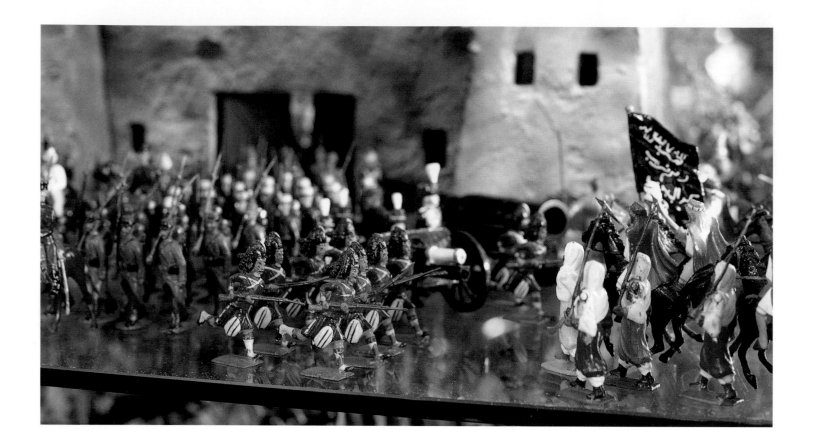

COLLECTING

Diana has amassed her impressive collection of soldiers over a long period of time. It is a passion she shares with her son Christopher and one that has taken her to auctions and shops in Europe and the United States on the search for specific pieces. She loves the excitement of going to auctions and seeing pieces that she never imagined existed. She cautions that it can be disappointing when prices skyrocket beyond one's budget, but finds that it's still possible to stumble upon an incredible find with a realistic price tag. Diana's advice: "Have fun collecting—collect more for the joy and the passion than the value of the pieces." The monetary value may increase over time, but unless a collector is really passionate and knowledgeable, the objects themselves can lose their appeal. The Internet has become an invaluable tool for collectors. The click of a mouse links buyers at home with sellers all over the world, at auction houses, galleries, independent dealerships, and even antique stores. While pricetags run to impressive heights, there's a category of collectible for every budget. It is quite possible to start a collection on a limited budget: Set price limitations on individual pieces and thrive on the challenge of the hunt.

Previous spread, left:
Two more cabinets in
the dining room are
laden with lead soldiers
and figurines.
Previous spread, right:
This massive Canadian
armoire dates to 1800
and features unusual
rat-tail hinges.

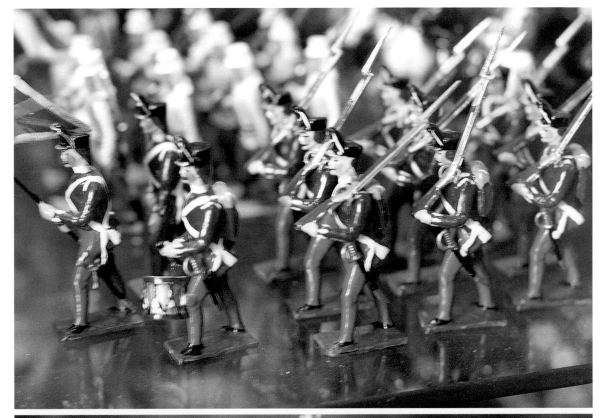

Opposite: Lead soldiers
from the Foreign Legion
fight Arab tribes.
Right, top: French
Mignot soldiers from
a Napoleonic regiment
stand in formation.
Right, bottom: A miniature
version of the Coronation
coach of George VI and
Queen Elizabeth reminds
Diana of her own journey
to the Coronation in 1937.

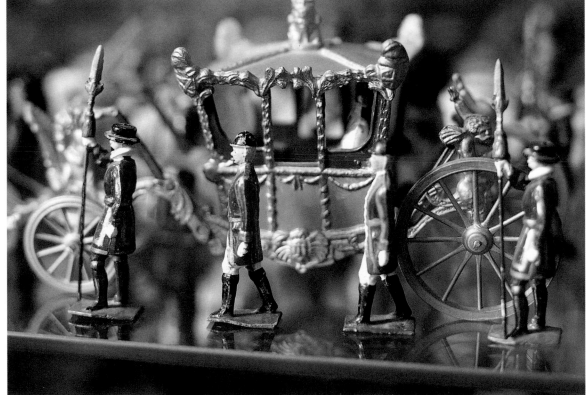

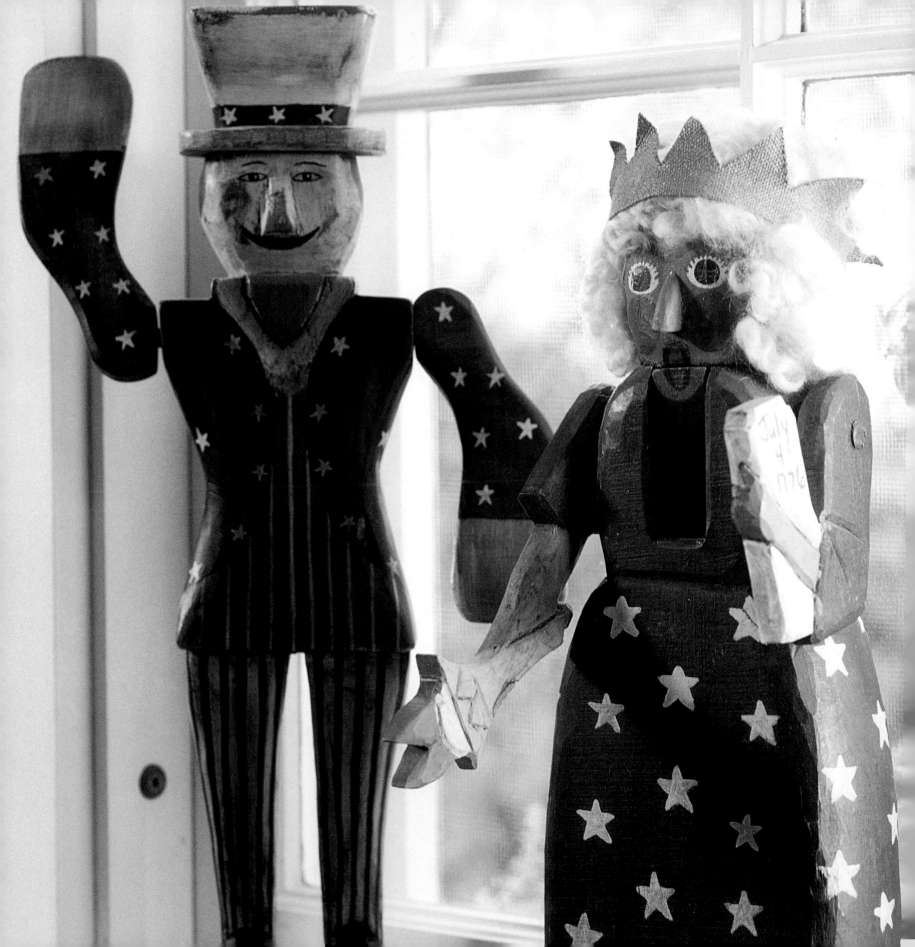

chapter two:
summer

Although Nantucket possesses wonderful character year-round, it is in the summer when the island truly comes alive. Ferries arrive packed with cars, bicycles, people, and dogs. Airplanes buzz in from Cape Cod, and stores and restaurants bustle with activity. Boats fill the harbor, and colorful sails dot Nantucket Sound. For three hectic months of barbecues, sailing trips, parties, and beach and sporting activities, a hum resonates throughout the island.

Surrounded by pine trees, Todd and Liz Winship's hacienda-style house is hidden from the summer crowds. Its open design provides ample sunlight and encourages cool summer breezes to blow through its spacious rooms. Near the center of town, Steven and Daisy Rapp have created an homage to Nantucket's showiest summer holiday—the Fourth of July. Their historic barn is decked out in red, white, and blue, a truly festive backdrop for good old-fashioned summer celebrations. At the other end of the spectrum, the converted carriage house of Eugenie Vorhees is painted in white from floor to ceiling, its calming interior a peaceful haven from all the summer activity. A bit outside of town, Geo P. Davis has built the retreat of his dreams. The design and decor make many references to seaside living, including a neutral palette that echoes that of the seashore, giving this truly original home great Nantucket charm.

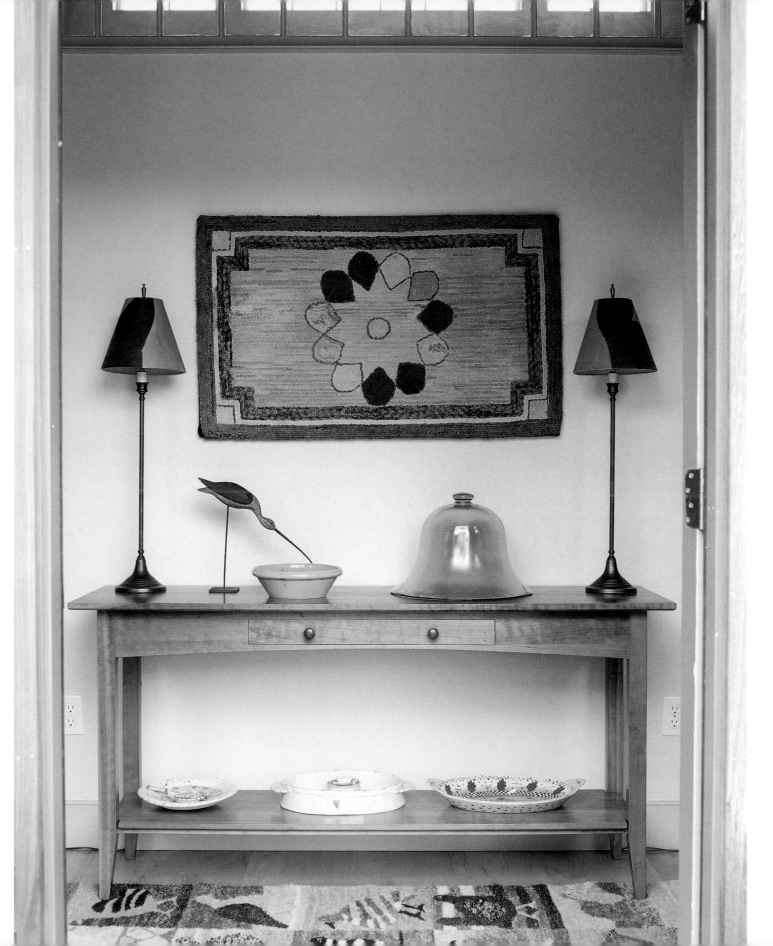

nantucket hacienda

Down a long drive, the house of Todd and Liz Winship is nestled quietly among the pines. A long wooden walkway leads from the drive to the glass front door. Inside, the living room opens up behind the entry wall. With high ceilings and a row of windows facing out onto the back deck, the room is filled with light. It is simple and uncluttered, yet throughout, intriguing objects by various artists lend subtle detail.

The Winships designed their one-story house in the shape of a U, to take advantage of the island's summer breezes. They built it all on one level to accommodate a hip condition that Liz has had since childhood. In case her condition deteriorates, wide doorways have already been installed to allow easy passage for a wheelchair.

The entrance to the house is at the base of the U. To the left are daughter Claire's room, a guest room, and the master suite. To the right are the dining room, the spacious kitchen, an office, and the den. The house is wrapped around a main deck in the center of the U, which inspired Todd and Liz to dub it their "Nantucket hacienda." For island dwellers, this kind of layout allows plenty of breezes to circulate throughout the house and keep things cool, a factor that is especially important during Nantucket's summer heat waves. Off the deck is

an expanse of lawn with a small pond and fountain, as well as a bench for quiet reflection.

Throughout the house are the beautiful and quirky works of art that Liz cherishes. Liz is the owner of Nantucket Looms, a retail landmark on Main Street downtown that offers items created in the store's own weaving studio upstairs, as well as others from both local and national artists, and home furnishings and accessories. Much of the Winships' home reflects the same aesthetic of simple furnishings mixed with fine examples of art and craftsmanship. On one dining room wall, several carved birds are displayed on shelves. In the hallway just outside the guest room there is a collection of intricate miniature Nantucket lightship baskets. Made for Liz by her dear friend Doc Magee, each basket includes a personal message just for her. Several hooked rugs hang throughout the

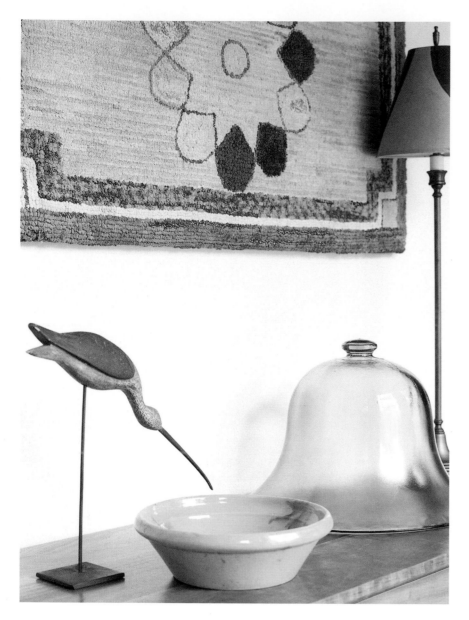

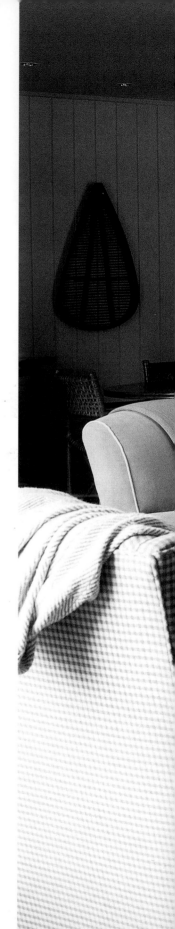

Left: On the cherry entry table, a sandpiper carved by Mike Bacle dips into a colorful bowl.
Opposite: In the living room, a painting by Sterling Mulberry hangs above the fireplace. In the foreground, the throw on the wing chair is a fine example of the woven pieces made at Nantucket Looms.

house, and unusual ceramic pieces sit on the kitchen sideboard and on a table in the entryway.

Although there is a lot to see, the house does not overwhelm. The artwork is subtly woven into the entire fabric of the house, creating a calm, peaceful place to come home to all year long. "It works so well with light and our lifestyle," says Liz. "We are still fine-tuning, but we love it a lot."

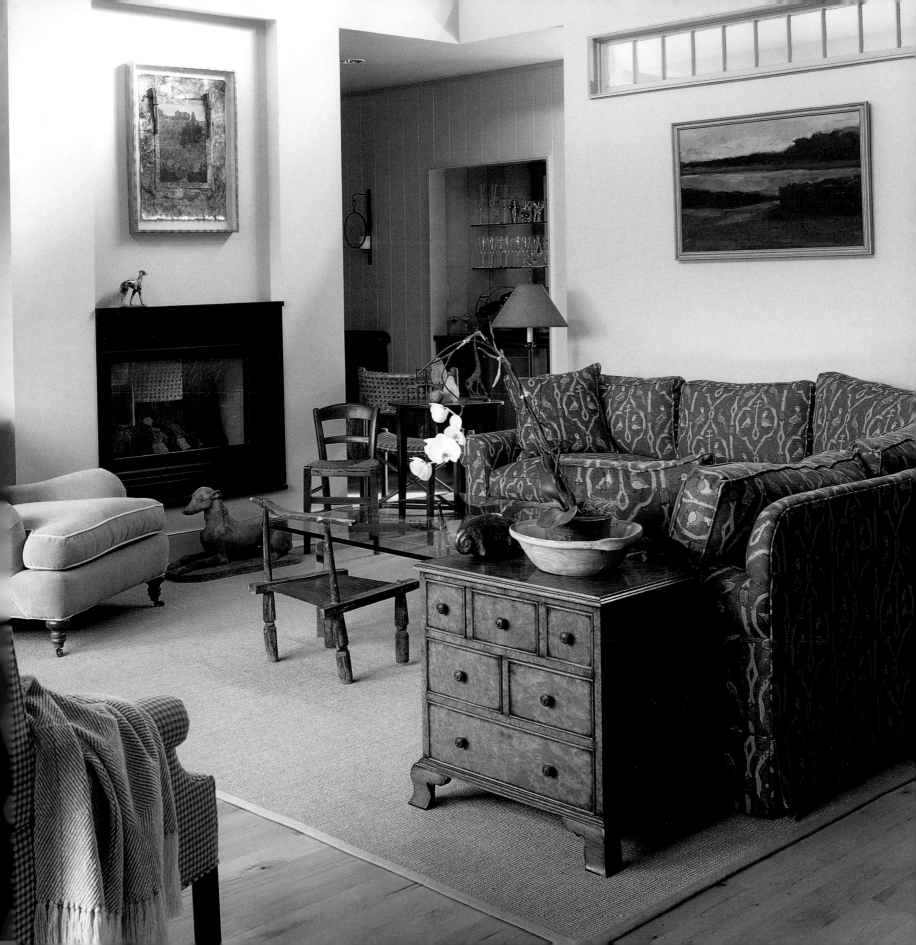

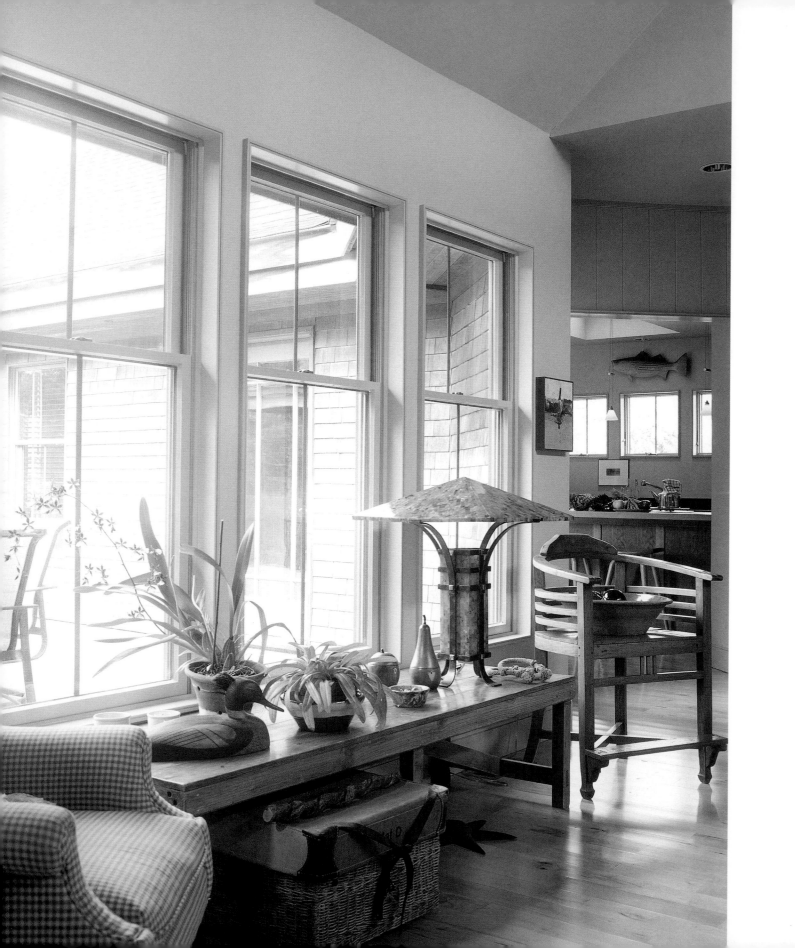

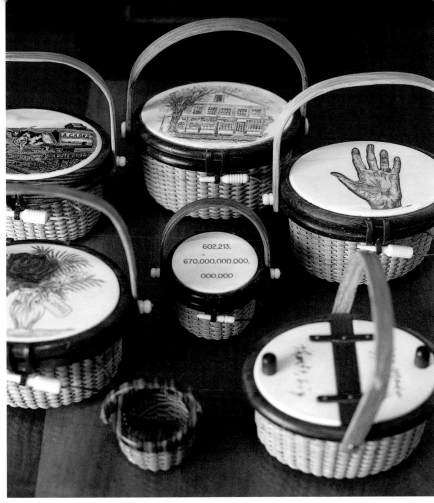

Opposite: Three windows overlook the deck. To the right, a hallway leads to the kitchen.
Left: Liz's special collection of miniature Nantucket lightship baskets.
Below: Sitting on an antique Chinese teak barber chair, a French glazed milk bowl holds old glass floats originally used in fishing nets.

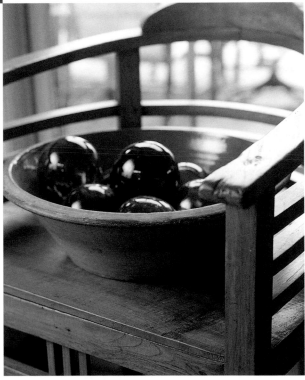

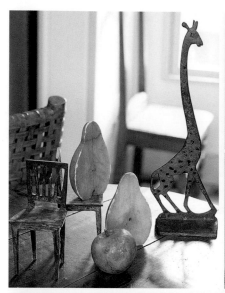

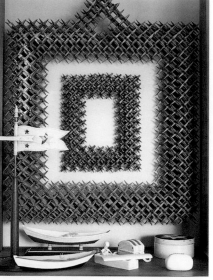

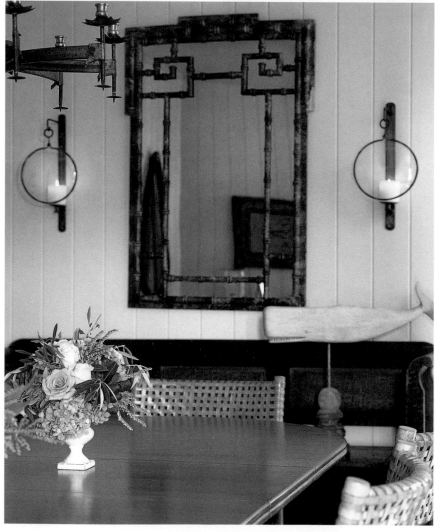

Top left: A still life on a side table includes three Victorian faux pears.

Top right: A quirky collection of carved ivory pieces includes a skeleton in a coffin.

Bottom: Mark McNair carved the white whale showcased here in the dining room, and Liz resurrected the faux bamboo mirror from the basement of her store.

Opposite: A trio of vases, from Liz's favorite island florist, Trillium, line the dining table. On the back wall are a collection of carved shorebirds by Mark McNair.

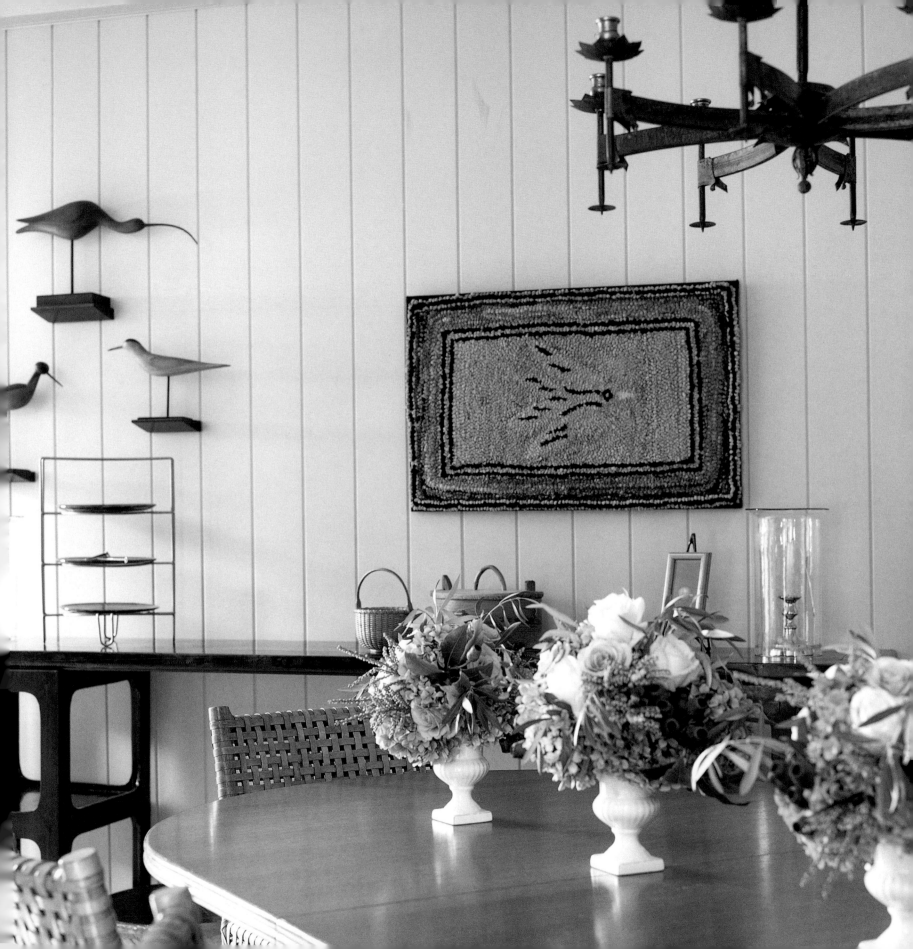

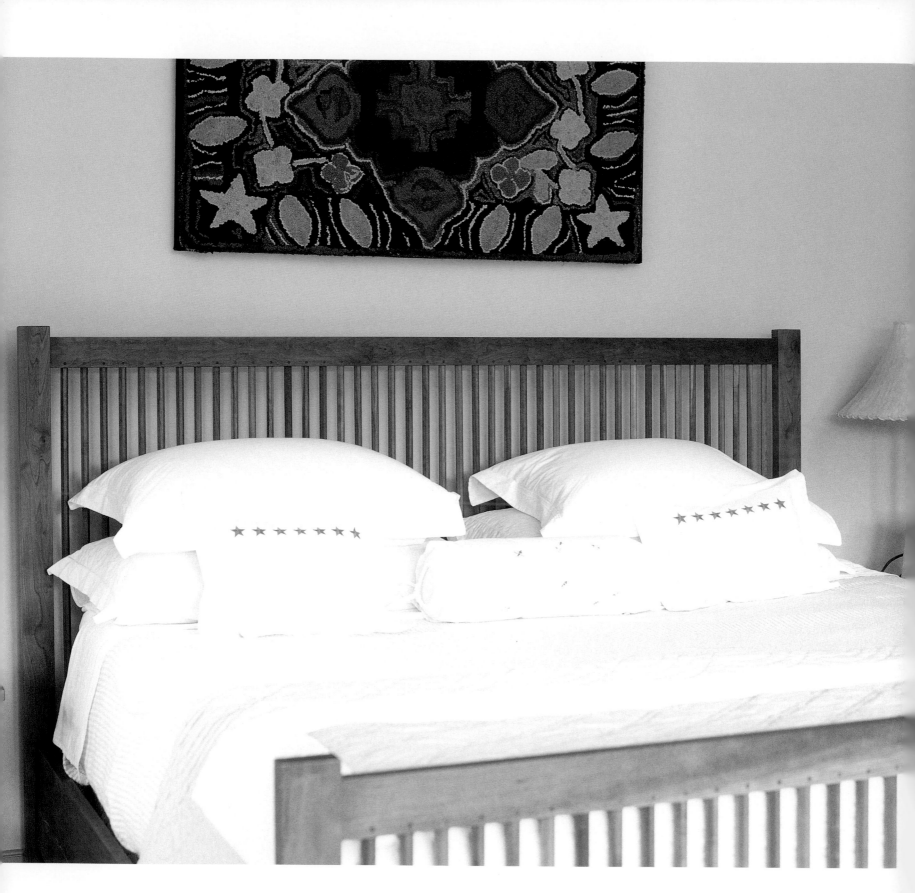

AT HOME IN NANTUCKET

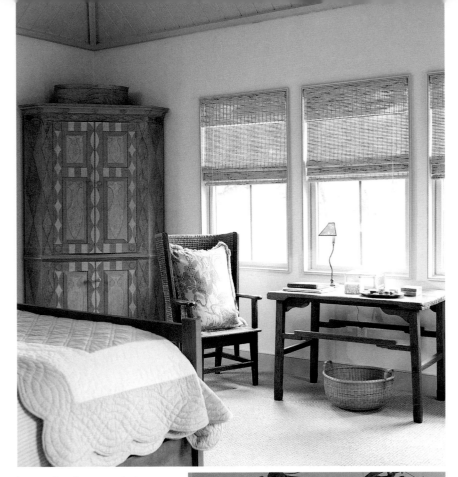

Opposite: The master bed, made of cherry and walnut, has a simple design.
Above: The inlay colors in the corner cupboard influenced the colors used throughout the house. A treasured chair comes from the Scottish isle of Orkney.
Right: An old dentist cabinet in the master bath holds treasured objects.

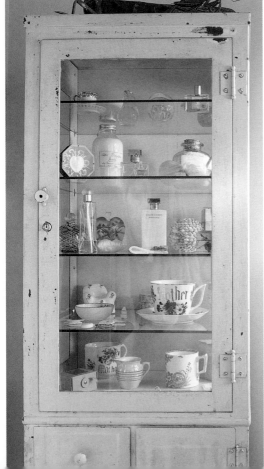

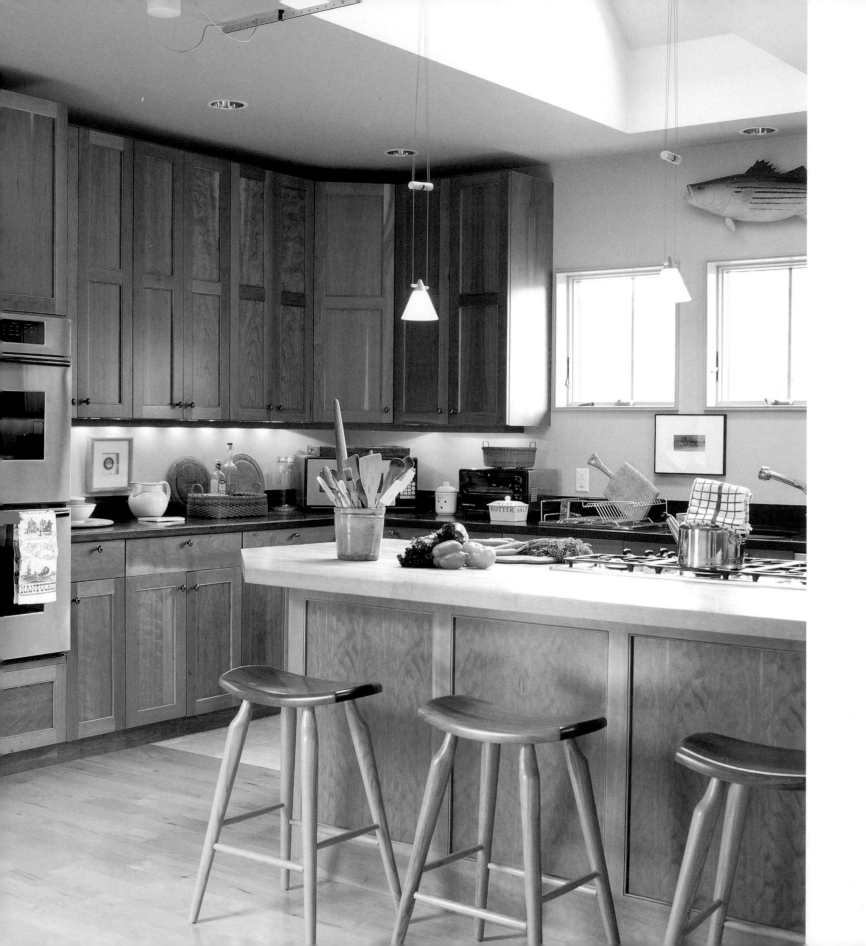

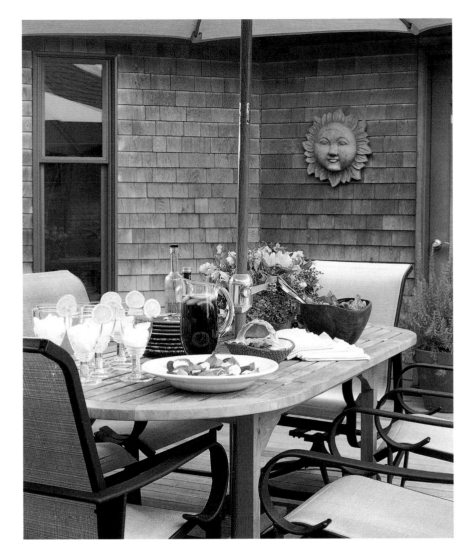

Captain Pentecost's Iced-Tea Punch

No summer gathering on Nantucket would be complete without this fizzy thirst quencher.

1 quart good tea (preferably Chinese Hu-Kwa)

2 – 3 sprigs fresh mint, plus extra for garnish

3 tablespoons sugar

Juice of 2 lemons, plus 1 lemon for garnish

4 ounces grenadine

Ice

1 quart ginger ale

1. Brew hot tea with mint for 5 minutes. Strain into a large pitcher, stir in sugar, and allow to cool for 2 hours, or until room temperature.

2. Add lemon juice, grenadine, and ice. Stir to combine. Add ginger ale just before serving. Garnish with fresh mint and lemon.

Makes about 2 quarts

Opposite: The kitchen cabinets and island are unstained cherry. The stools are from Stephen Swift and the carving of a bass above the sink is by Franck Finney.
Left: On the deck, a summer lunch of farm-fresh tomatoes with mozzarella, a garden salad, and iced tea stay cool under a market umbrella.

FARM FRESH

One of the best things about summer on Nantucket is the delicious produce available. Bartlett's Ocean View Farm, which has been in business for more than thirty years, has a truck on Main Street every day filled with fresh-picked corn and tomatoes and simple bunches of flowers. The farm, out on Bartlett Farm Road, has several greenhouses with plants and flowers for sale, and also offers a wide selection of home-made, take-away meals.

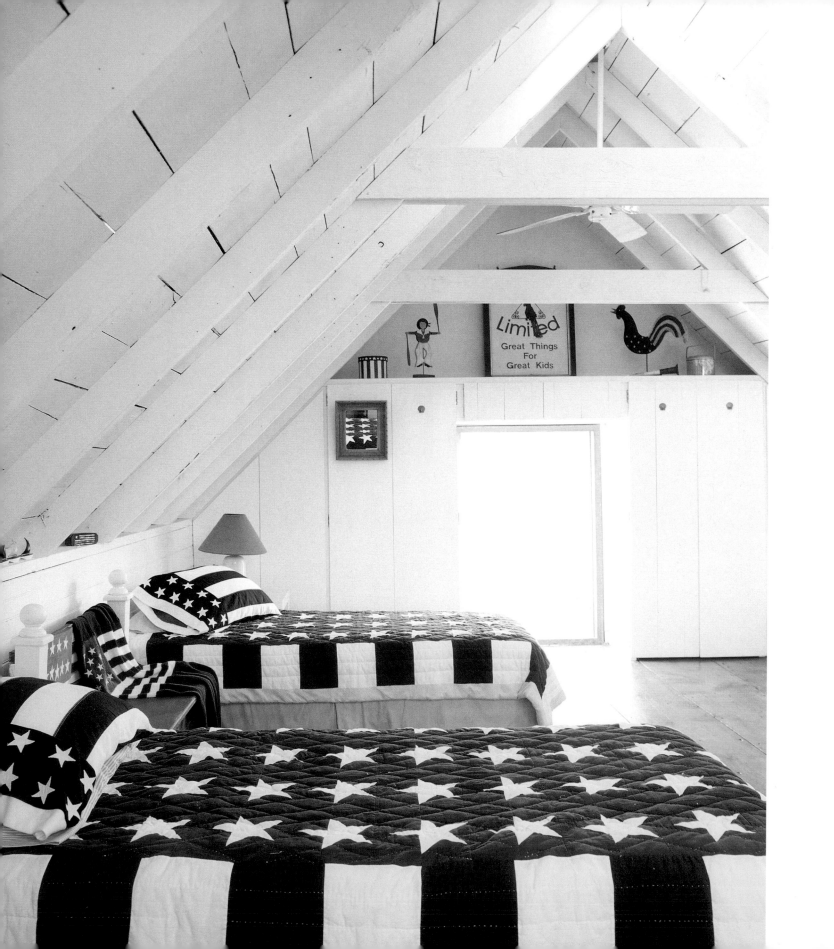

a patriotic barn

At the back of their property, near the center of town, Daisy and Steven Rapp have filled an old barn with a wonderful dose of patriotism. "It's hard to say how this red, white, and blue theme happened," says Daisy. "I guess it has something to do with the way Nantucket gets all decked out for July Fourth, with the water fights on Main Street, the pie-eating contests, and all that. We just love old-fashioned hometown celebrations."

Their barn is perfectly suited for just such celebration, especially one in honor of the Fourth of July. Like the annual fireworks display, the inside of the barn explodes with color and life. The Rapps' extensive collection of flag-based objects includes whimsical folk-art pieces; flag pillows; rugs; a bench; furniture covered in red, white, and blue; and plenty of tableware. "We just love flags, pure and simple, and anything with flags on it," Daisy says. "Once I started, the collection of flag stuff kept growing."

The barn actually played an important role in the history of the island. It used to be the workshop of renowned local artist William Chase, who lived from 1850 to 1931. It was here that he made his famous weather vanes, or "whirligigs," often crafted in the shape of a sailor boy whose arms rotate or whirl in the wind. When the Rapps bought the barn in 1987, they wanted to keep the look inside clean and simple. They achieved that easily with several coats of white paint. They still needed some basic renovations, however, to transform it into a more convenient space. A staircase, originally located at the front of the building, was moved to the back, and a kitchen and bathroom were added. In summer their barn becomes a family room, guest house, and the perfect place for entertaining.

The ground floor of the barn has an open floor plan, with comfortable seating and lots of light. The room can easily be rearranged for parties and even can accommodate a long buffet table. In inclement weather, the Rapps forgo July Fourth on their boat and host the celebration indoors, with red, white, and blue tablecloths, plates, napkins, and silverware, and food suited perfectly for the occasion (see pages 71–73).

Opposite: The beds in the upstairs sleeping loft are outfitted with quilts and pillowcases made out of old flags by Ann Lee in Kentucky.

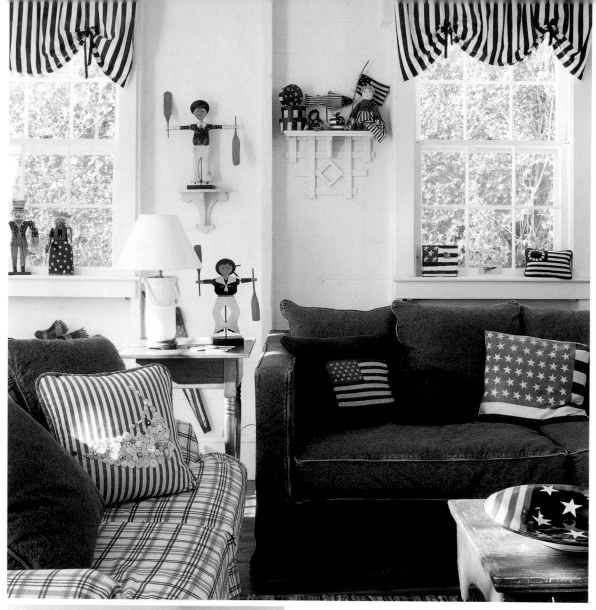

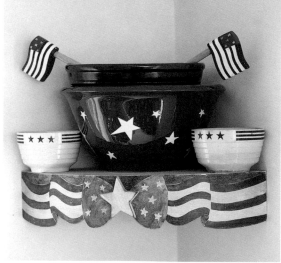

Summers on Nantucket provide a wonderful outlet for the Rapps. "We love the architecture, the water, the wonderful restaurants, and the great husband-and-wife teams that run most of them," Daisy says. "We love the adventure of getting to the island, and we love that when you get here it feels like you are in another country. Nantucket has a certain old-fashioned way of celebrating holidays that gives a strong sense of tradition. In the summer the gardens are overflowing with flowers and vegetables and the air is filled with the refreshing scent of the sea."

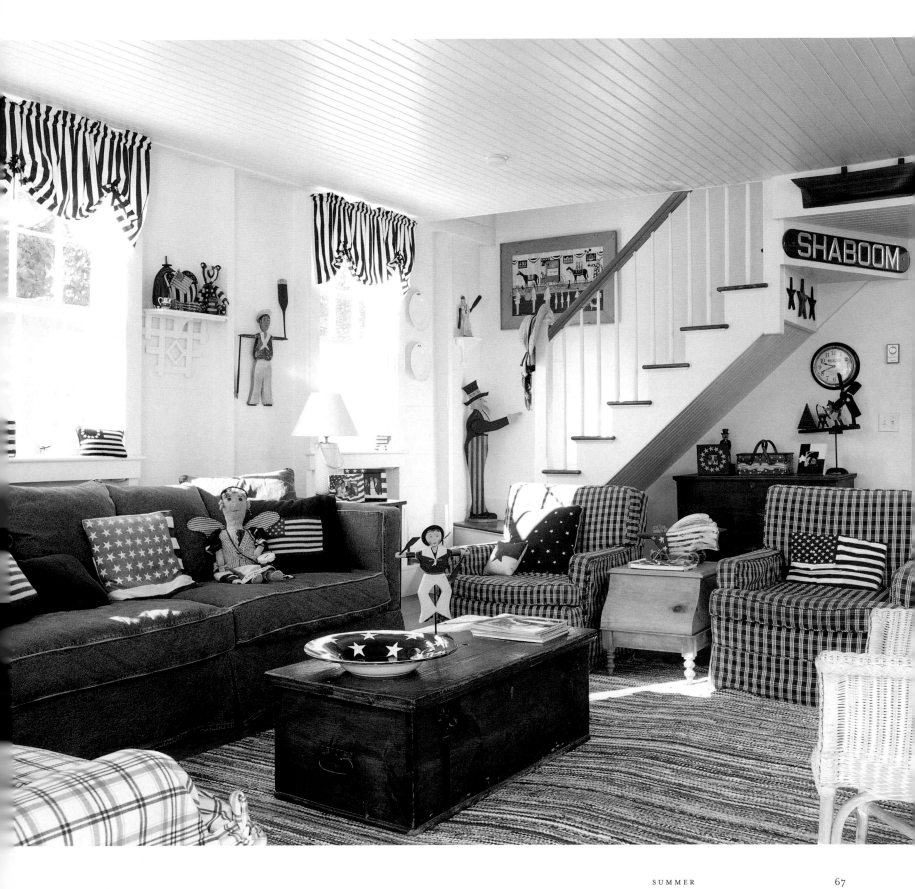

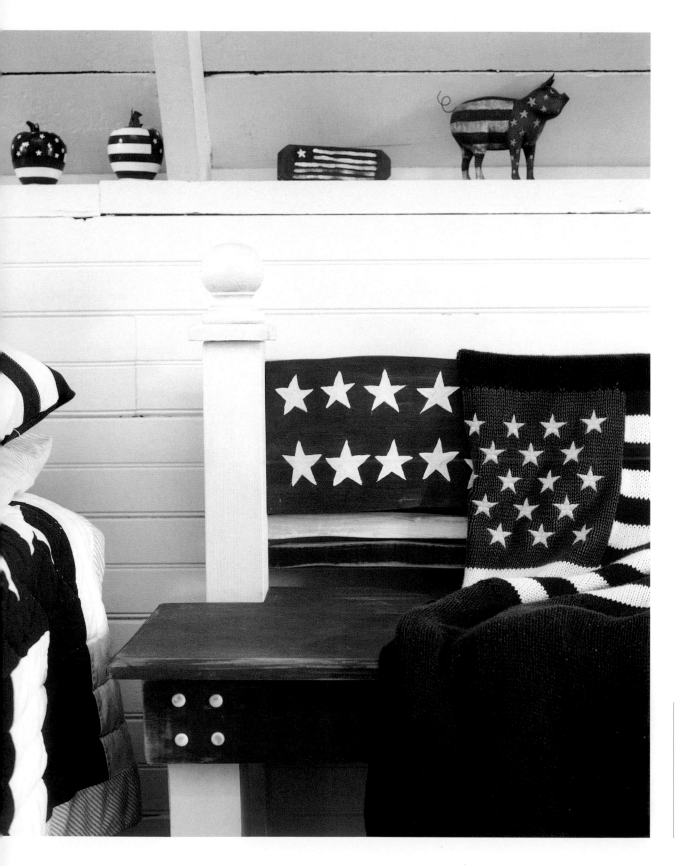

Left: Artist Ken Ferris made the flag bench, and the pig was made by famous folk artist Bush Prisby.
Opposite: Daisy's latest acquisition, a wooden windmill, stands tall near the door.

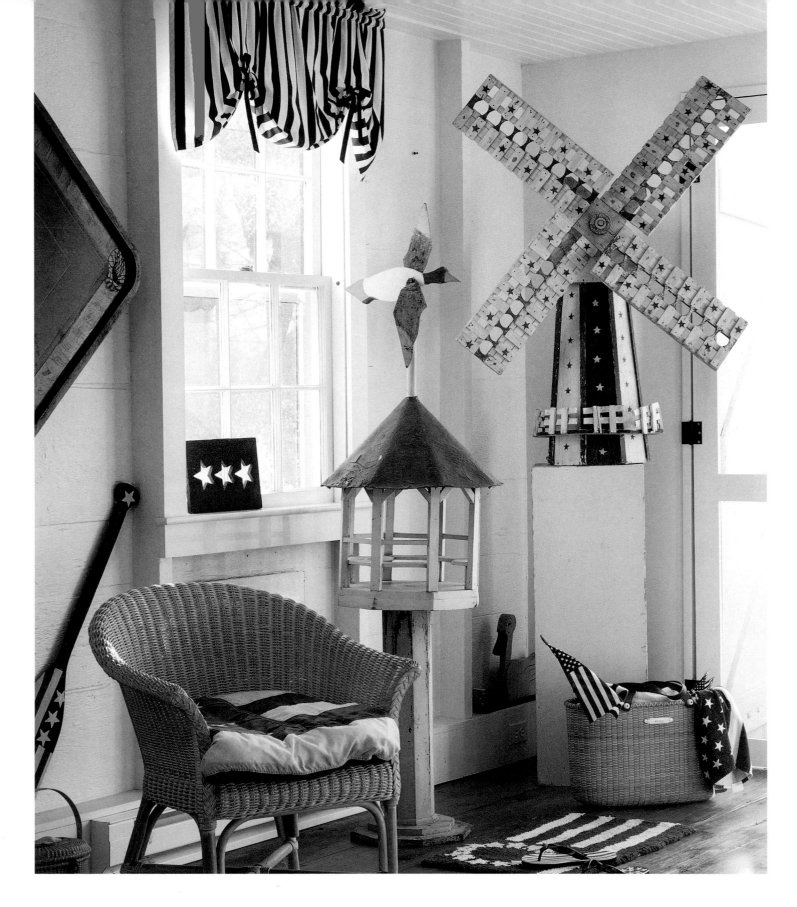

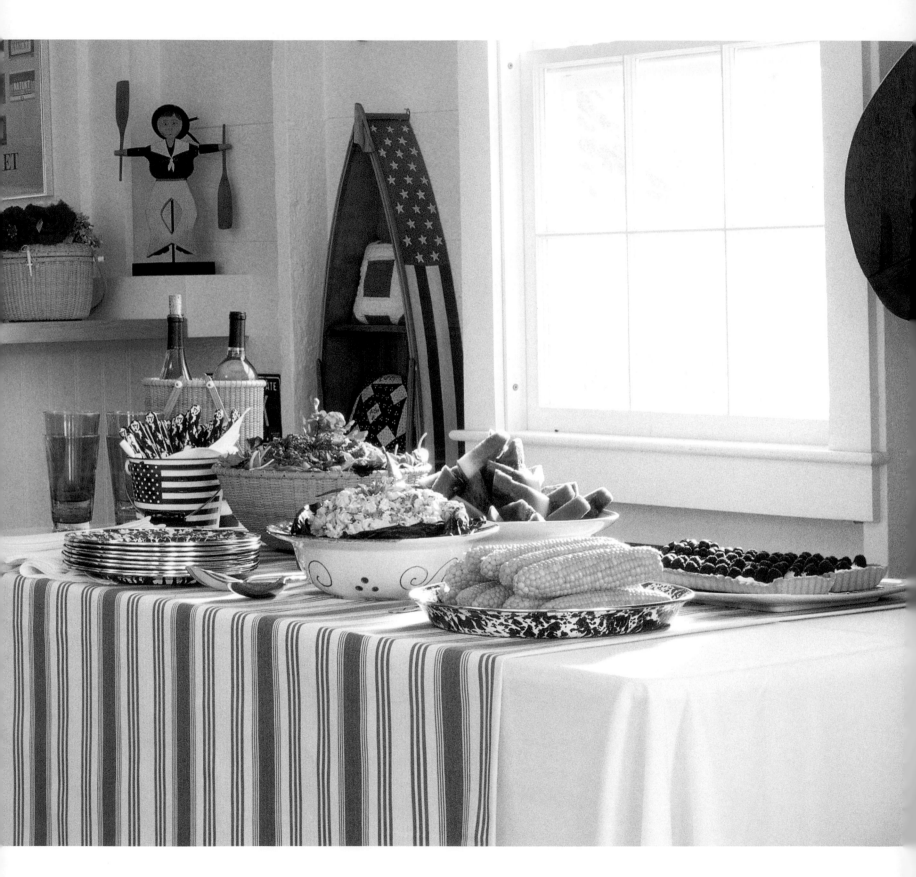

Summer Salads

July Fourth weekend is the time when the Rapps exhibit the height of their patriotic pride. In good weather they can be found out on their boat with friends and family enjoying a sumptuous picnic lunch. Michael Getter, of the restaurant American Seasons, offers these two salads, perfect for a summer picnic at Great Point. Getter and his partner, Bruce Miller, have owned the restaurant on Centre Street in the heart of downtown Nantucket since 1995. It offers a warm and casual atmosphere and delicious Nantucket fare.

Caramelized-Onion Potato Salad with Pommery Vinaigrette

For the onions:

3 tablespoons olive oil

4 medium Spanish white onions, thinly sliced

1/4 cup water

2 tablespoons sugar

For the vinaigrette:

2 teaspoons sugar

1 tablespoon kosher salt

1/4 cup fresh lemon juice

1 1/2 cups rice wine vinegar

3 teaspoons honey

2 cups good Pommery or wholegrain mustard

2 1/2 cups olive oil

1/2 cup water

3 pounds small red bliss potatoes, unpeeled

3 tablespoons kosher salt

1 large red bell pepper, seeded and finely diced

1/2 cup chopped Italian (flat-leaf) parsley

1. To make the onions, heat olive oil in a sauté pan over high heat until a slight smoke appears. Add onions and sauté, stirring constantly, until they start to brown, about 2 minutes.

2. When onions begin to stick to the pan and caramelize, add water, scrape the brown bits from the bottom of the pan, and continue to caramelize.

3. Add sugar and continue to caramelize until onions have turned dark brown about 2 to 4 minutes. Add more water as needed to prevent onions from burning. When finished, remove from pan and cool.

4. To make the vinaigrette, combine sugar, salt, lemon juice, and vinegar in a bowl. Whisk until sugar is dissolved.

5. Add honey and mustard and whisk well.

6. Slowly drizzle in oil while whisking to combine. If the vinaigrette starts to get too thick, add a little water. Set aside.

7. Cut each potato into quarters or eighths, depending on their size. Place in a saucepan, cover with cold water, and add salt.

8. Bring to a boil over high heat, then reduce heat and simmer until potatoes are easily pierced with a fork. Drain and transfer to a tray to cool.

9. Place cooled potatoes, caramelized onions, half the diced bell pepper, and parsley in a large bowl and mix well. Be careful not to smash the potatoes. Add half the vinaigrette, toss gently, and then add remaining vinaigrette, until the salad is fully coated. (If the onions are quite moist, you need not add all the vinaigrette.)

10. Turn out onto a platter in a high pile. Sprinkle with remaining bell pepper for garnish.

Serves 10

Classic Summer Lobster Salad

In a large bowl, combine lobster, celery, green onions, and parsley. Mix well. Add the mayonnaise, lemon juice, celery salt, kosher salt, and pepper and mix thoroughly. Cover and refrigerate until chilled, at least 2 hours. To serve, make a bed of mesclun greens on a platter and arrange the salad on top.

Serves 10

Opposite: This festive table is set for an outdoor summer picnic. In the background, an original William Chase whirligig sailor boy sits on a ledge accompanied by a delicate Nantucket lightship basket nearby, woven by Daisy.

3 1/2 pounds cooked lobster meat, roughly chopped

1 cup finely chopped celery

3/4 cup green onions, thinly sliced

1/2 cup finely chopped Italian (flat-leaf) parsley

3 cups best quality mayonnaise

2 tablespoons fresh lemon juice

2 tablespoons celery salt

1 tablespoon kosher salt

1 teaspoon freshly ground pepper

8 ounces mesclun greens

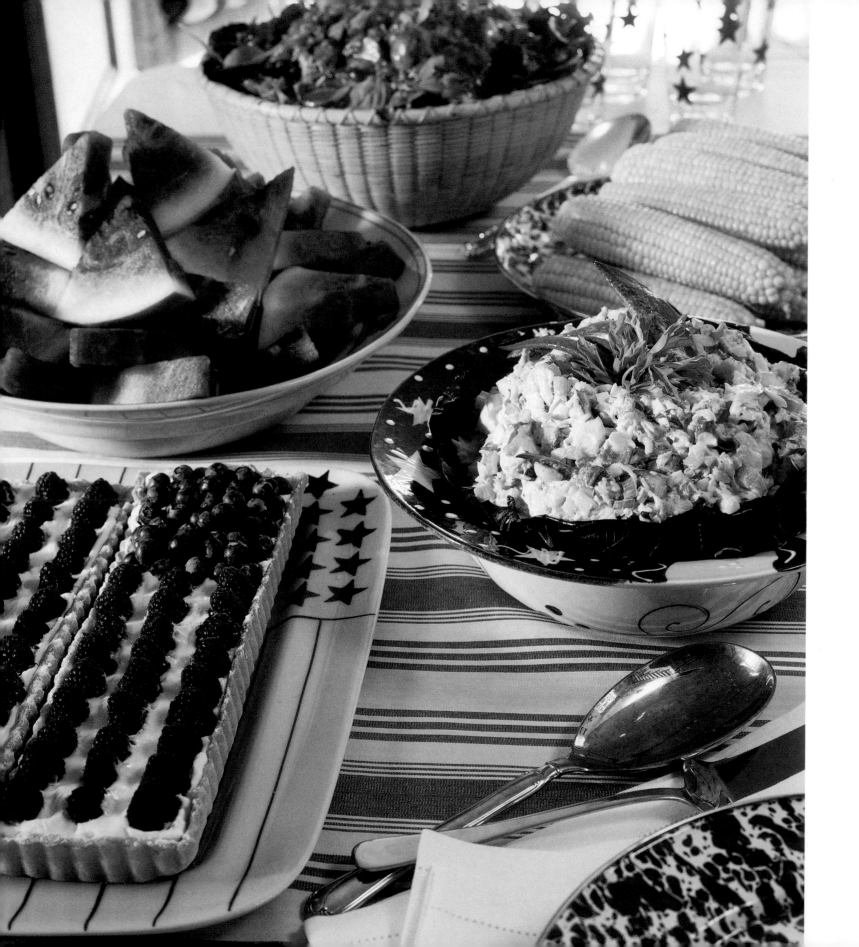

Flag Berry Tart

For 2 tart shells:

2 ½ cups all-purpose flour

3 tablespoons sugar

Pinch of salt

1 cup (2 sticks) chilled
    unsalted butter, cubed

2 large egg yolks

¼ cup very cold water

For the filling:

8 ounces cream cheese, at
    room temperature

1 teaspoon vanilla extract

4 ounces crème fraîche

½ cup confectioners' sugar

4 ounces semisweet chocolate

1 pint plump blueberries

2 pints large plump raspberries

½ cup raspberry jam

1 tablespoon hot water

2 cups fresh whipped cream

1. To make the shells, place flour, sugar, and salt in a food processor fitted with the metal blade and pulse to combine. Add butter and process until the mixture resembles coarse meal.

2. In a small bowl, lightly beat together egg yolks and water. With the food processor running, add the yolk mixture to the dry mixture just until it all holds together.

3. Divide the dough in half and form into flattened balls. Wrap in plastic wrap and chill for at least 2 hours.

4. Preheat oven to 375 degrees F.

5. On a lightly floured work surface, roll out one ball to fit a 4-by-14-inch fluted tart pan with removable bottom. Carefully transfer dough to tart pan, pressing it into the edges and sides. Trim off excess dough. Prick the bottom with a fork, cover with plastic wrap, and refrigerate for at least 1 hour. Repeat with the second ball of dough and another pan.

6. Place both tart shells on a baking sheet. Line each with aluminum foil, letting it hang over the edges. Fill the foil with pie weights so that the foil tucks in along the insides of each shell; make sure the shells' edges are supported by the foil and the weights.

7. Bake until the edges of the shells are just starting to turn light brown, about 25 minutes. Remove weights and foil and continue baking until crust is lightly browned, about 10 more minutes. Transfer to a wire rack and let cool.

8. To make the filling, beat cream cheese and vanilla in a bowl until soft.

9. In a separate bowl, whisk the crème fraîche until it forms peaks.

10. Whisk one-third of the crème fraîche into the cream cheese mixture. Gently fold in the remaining crème fraîche while gradually sifting in the confectioners' sugar. Cover with plastic wrap until ready to assemble the tarts.

11. Melt chocolate in a small double boiler. Spoon several scoops of chocolate into each tart shell, spreading evenly with a knife until the bottom of each shell is covered. Refrigerate for 5 minutes to set.

12. To assemble the flag tarts, spread half the crème fraîche mixture over the chocolate layer in one tart shell. Use the rest to cover the chocolate in the second shell.

13. Starting in the corner of one shell, make the blue field of the flag using a double layer of blueberries to fill about one-third of the shell.

14. Arrange raspberries in 6 rows, lengthwise, from blueberries to opposite edge of the first pan and edge to edge of the second pan, leaving a stripe of crème fraîche of equal thickness exposed between each row of raspberries.

15. Heat raspberry jam in a small bowl with hot water. Brush the raspberry hole and blueberry field with jam. Chill until ready to serve. Just before serving, fill in the stripes between the raspberries with whipped cream, release the pan sides, and arrange the two tarts side-by-side on a platter to create the flag.

Serves 8—10

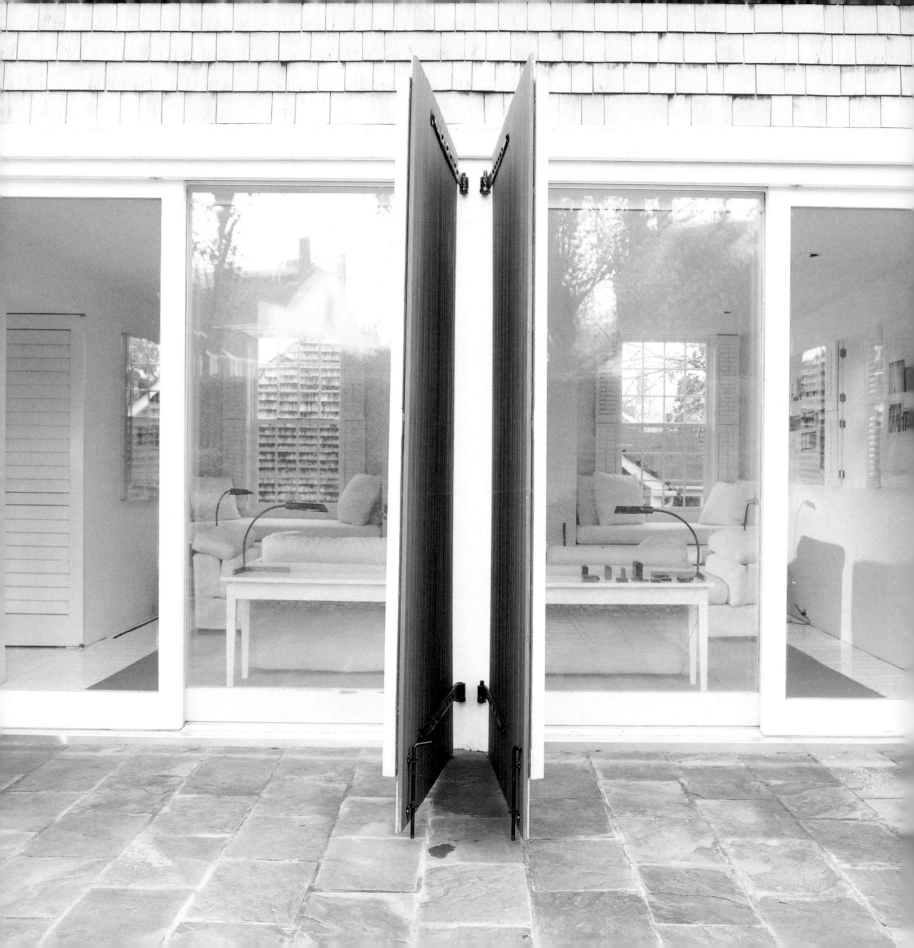

sanctuary in white

Along a narrow cobbled street in the historic district of town is the converted carriage house of Eugenie Vorhees. Dating to 1840, it was part of one of the big traditional homes built during Nantucket's whaling heyday. When it came up for sale in the 1990s, it was in surprisingly good condition. Eugenie had specific ideas for how she wanted to renovate the space and hired renowned architect Hugh Newell Jacobsen to help execute her ideas.

Eugenie did not want the exterior changed in any way, but the inside has been completely transformed. Every surface in this humble carriage house—floors, walls, ceilings, most of the furniture, bookcases, and even the staircase—is completely white. The floorboards, which are original, have been coated with several layers of high-gloss paint, giving them an enamel-like finish.

In the living room, on the ground floor, a sofa and boxy white chairs encircle a blue Brazilian granite coffee table—literally the only piece of furniture in the room with any color. Two giant glass doors were added inside the original carriage doors and provide plenty of light. In the summer, added screens allow breezes to circulate.

Along a short hallway at the other end of the first floor is the dining room, with a table designed by Jacobsen at its center. Bookcases fill the walls on two sides and give the room a small amount of added color. Just off the din-ing room, the kitchen is equally minimalist. Sparkling white counters are devoid of the usual clutter. A shiny chrome stove and dish-washer reflect light from the single window.

Open stairs lead up from the dining room to the second-floor hallway, which runs along the length of the house. Light from a window bounces off the shiny painted floors. The sparse guest room has two twin beds dressed in linens with a subtle graphic design. The only color in the room is a steel support rod that has been painted a bright glossy red. In the master bedroom are bookcases that mimic the ones in the dining room below. A desk sits in front of a window that overlooks the next row of houses.

With its minimalist furnishings and acces-sories, the house is quite peaceful. The all-white decor makes other elements, such as books, food, and even people, the focus inside the house. Eugenie believes they've all got plenty of color to balance things out.

Opposite: With the large doors open, light streams into the pristine living room.

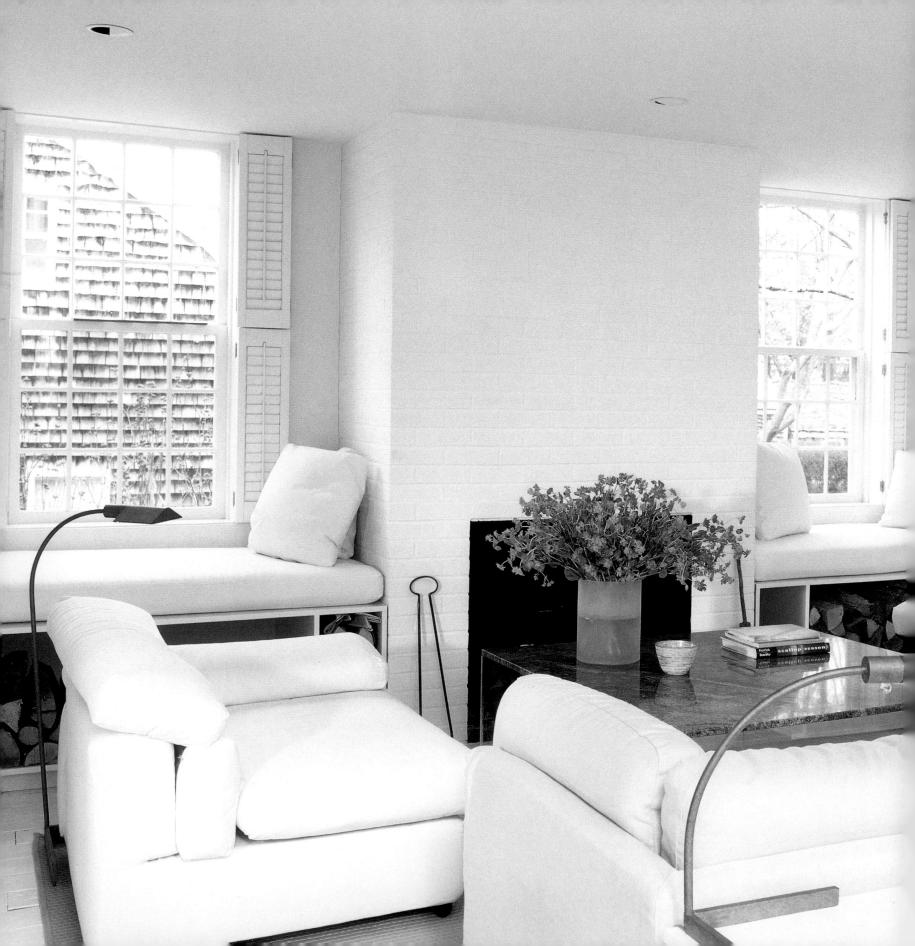

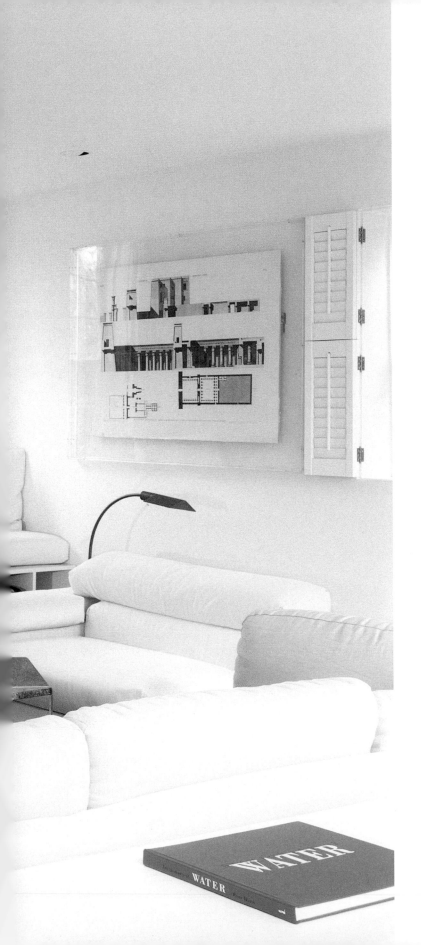

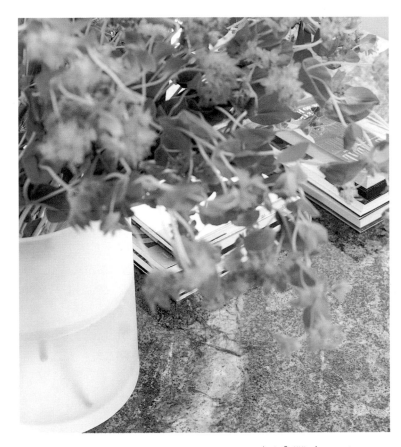

Left: Window seats, a sofa, and two chairs, all outfitted in white, provide ample seating space. On the wall is one of several lithographs from the Louvre, commissioned by Napoleon to document Egyptian antiquities.
Above: In the living room, the coffee table, designed by Jacobsen, provides a touch of color with its Brazilian granite top.

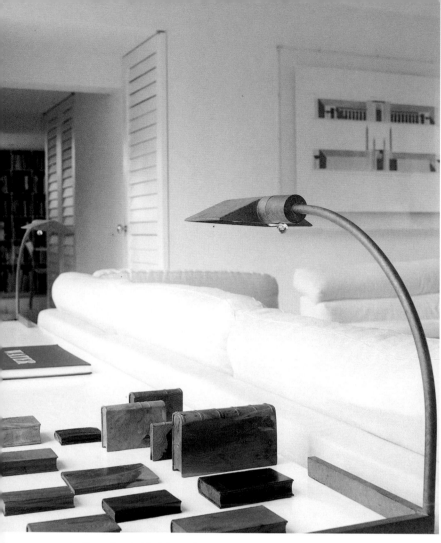

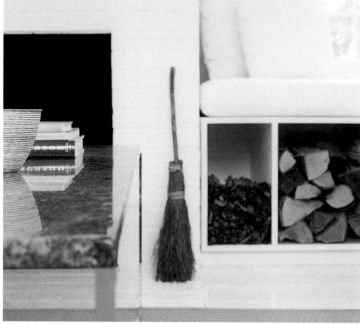

Above: Just behind the sofa, a collection of wooden books carved from exotic woods decorates the table. The lamps, made by Cedric Hartman, Inc., have a special Jacobsen finish.
Right, top: The window seats come with convenient storage space underneath.
Right, bottom: Just outside the living room, behind a slated door, a well-stocked bar awaits the next cocktail party.

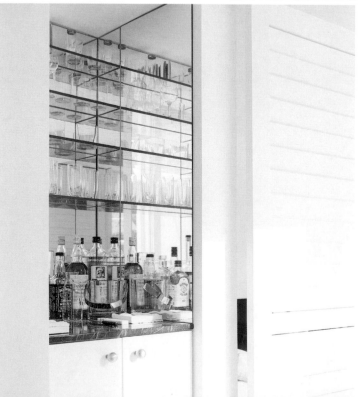

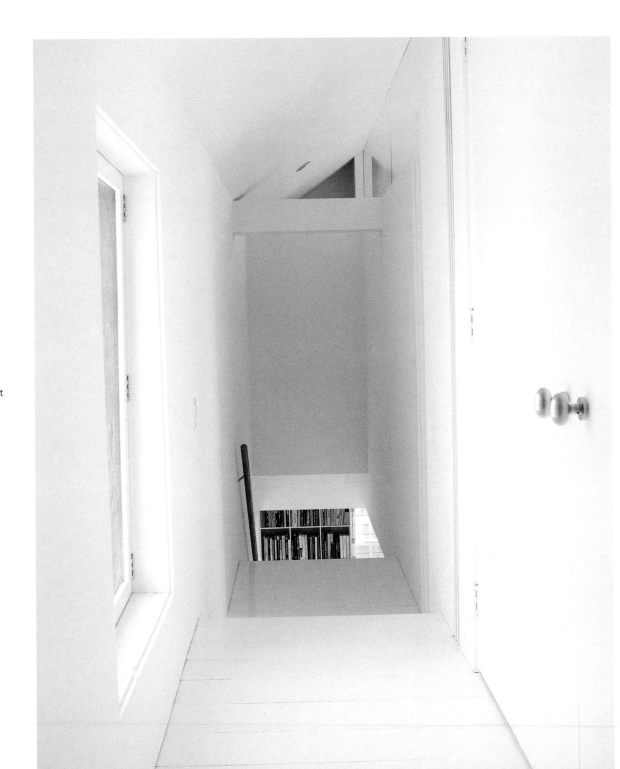

Right: The upstairs hall-way leads along the front of the house.

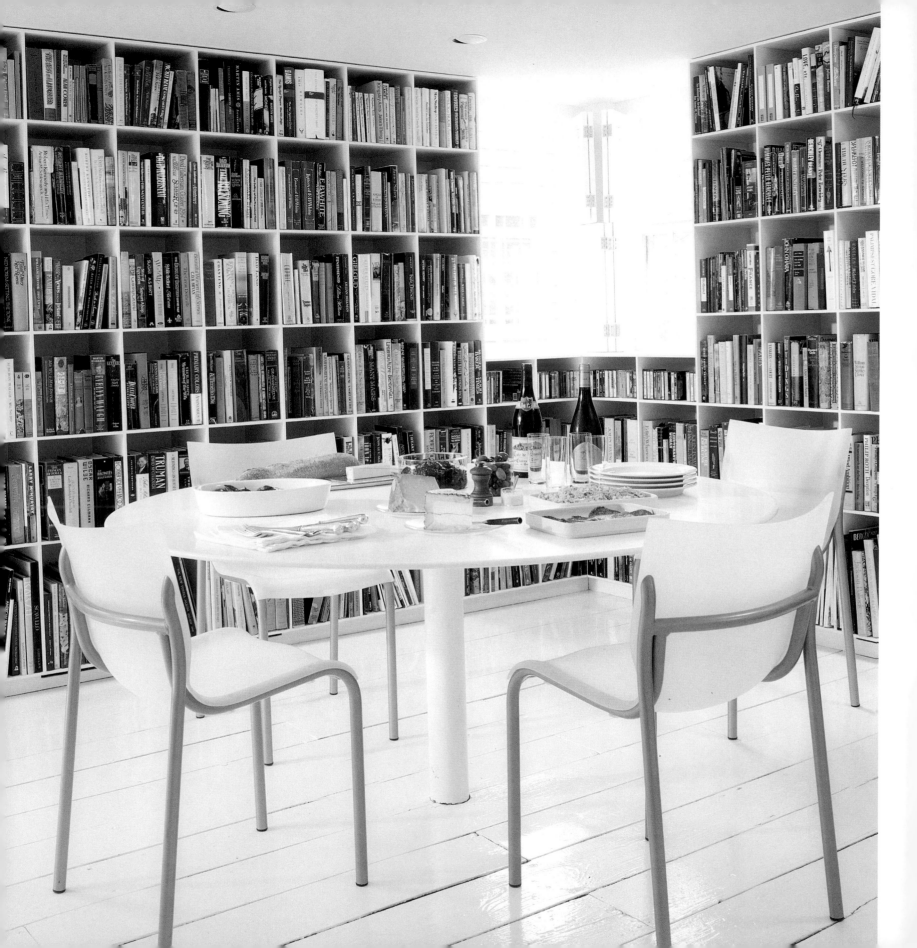

Opposite: The dining room has been outfitted with floor-to-ceiling bookcases. The table, designed by Jacobsen, is surrounded with plastic chairs by Philippe Starck.
Right: The open stairs lead from the dining room to the second floor.

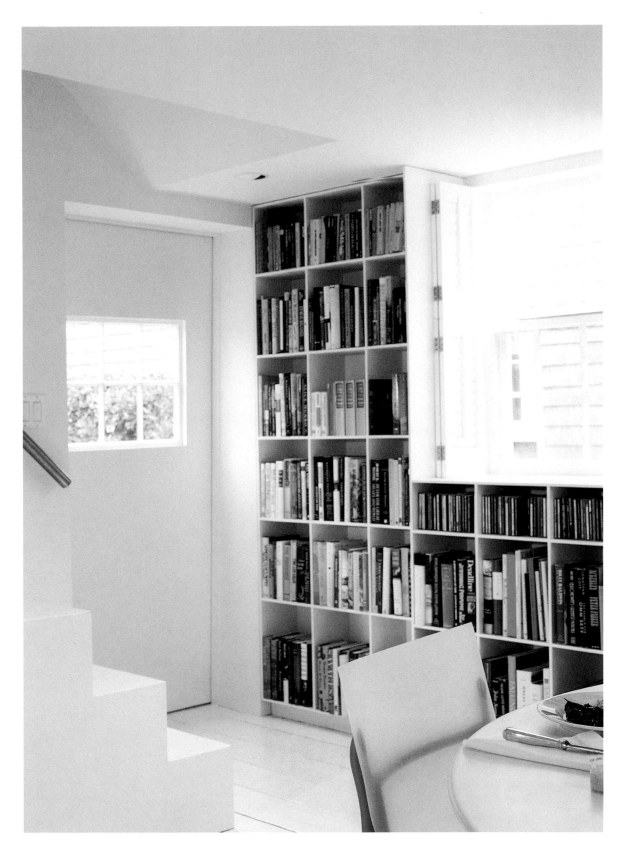

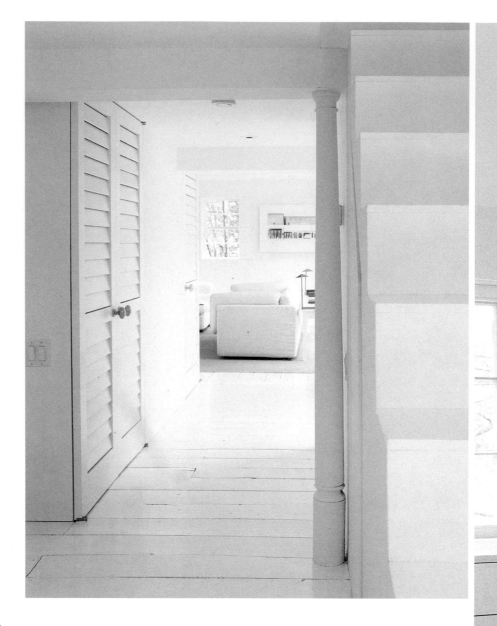

Above: The view from the dining room back into the living room.
Right: The simplicity continues in a restful guest bedroom where the bedding mimics the multi-paned windows.

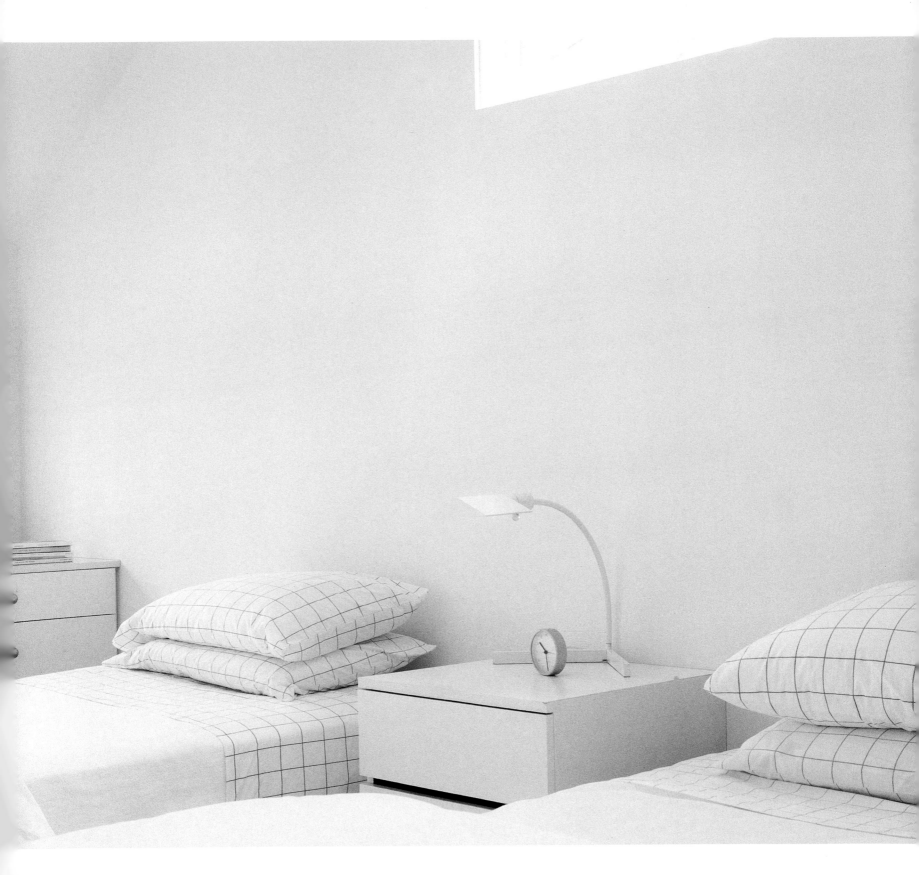

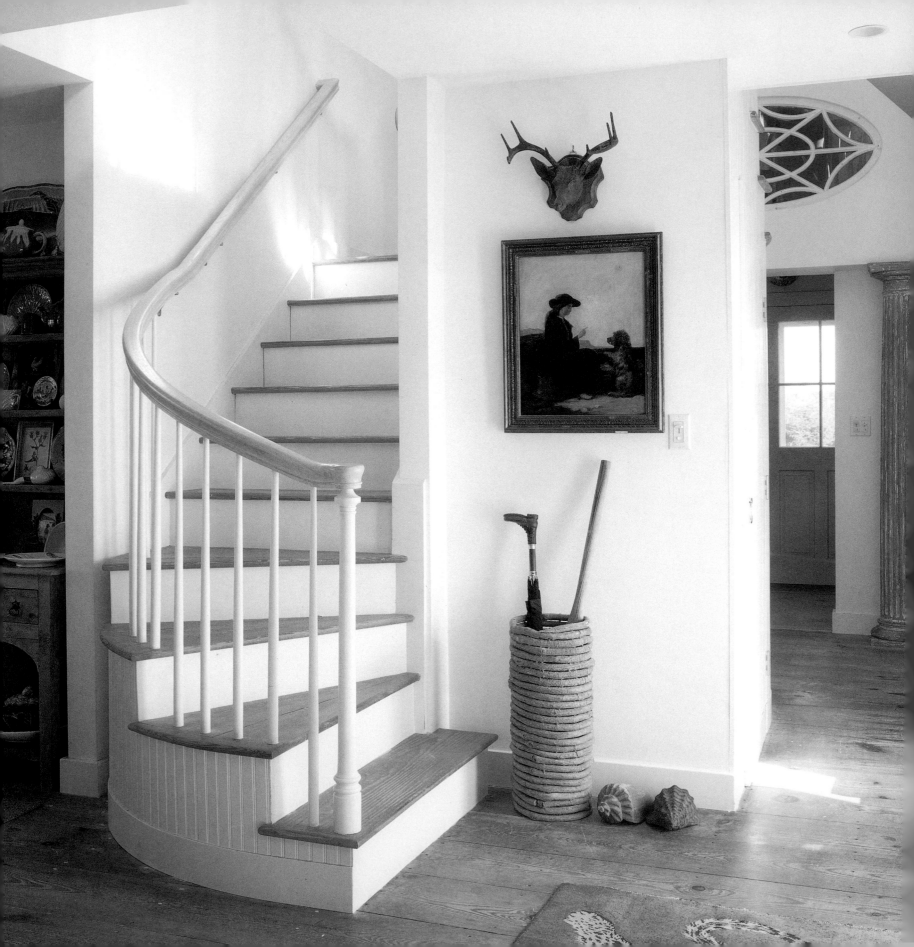

stylish simplicity

At the top of an unassuming shell driveway sits the house of Geo P. Davis, which embraces its visitors with seashore tranquility as soon as they enter. Stepping through the front door, you see the view of a pond and the ocean beyond through the dining room windows. Warm Nantucket light filters throughout the house.

"The house was designed by the sunrise and sunset and the influence from the pond and the ocean," Geo says. "I wanted to incorporate many of my favorite architectural features, and elements such as columns, vents, and molding. Because the site faces northwest, I wanted some morning sun in the kitchen, a big sunny master bath, and a big view from the master bedroom."

Geo's initial plans for the layout of the house came to fruition perfectly. To the right of the front door, toward the back of the house, is the all-white kitchen. In the morning, the sun streams through the windows, and the large island is an ideal spot for a cup of coffee. Just outside the kitchen is the dining room, to which an oval wooden table and rush seats give a natural look. All-white bookcases fill the walls on either side of the stripped-wood fireplace surround.

"The dining room firebox had been set in stone when I went off to England to restock my shop, Weeds [on Centre Street in downtown Nantucket]," Geo says. "I wandered into a favorite shop on Portobello Road to find it was going out of business. As I was leaving, the fireplace surround caught my eye. I bought it with the vague feeling that it was close to the proportions of the existing firebox. It was a perfect fit and set a style for the room." The piece gives the dining room a strong focal point.

Down several stairs to the left of the front door is the spacious, light-filled living room. Here Geo's palette of whites and beiges blend beautifully, mimicking the sandy shores of the island. Two matching white sofas face each other in the center of the room. An old zinc-lined potting table has been given new life as a coffee table. A pair of wing chairs adds texture, and several pieces, such as an antique wooden horse

Opposite: A sensuous curved stairway leads to the second floor. The painting of the girl and dog was picked up in England from the back of a battered Citroën.

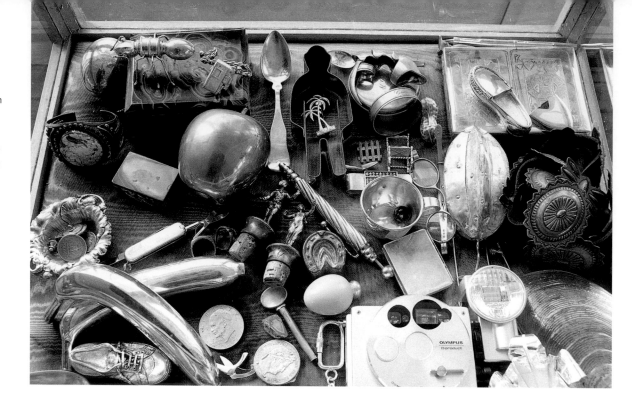

Right: Geo's "magpie" collection.

Opposite: The living room fills with light at the end of the day. An old zinc-lined potting table serves as a coffee table between the two sofas.

and part of an old canoe, add interesting visual elements. In a small glass-covered case is Geo's "magpie" collection of silver objects. "The inspiration came from a gentleman at Sotheby's who had a glass-top display filled with gold objects that had no central theme, other than the precious metal itself," Geo says. "I found a beat-up vitrine and filled it with a lifetime of small silver objects—an Indian belt from my hippie days in Aspen, an Olympus 'O' camera, old coins, silver bananas from Hawaii, stickpins, buttons, and bottle stoppers."

Upstairs in the master bedroom, Geo has a lovely view, looking down on the pond and the ocean. For added connection to the sea, he has two model yachts on stands in the corner of his bedroom. "I love gaff-rig sailboats," Geo says, "particularly large pond yachts that fathers and sons used to sail in park ponds created for just that pastime. They were the Lionel train sets of their day. They didn't whistle, toot, or scare the cat, but they did crash, sink, and need constant

repair. One of mine has its original sails, quilted with patches and tear repairs. They look more like ships with a history than the hybrid models, with their sparkling varnish and protective glass cases." The boat and sailing theme is reiterated throughout the room. Hanging above the bed is a painting of the yacht *Magic* by an English sign painter; sitting above a diorama of a catboat is a porcelain piece of three drunken sailors.

It seems Geo has put together the ideal house for his island life. "I've been a nester all of my life," he says. "I began to understand the principles of a good house from the chapters on the Swiss family Robinsons' construction of their wonderful tree house. I have always chosen to live in places with a wonderful environment over places of easier opportunity or advancement. I love the great beauty of the mountains and sea, joined with seasonal changes, mists, and histories, vistas rather than sprawl. Air over exhaust. Nantucket has always seemed to be the place for me."

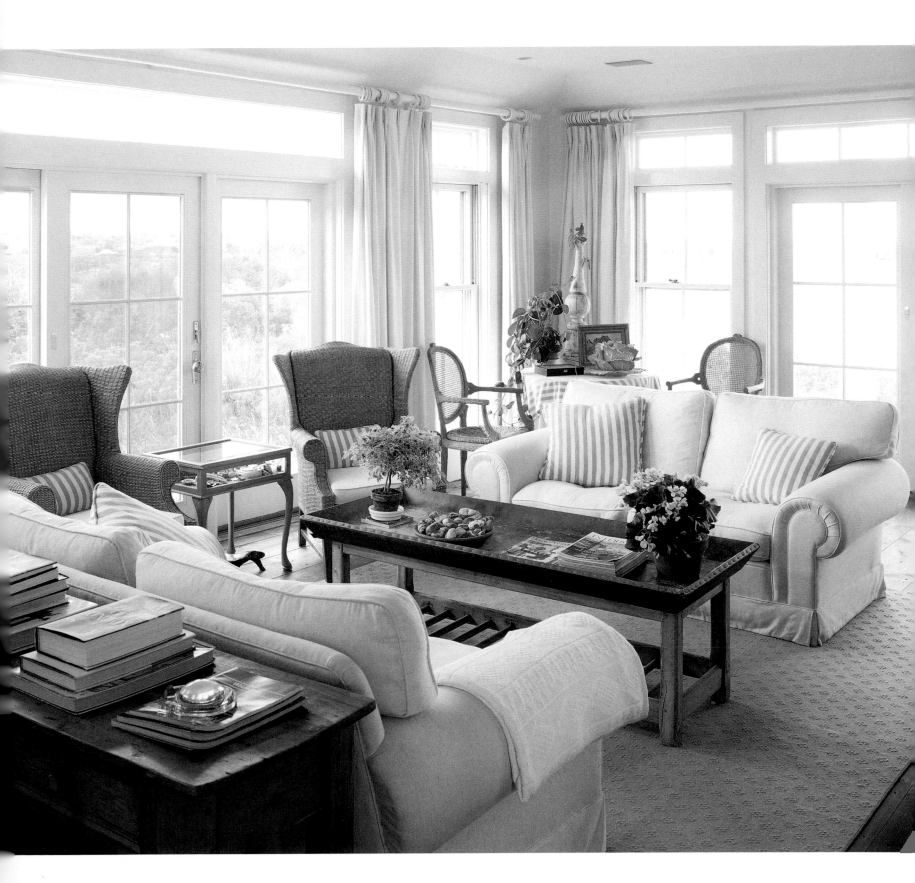

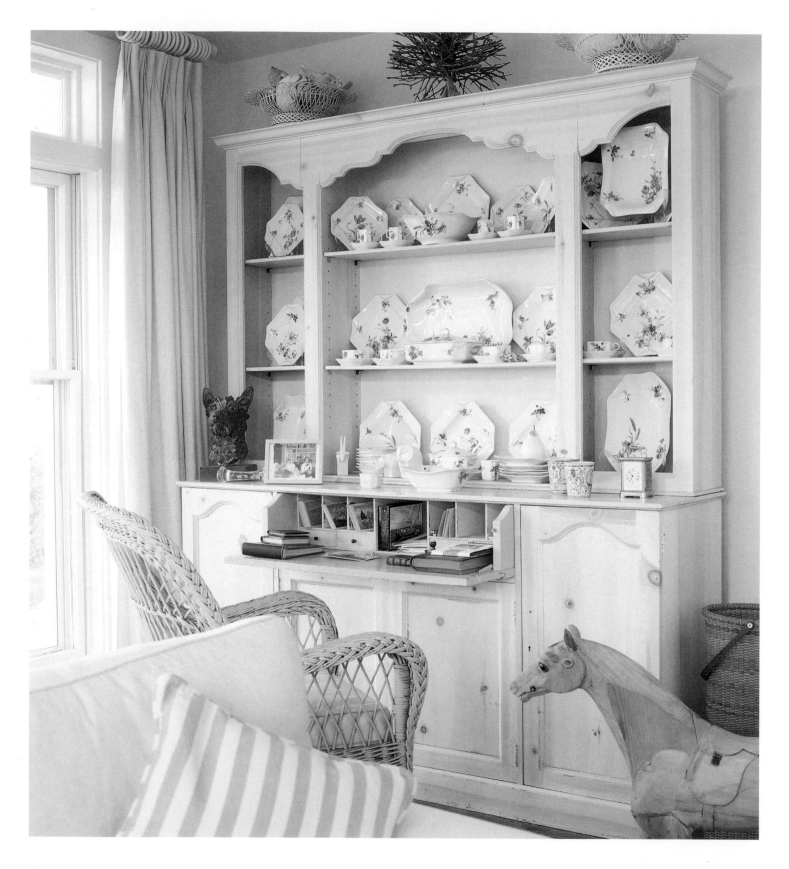

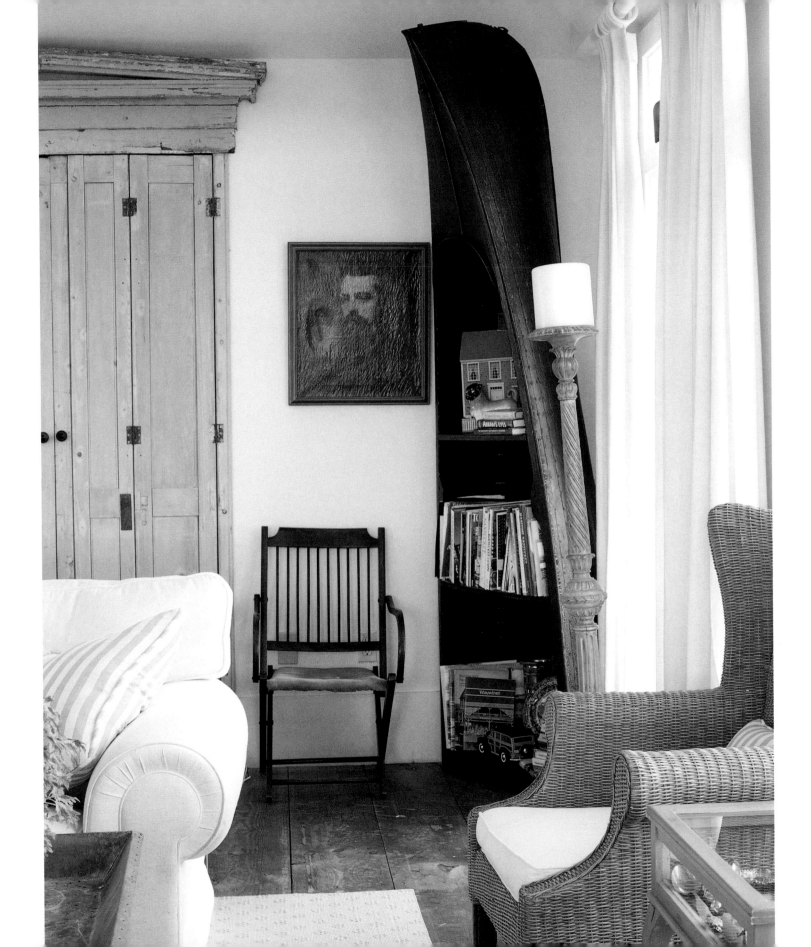

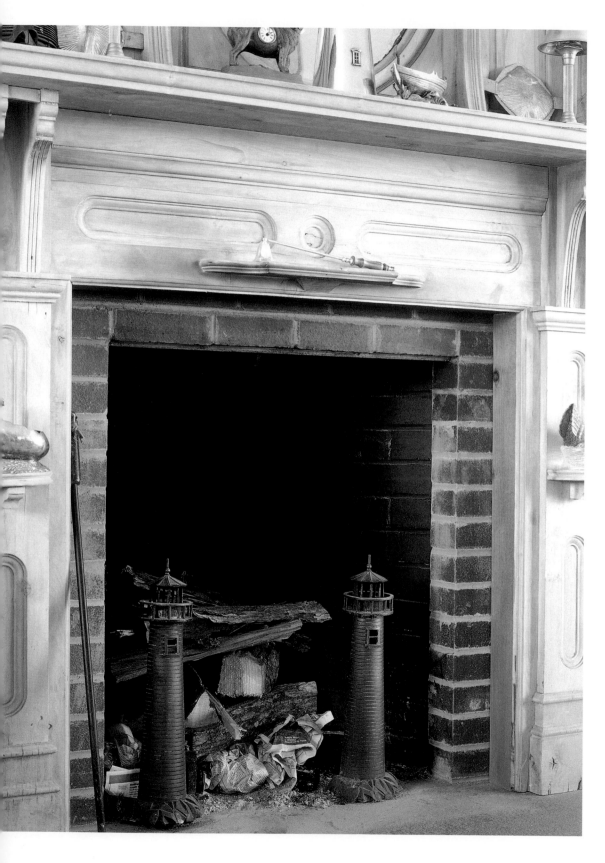

Previous spread, left: Painted by artist friend Bruce Dilts, the secretary in a corner of the living room houses Geo's great-grandmother's collection of Haviland Limoges.

Previous spread, right: Adding visual height, half of an old wooden canoe provides creative storage space for books.

Left: The unusual lighthouse andirons were discovered at a summer island antique show.

Opposite: Just outside the kitchen, an English dresser is filled with a vibrant Majolica collection; the Wedgwood fish platter on top was found for a mere fifteen dollars at a Key West rummage sale.

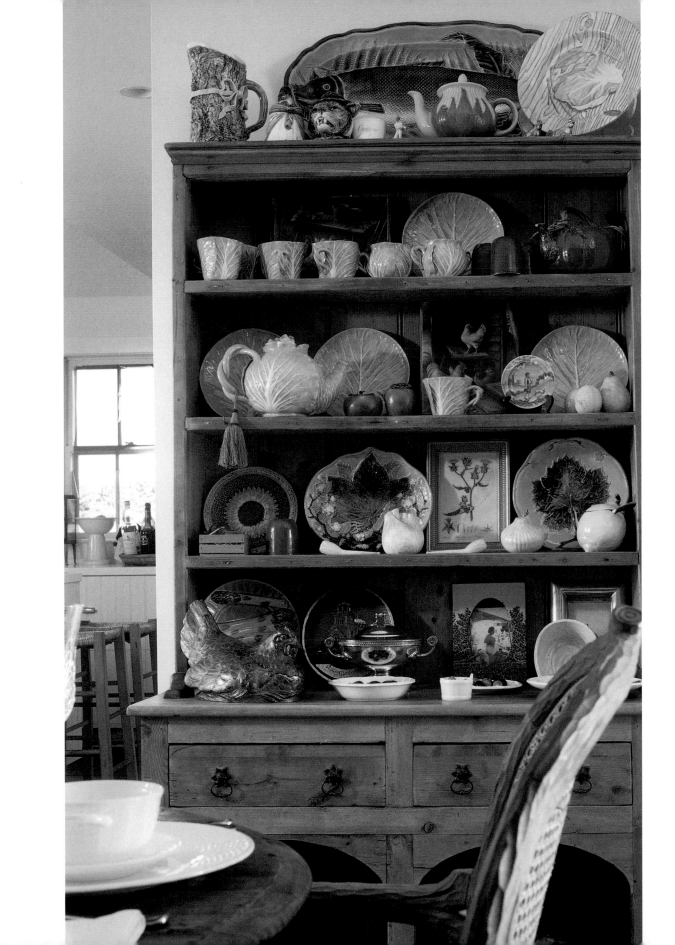

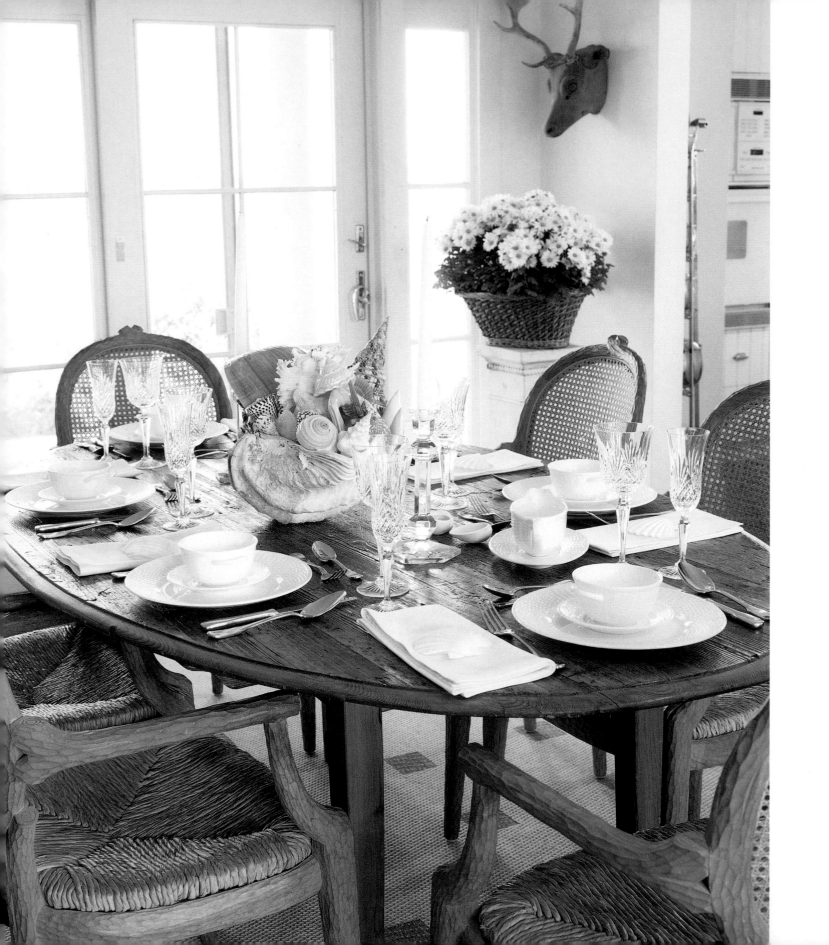

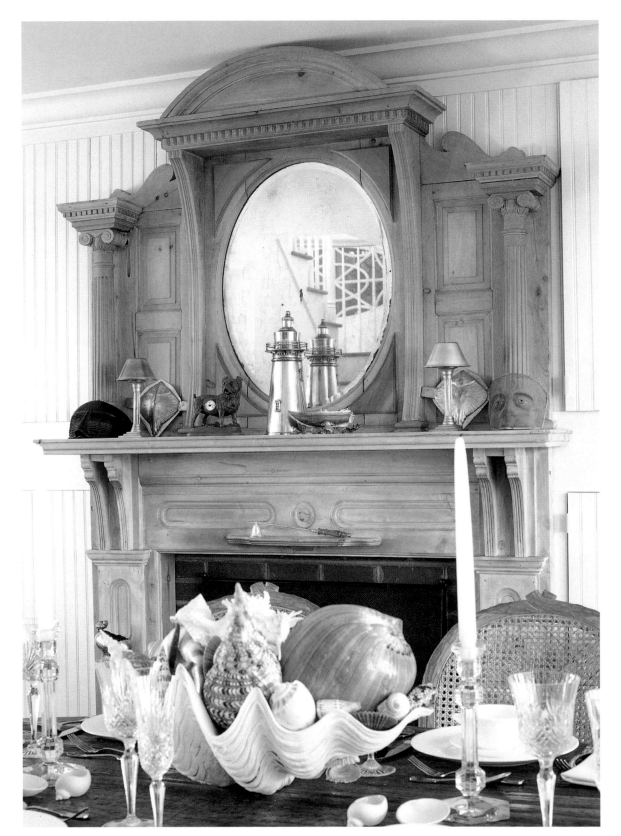

Opposite: The dining table is set with Geo's own Wedgwood "Nantucket Basket" bone china and a large clamshell has been filled with a colorful collection of seashells.
Right: The stunning mantelpiece comes from Portobello Road in London.

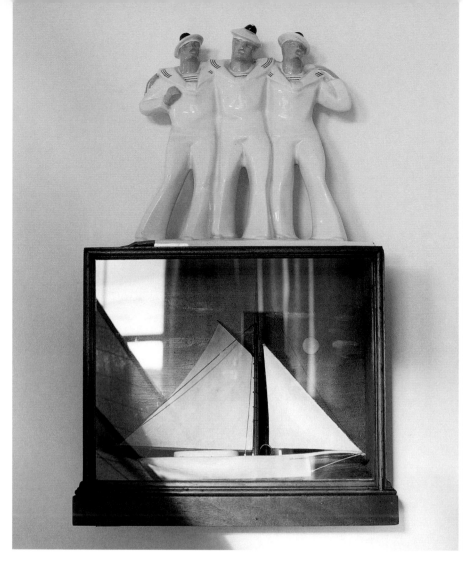

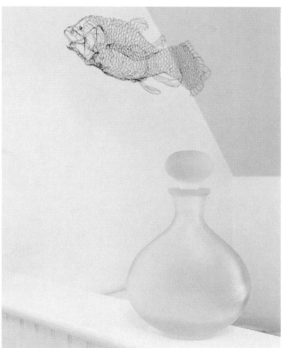

Left: Geo found the trio of drunken sailors in Covent Garden, England, and placed them above the mysterious catboat diorama.
Below: A wire fish floats in the corner of the master bath.
Opposite: The yacht *Magic* sails above the master bed. On a side table a 1950s French swimsuit manufacturer's "surfer dude" advertising figurine dons his own suit; Geo found a new surfboard to replace the lost original.

CASTLES IN THE SAND

In August, the island is filled to capacity. The summerhouses are all rented out, hotels are booked, and reservations at restaurants are in great demand. Nantucket Sound and its surrounding waters brim with sailing and fishing boats, and swimmers and surfers enjoy the waves on the south side of the island. Landlubbers bicycle along the many bike paths or walk the picturesque streets. August is when the island hosts, among other things, its annual Sandcastle and Sculpture Day on Jetties Beach. Since 1973, eager participants have worked side by side all afternoon, creating masterpiece sandcastles and sand sculptures. Ribbons are awarded in various categories, but it is more the spirit of competition and camaraderie that draws participants.

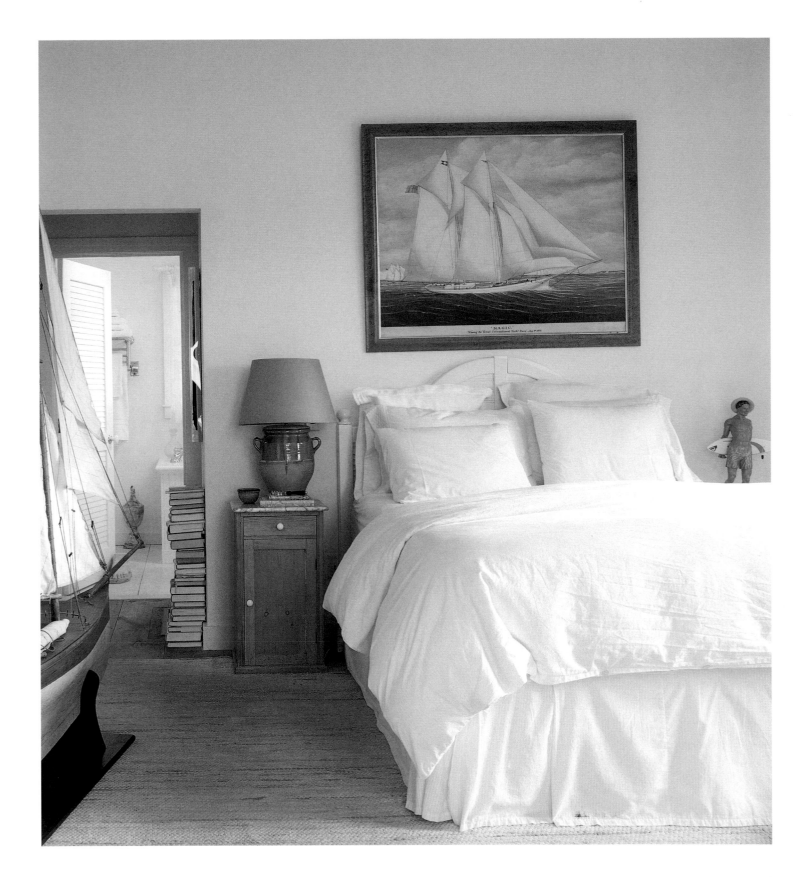

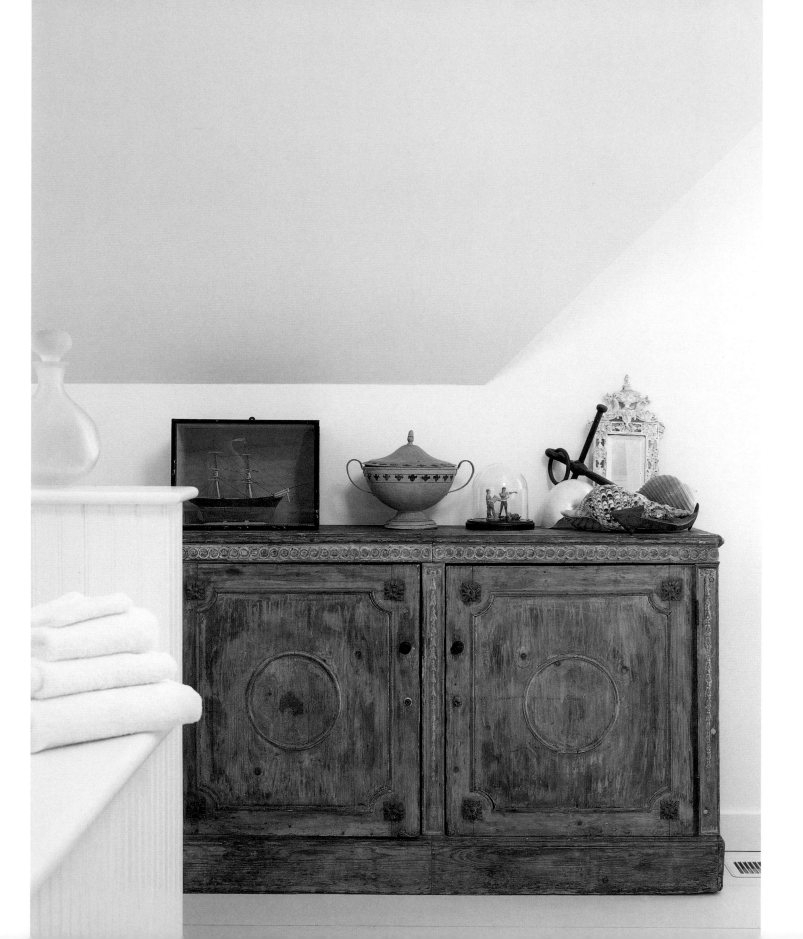

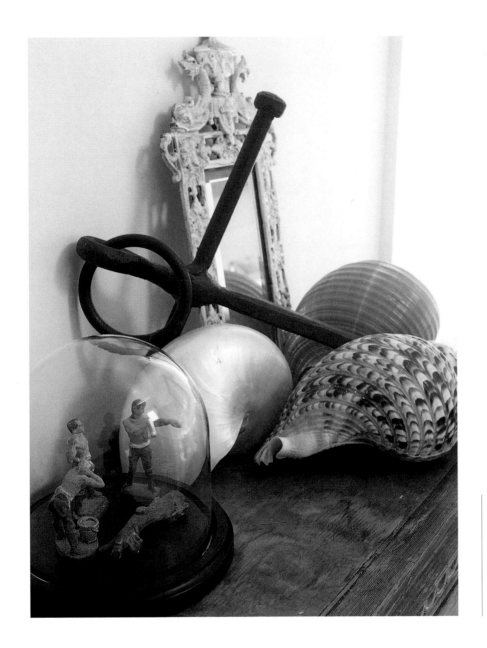

Opposite: In the spacious
master bath a hand-
painted cupboard pro-
vides storage for towels.
Left: Three bathing figures
stand under a glass dome
in a still life on the bath-
room cupboard.

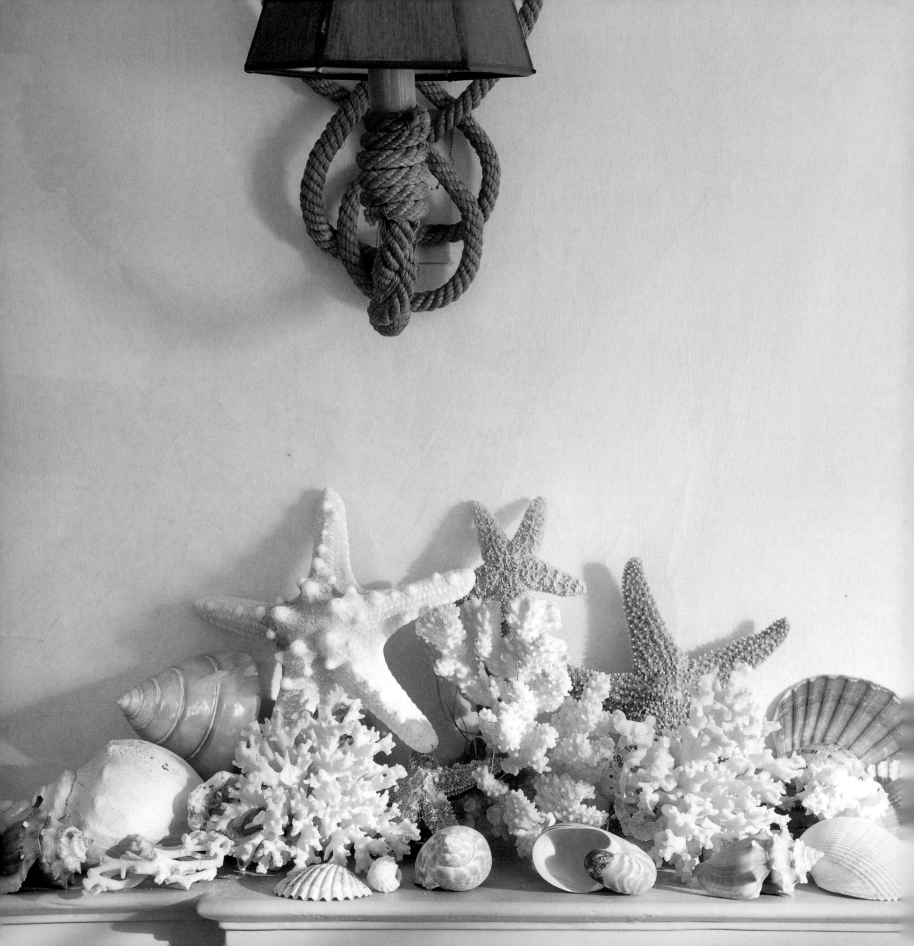

chapter three:
autumn

Autumn brings a much-welcomed calm following the busy summer months. Although tourist season lingers well into October, the crowds begin to thin after Labor Day. The air gets a slight crispness to it, and the moors and cranberry bogs turn brilliant shades of red and orange. The island celebrates autumn with the opening of scallop season, the annual Chowder Contest, Halloween, Thanksgiving.

Rich with deep fall colors, Connie Umberger's converted horse barn provides a tranquil refuge year-round. Filled with family possessions, her home has a comfortable, time-worn patina. The 1828 cottage of Gary McBournie and Rob Geary bursts with warm colors. Featuring an eclectic mix of furniture and fabrics, each charming room has a personality of its own. Cam and Gardiner Dutton worked closely with their architect and builder to create the perfect home for their family and their art and antiques collections. Cam's birthday falls on Halloween, and their extensive collection of vintage Halloween mementos is always a feature of their annual celebration. On the other side of town, the home of Bill and Susan Boardman is a prime example of successful historic preservation. As autumn gives way to winter, the couple looks forward to a houseful of guests for Thanksgiving dinner.

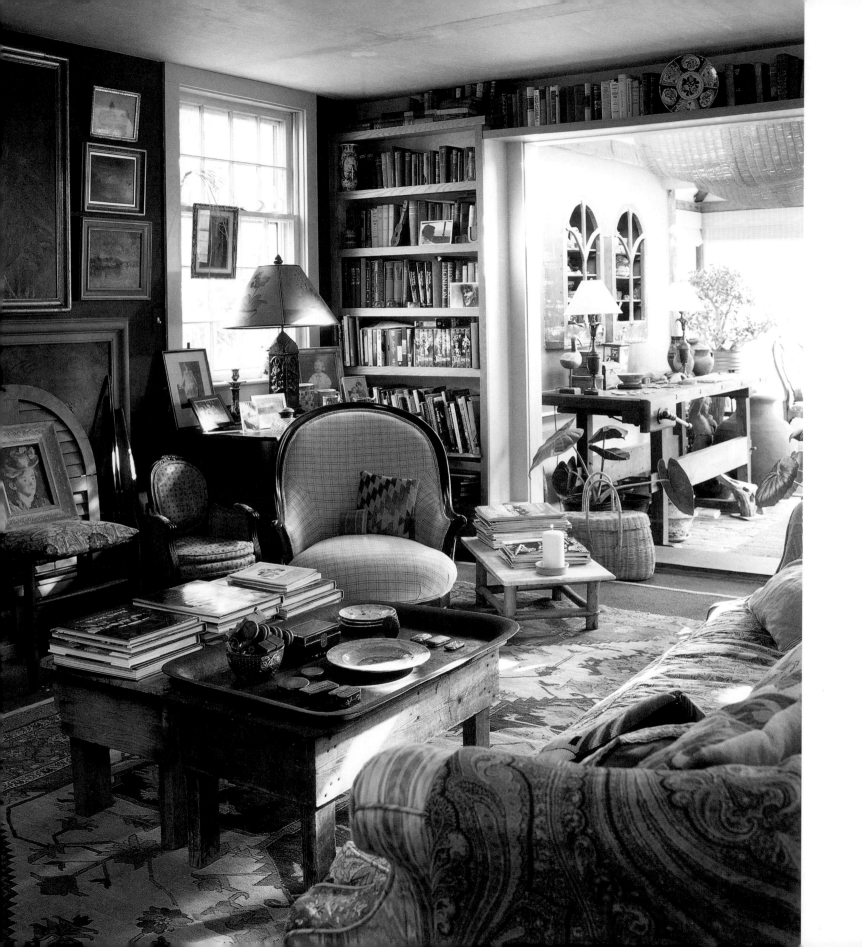

european treasure

Along one of the main routes to the beach, in a house hidden from the road, Connie Umberger has created a haven with a rich, old-European feel. The house itself is a horse barn that Connie bought in 1982 and converted over the course of a year into her permanent residence. With the help of possessions collected by her family over many generations, however, it feels as if it has been around for decades.

Through an arched gateway, a path meanders across a delightful rambling garden to the front door. The entire house is surrounded by a series of gardens, each separated from the other by a fence and gate. It feels as if the house is an island in a sea of gardens that surround and protect it. "I love Nantucket for the climate, seclusion—especially during the off-season—freedom, and distance from the notions and conventions of the establishment," Connie says.

The front door opens into a small foyer, and the kitchen lies just beyond. With simple, open shelves and a large island to congregate around, the kitchen suits the house well. It opens onto the living room, where floor-to-ceiling bookcases fill an entire wall. They are laden not just with books but also with small paintings and other treasured objects. The far wall has been painted black, which, contrary to what one might expect,

gives the room an added aura of warmth and coziness. To add visual richness, the sofa and chaise longue have been layered with pillows and a colorful selection of fabrics. Reds and oranges from the paisley shawl draped over one arm of the sofa and an old kilim rug given new life as a pillow cheer the room with autumn colors.

Off the living room is a sunlit dining wing, which offers a tranquil spot for eating a meal or reading the paper over a cup of tea. Not part of the original home, this addition, added in 2000, has windows on three sides that look out onto the front garden. In fact, the gardens practically surround this wing, reinforcing the feeling of serenity.

Throughout the house, Connie has implemented several inventive ideas to create visual interest, especially above the beds. In a cozy downstairs guest room tucked behind the back

Page 98: Below an unusual rope sconce found in Paris, a meticulous arrangement of shells creates the right balance.
Opposite: The living room is filled with rich, warm colors that bring the Nantucket fall inside. Through the opening is the new dining wing, added in 2000.

Right: On the living room sofa, a whimsical mermaid pillow is a reminder of the important role the sea plays in life on an island. In the back is a pillow made from an old Turkish kilim rug.
Opposite: In the corner of the living room, a chaise longue has been covered with a colorful mix of textiles. On the wall, a portrait of Connie's grandfather, at age twelve, was painted by Frank Fowler.

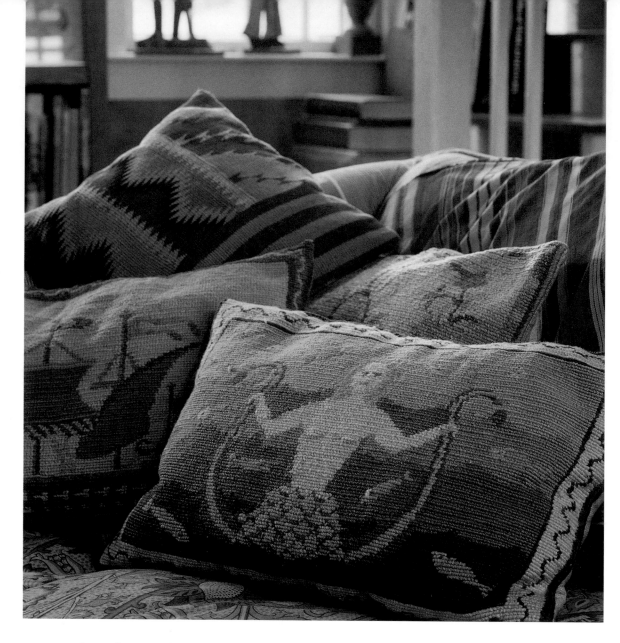

staircase, she took apart a French children's book on the Napoleonic Wars, laid it out from start to finish above the bed, and covered it with Plexiglas to keep it preserved. In the upstairs guest room, with its lofty ceilings, Connie took the canvas off an old wooden screen and hung the bare framework above the bed. This diminishes the effect of the high ceilings and ties the various elements of the room together. Above her own bed, Connie hung a piece of blue-and-white fabric from a dowel. Not only does that

create a greater sense of intimacy, it also tones down the stark white of the slanted ceiling and complements the colors of the bedclothes.

As Connie puts it, her house represents the joyful accumulation of several generations of collectors. No one in her family was ever able to part with anything, so her home has a wonderful lived-in quality that normally would take years to acquire. She has successfully combined the many elements to create a private world, enriched by things that she loves and that inspire her.

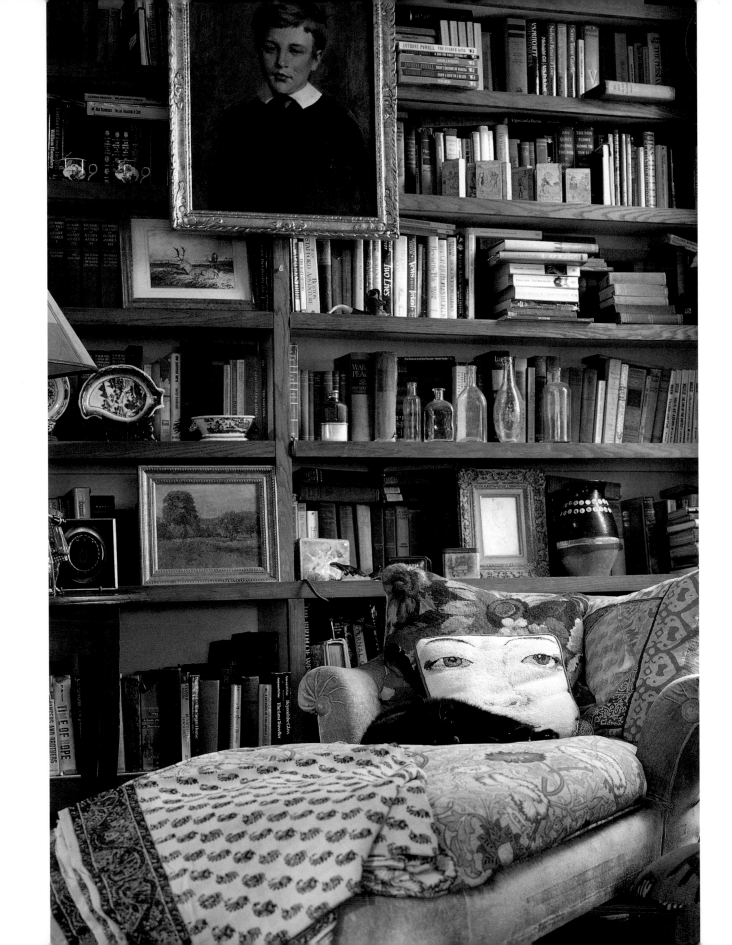

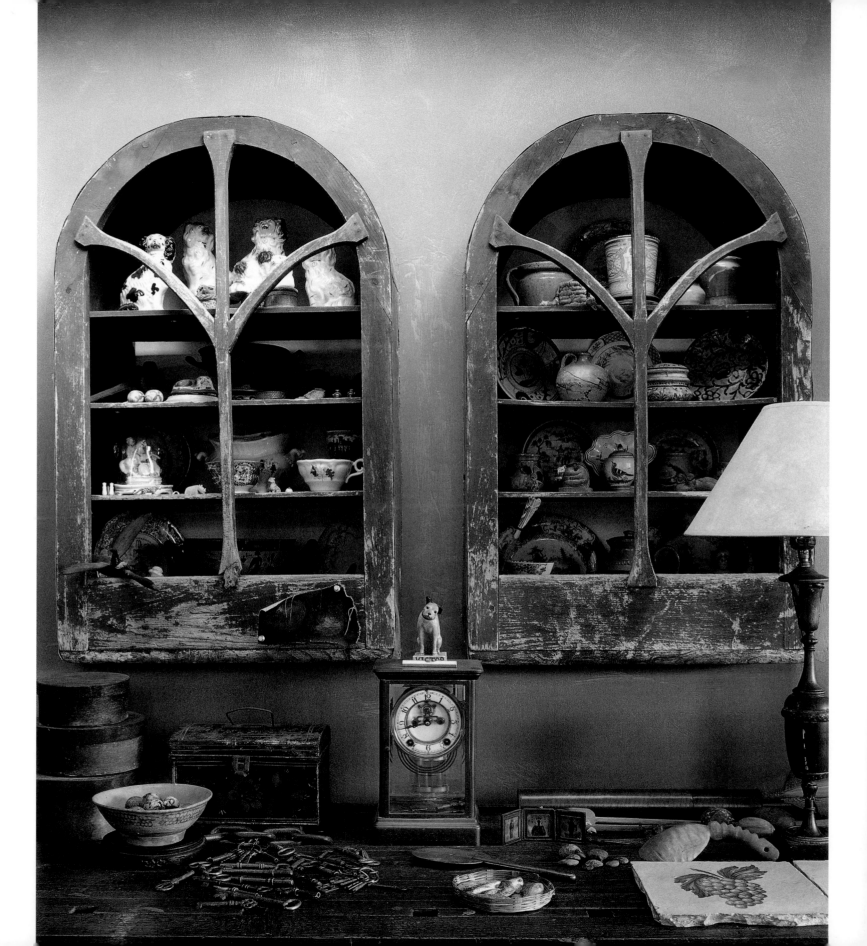

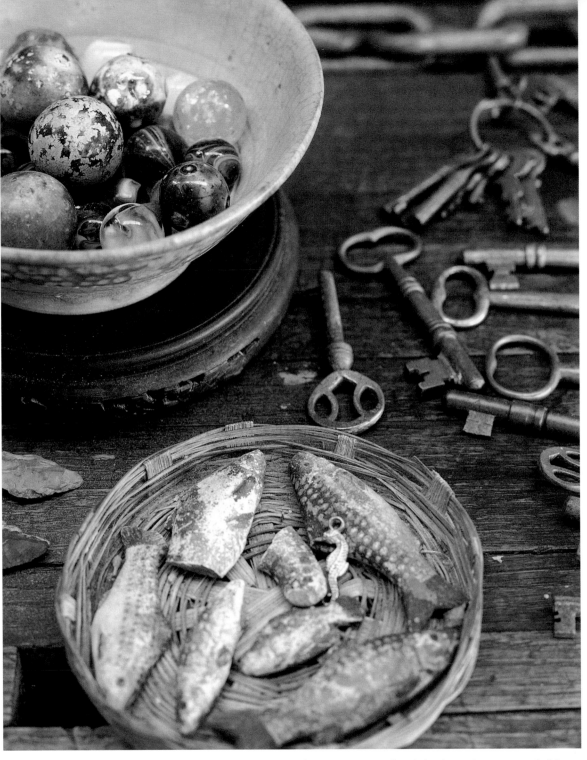

Opposite: A pair of English cabinets houses a wonderful collection of objects such as miniature ivory animals, an old baby rattle, and pottery fragments.
Above: Odd collections of tiny plaster fish, a bowl filled with marbles, and keys from several generations of family houses make for an interesting visual display.

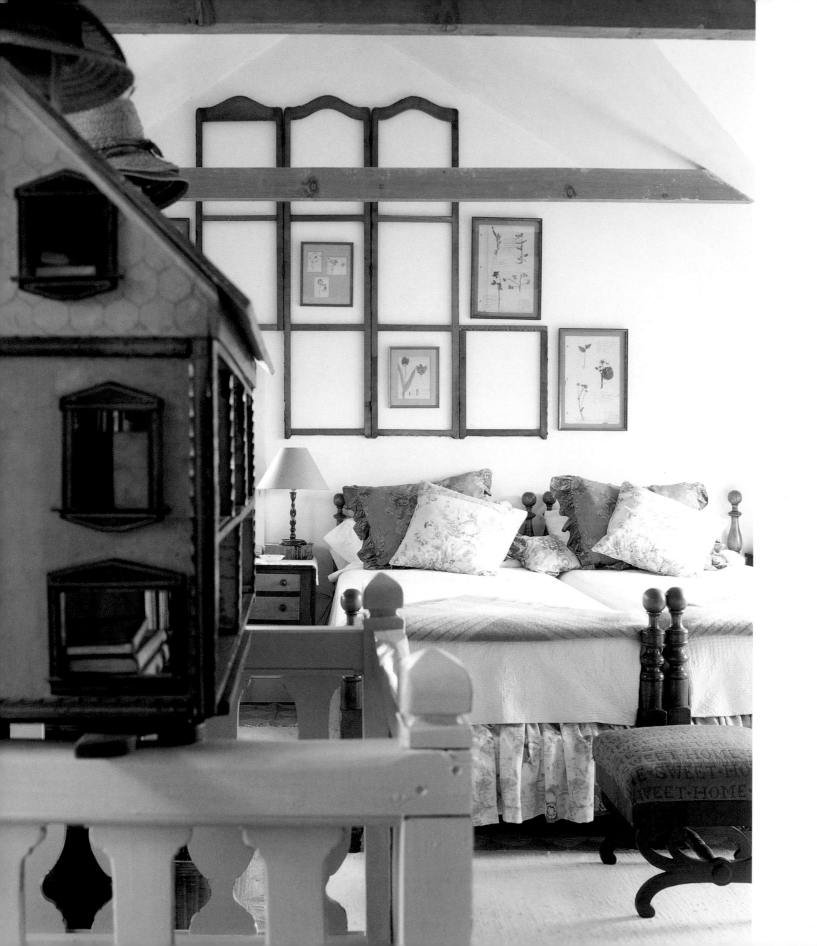

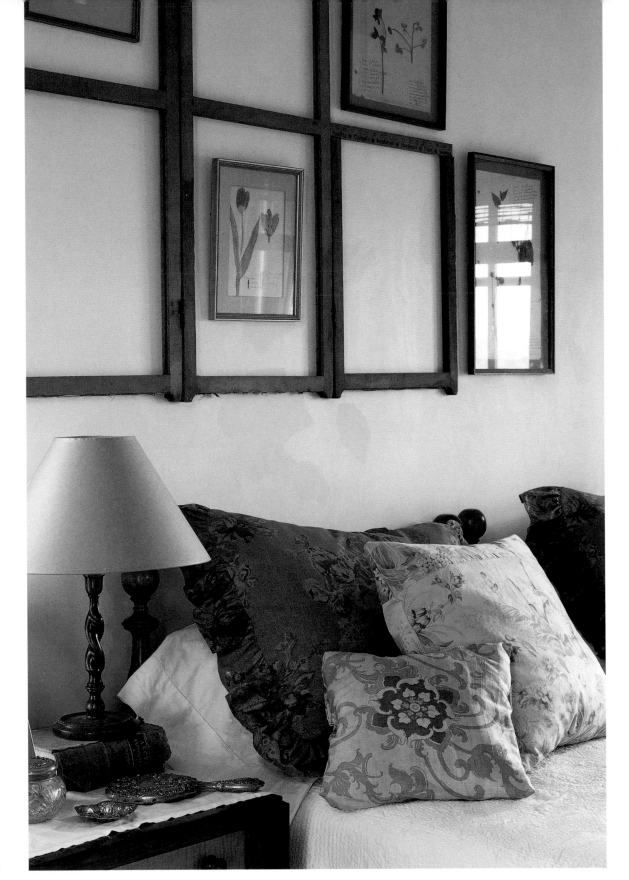

Opposite: In the upstairs guest room, Connie took an old wooden screen, stripped the fabric off, and laid the frame out above the two beds for an interesting focal point. *Right:* Bringing the outdoors in, in the space above the beds, Connie hung pressed botanicals and watercolors painted by her great grandmother.

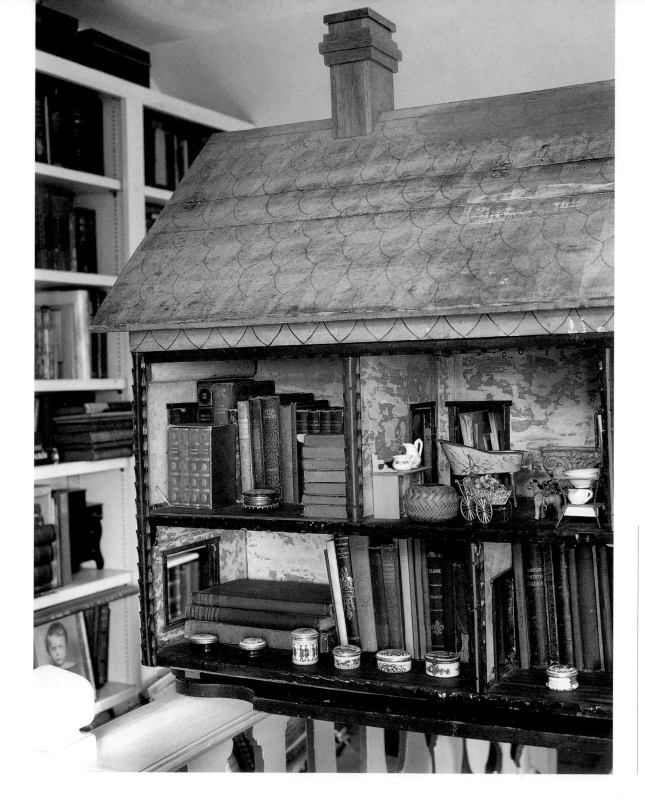

Left: The dollhouse was made for Connie's sister by their grandfather. It now offers ideal storage for small books and enameled boxes from halcyon days.

Opposite: To create a more intimate space in her bedroom, Connie hung simple blue-and-white fabric from a dowel on the sloped ceiling. It coordinates with the old batik sarongs used to upholster the headboard.

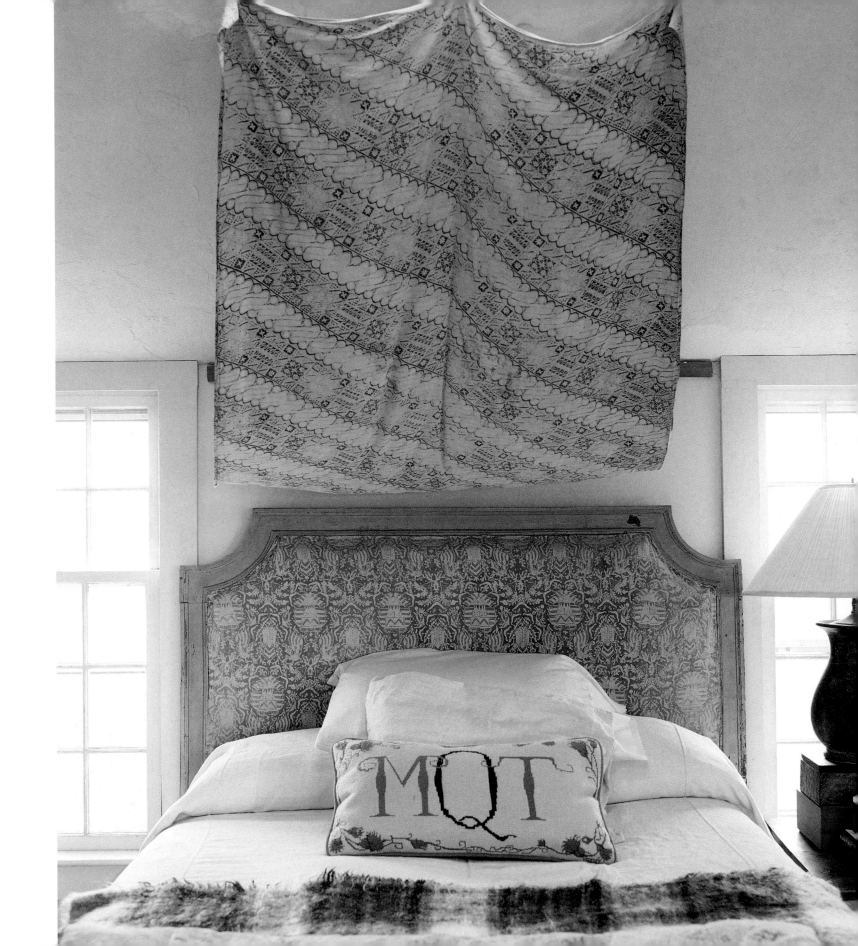

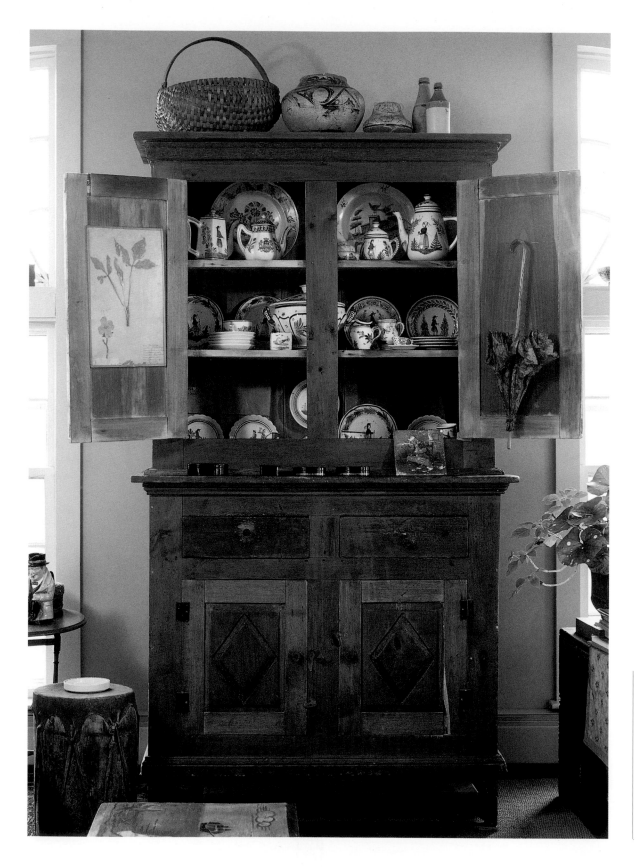

Left: In a large upstairs room that houses Connie's office, a cupboard displays a beautiful collection of French Quimper ceramics.
Opposite: Gold pocket watches hang under glass domes and an Austrian cow pull-toy stands behind.

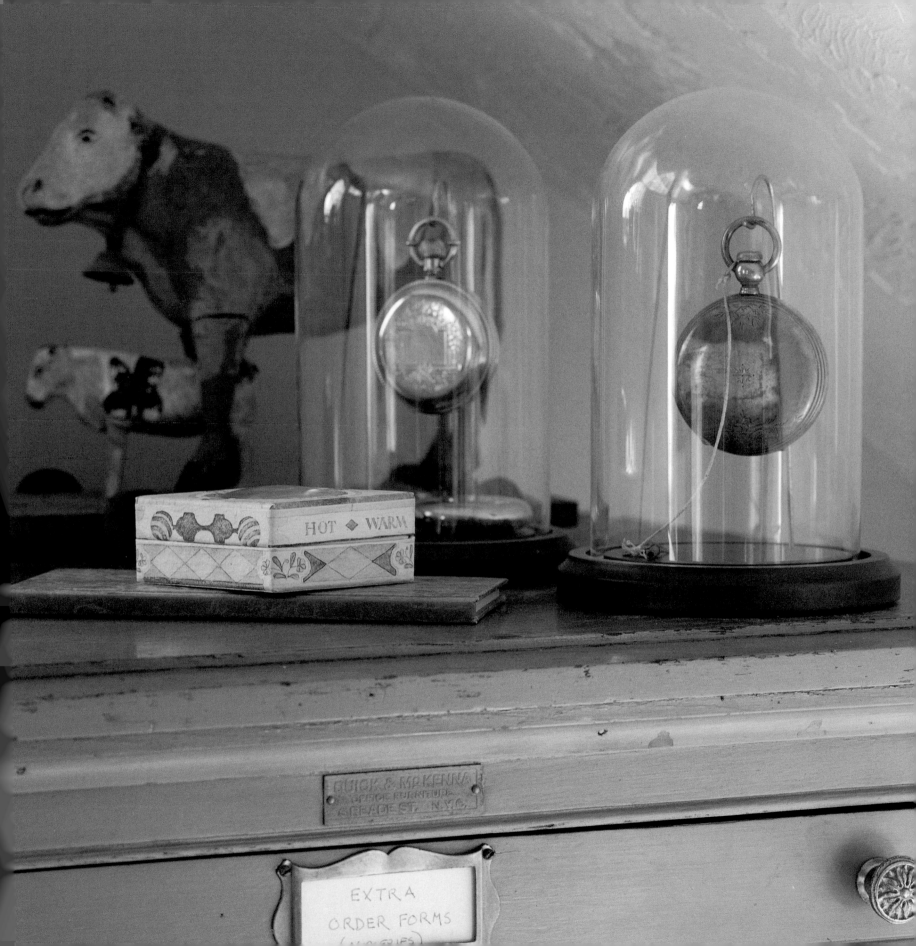

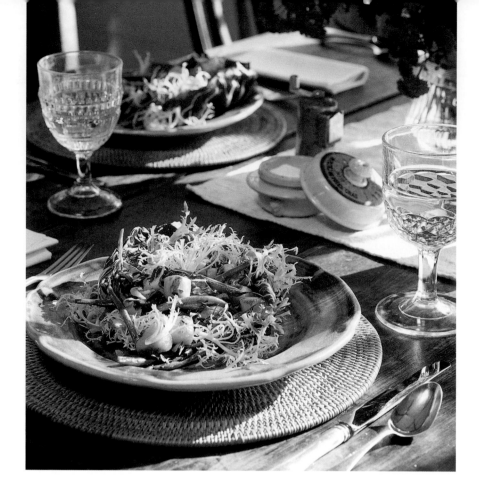

Seared Bay Scallops with Frisée

When scallop season opens at the beginning of October, local restaurants feature this delicacy in their dishes. Jaime Hurley, the chef at the West Creek Café, on West Creek Road near the main rotary, created this delicious dish of seared bay scallops served over a frisée salad. It is light yet hearty and ideal for lunch or dinner.

1 pound trimmed haricots verts (green beans)

1 head each frisée and radicchio, separated into leaves

1 tablespoon olive oil

¹/₂ pound Nantucket bay scallops

Salt and freshly ground pepper to taste

¹/₃ cup sliced almonds, toasted

4 tablespoons butter

Juice of 1 lemon

1. Blanch the haricots verts in salted boiling water, then cool quickly in ice water; drain and set aside.

2. Wash frisée and radicchio in cold water and spin dry. Separate some of the larger leaves of the radicchio to make cups to hold the finished dish. Thinly slice additional leaves and add them to the frisée. Set aside.

3. Heat the olive oil in a sauté pan until it's very hot, about two minutes. Season scallops with salt and pepper, add to pan, and sear for a minute on one side. Add haricots verts and toss for a minute, to heat the beans.

4. Add almonds and butter. Cook for a minute or two, until the butter melts and begins to brown a little. Add lemon juice and season to taste with more salt and pepper if necessary. Add the hot items to the frisée mixture, toss together, and serve in the radicchio "cups."

Serves 2

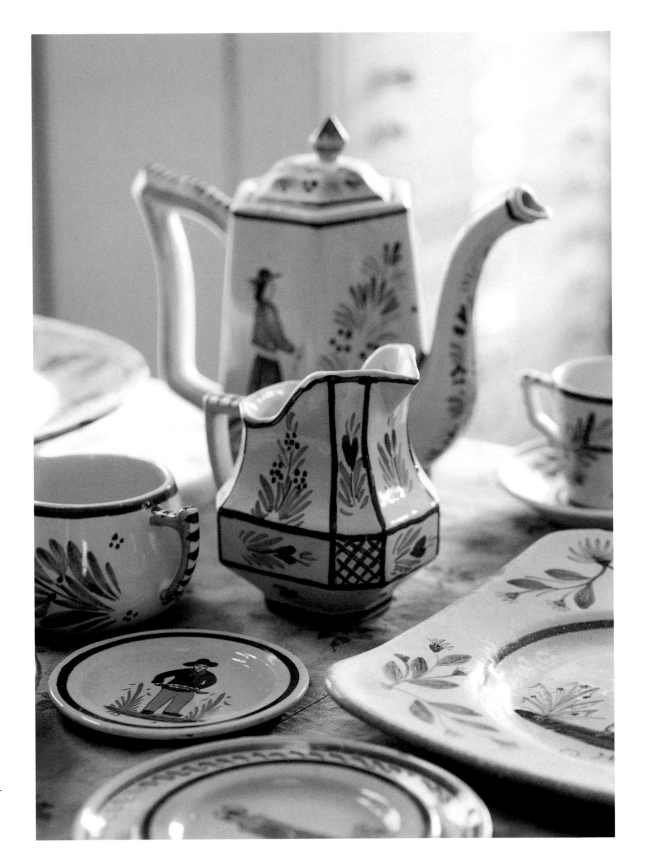

Right: Favorite pieces from Connie's forty-year-old Quimper collection sit on top of a trunk in her office.

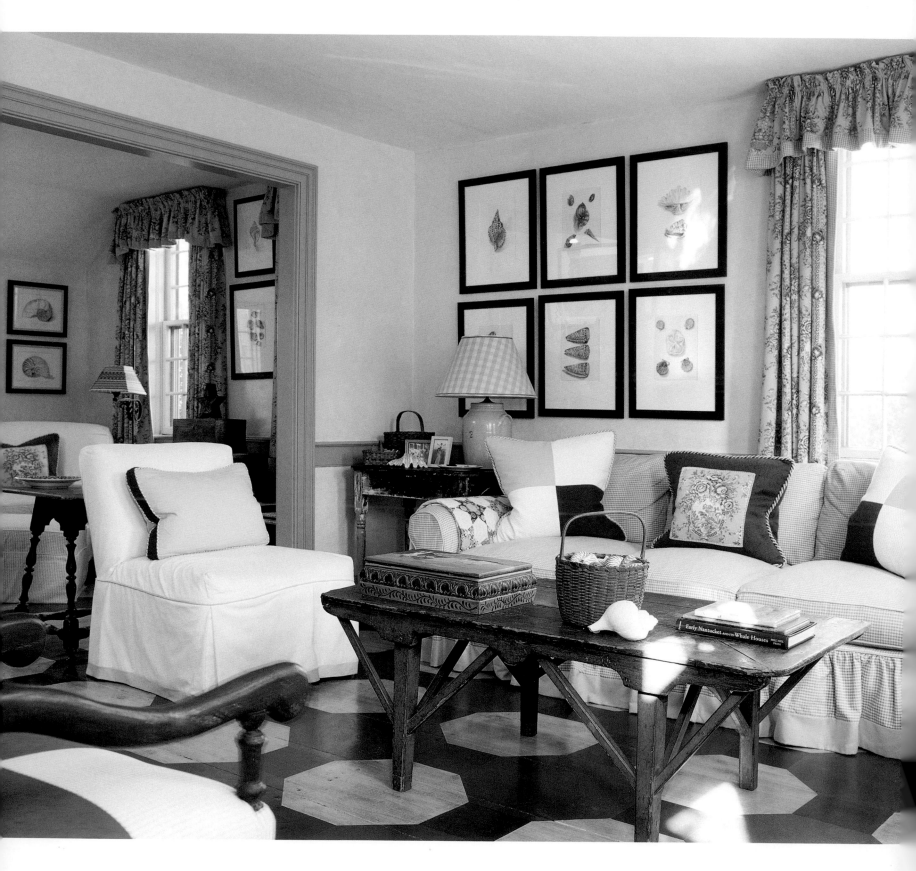

AT HOME IN NANTUCKET

painted cottage

Near the center of town, on a quiet side street, Gary McBournie and Rob Geary have transformed an 1828 cottage into an idyllic retreat. Deceptively small when viewed from the front, the house rambles back from the street in a series of charming rooms.

Gary, an interior designer, didn't want the house to feel too much like a beach cottage, and he especially did not want it to be too fussy. With that in mind, he used an eclectic mix of French furniture and fabrics accompanied by flea-market finds to create an American look with a European feel.

Color is an important element throughout. In the living room, at the front of the house, Gary added saffron, yellow, and red with curtains, throw pillows, and even the floor, on which, over several long weekends, he and Rob painted a geometric design. The dining room, across the front foyer, has mustard-yellow plaid fabric upholstered onto the walls. A series of thirty-four French bird engravings by Martinet fill much of the wall space in the room.

The kitchen, between the public rooms and the private master suite, has a blue-and-yellow color scheme. A collection of blue-and-white English china complements the vivid yellow woodwork. Again the floorboards have been painted, this time in black and white checks. Outside the kitchen's side door is a spacious deck, which in the warmer months becomes an outdoor room for entertaining. A raised trellis runs along one side, providing much needed shade, and an umbrella and yellow cushions with blue stripes lend a boost of color.

At the back of the house is the master suite, where the dominant color also is blue. The room is calm and peaceful, with simple furnishings. Natural-wood blinds hang on the windows, accompanied by long white panels. A nineteenth-century hand-painted bureau, found in Paris, has an effective antiqued patina, and on the walls on either side hang a series of twelve sailors' valentines, which Gary made himself, modeled on the traditional art form.

Opposite: The living room wall features a series of watercolors painted by Gary. Warm colors in the curtains and throw pillows fill the room with cheer. Gary and Rob painted the floor over several long weekends.

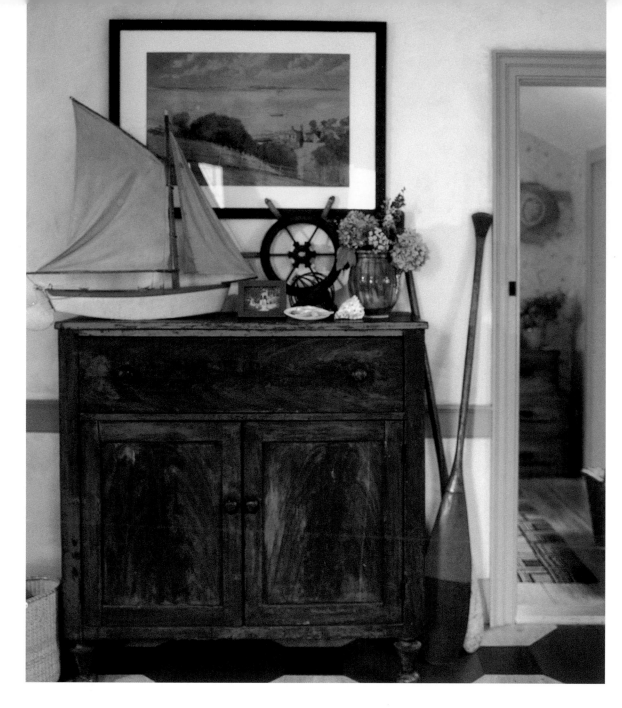

Left: On top of a nineteenth-century cupboard sits a vintage pond boat. Above it hangs a John Harlow painting of Gloucester Harbor rom the 1920s.

Opposite: Above the fireplace hangs one of Gary's watercolors. The chair to the left is a Dutch piece from the seventeenth century and the delightful shell side table in the foreground was discovered in a shop in West Palm Beach.

The colors and furnishings suit the cottage year-round, so Gary and Rob, who spend most of the summer in the house, also take advantage of it on long weekends and during the off-season. Gary says, "We like being away from the mainland, in an island setting. It's friendlier and warmer than life on the mainland."

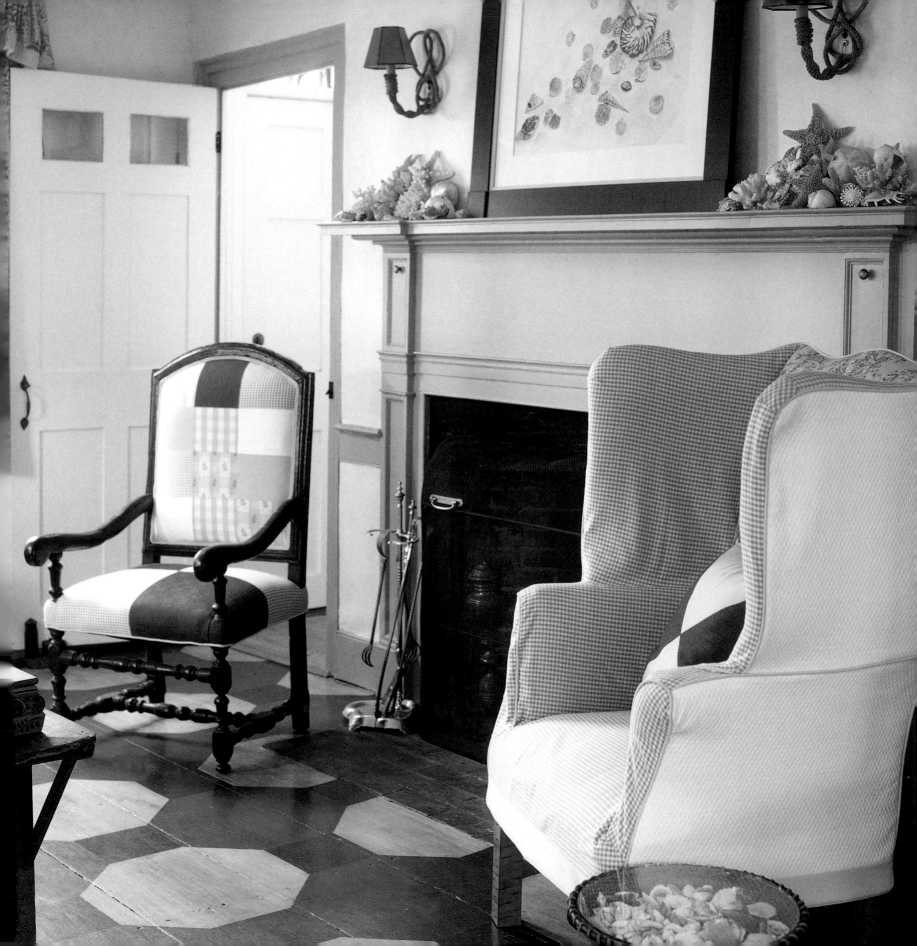

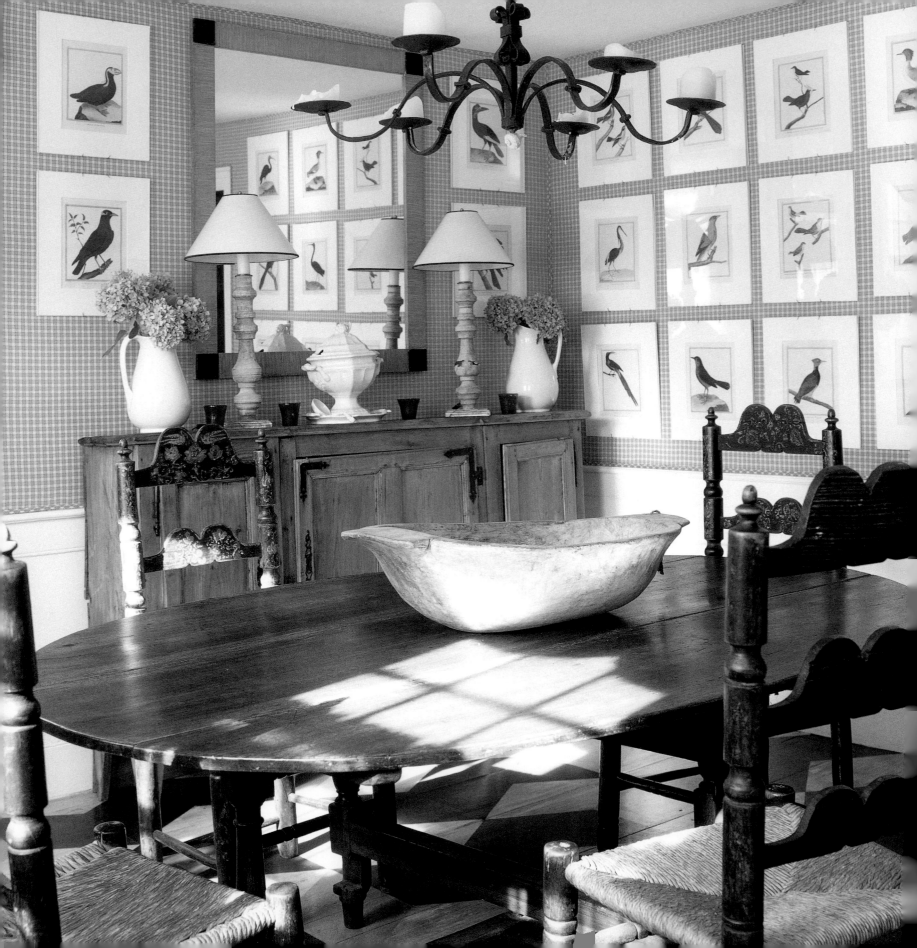

Opposite: A series of French bird engravings by Martinet hang in the sunny dining room. They are part of a larger series that Gary bought and used in a client's house. *Right:* A detail of the fabric-covered walls shows the basic edging used to finish off the look. Paired with the engraving behind, a jug of fresh hydrangeas creates a simple still life.

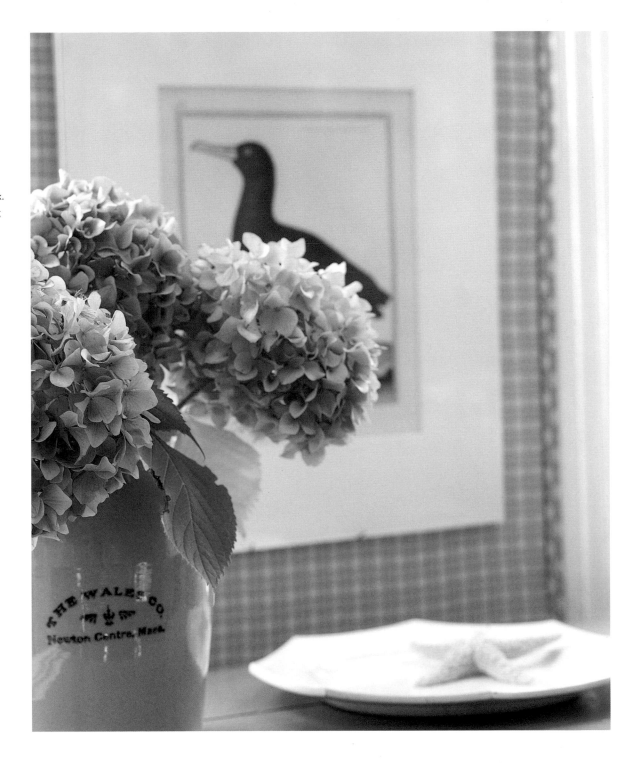

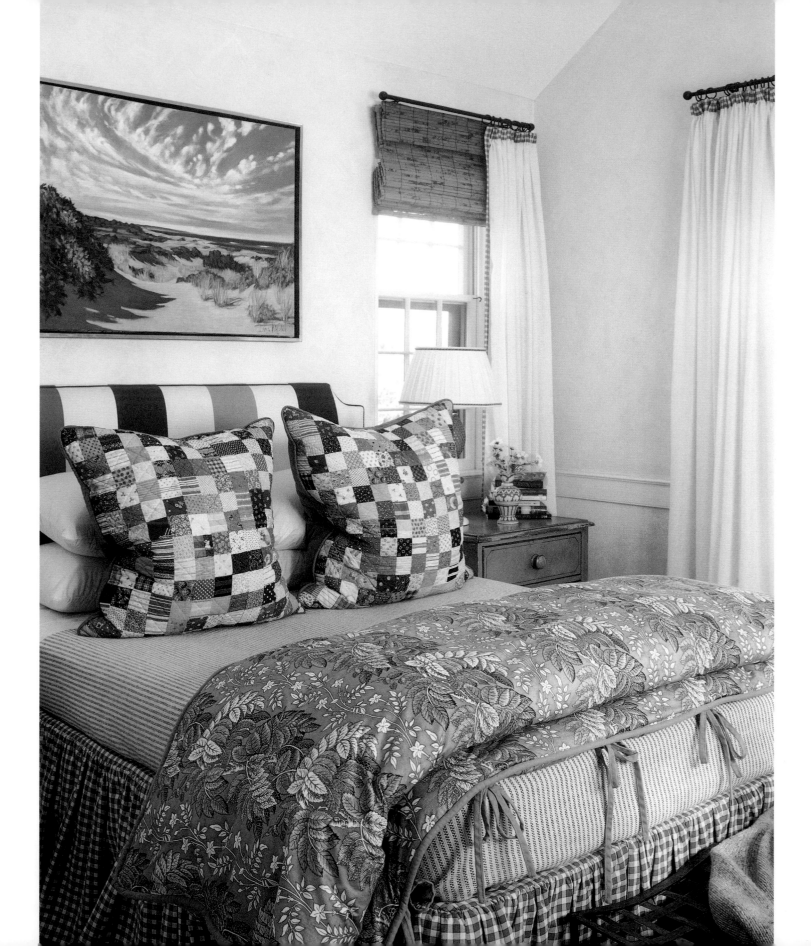

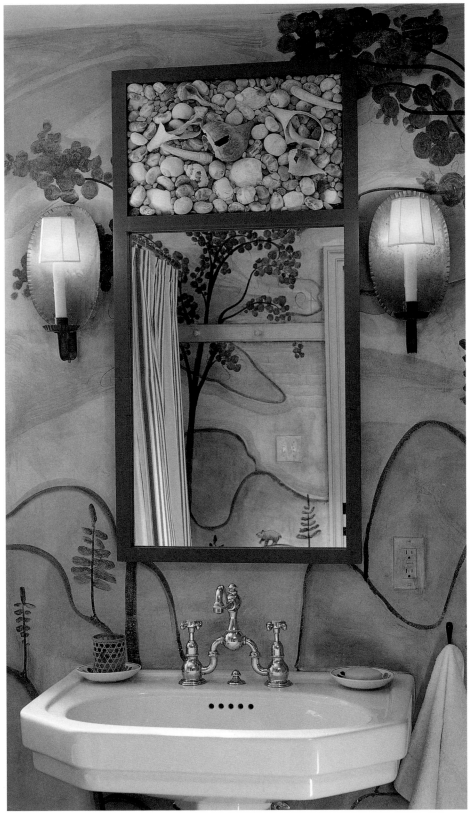

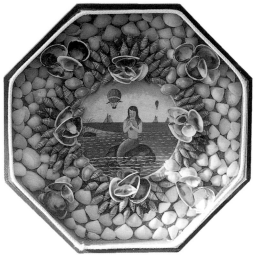

Opposite: In the master bedroom, a painting by local artist Illya Kagan hangs above the bed. The room is infused with the color of the ocean; simple window treatments using bamboo shades and white curtains keep the look clean.

Left: In the bathroom, artists Kevin Paulsen and David Wiggins painted the whimsical mural. Gary created the mirror by hot-gluing rocks and shells found on the island into the decorative top. *Above:* Armed with his glue-gun, Gary completed the intricate design on this sailor valentine.

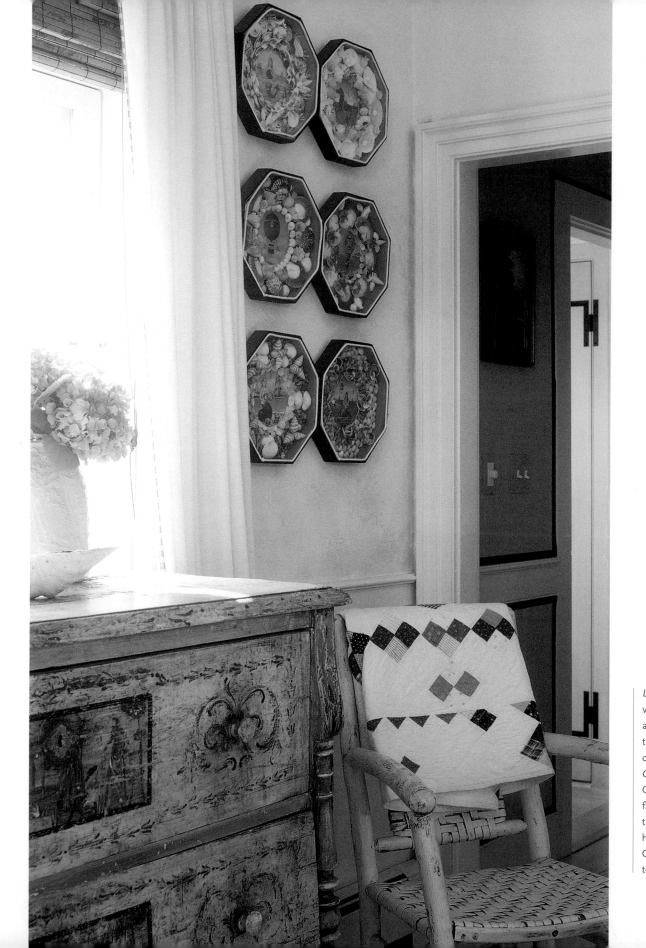

Left: Six of twelve sailors' valentines Gary created adorn a corner wall; on the chair lies an American quilt from the 1930s. *Opposite:* In the kitchen, Gary and Rob painted the floor themselves. A collection of English china hangs above the fireplace. Out the door, the deck lies to the right.

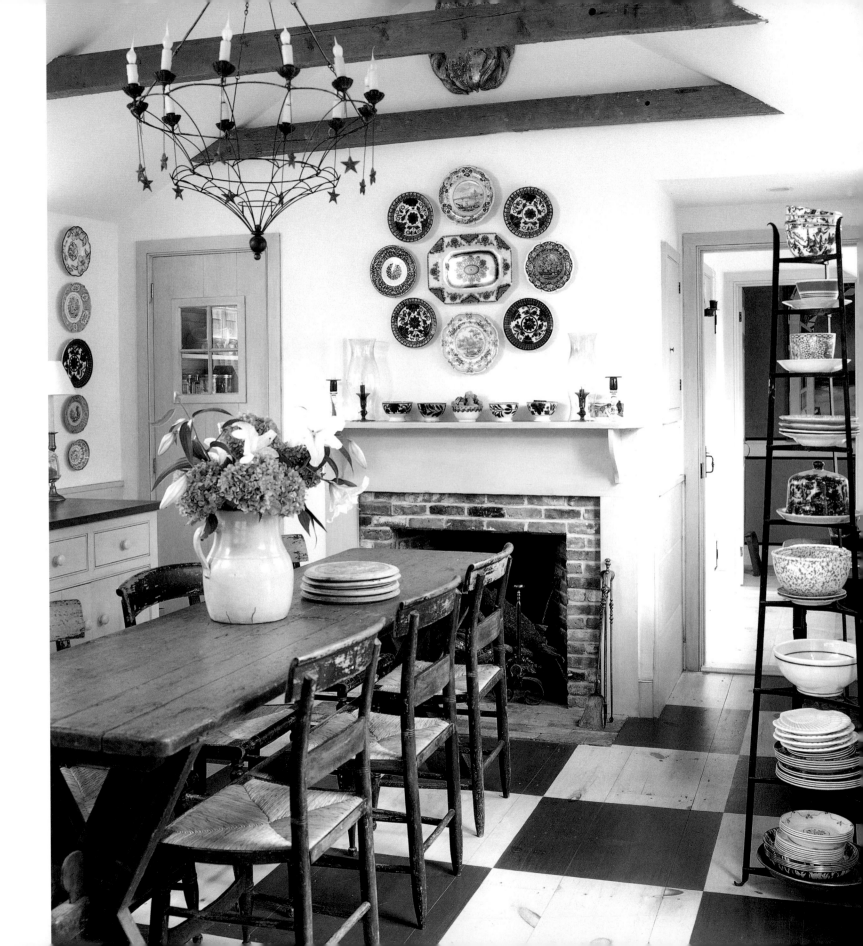

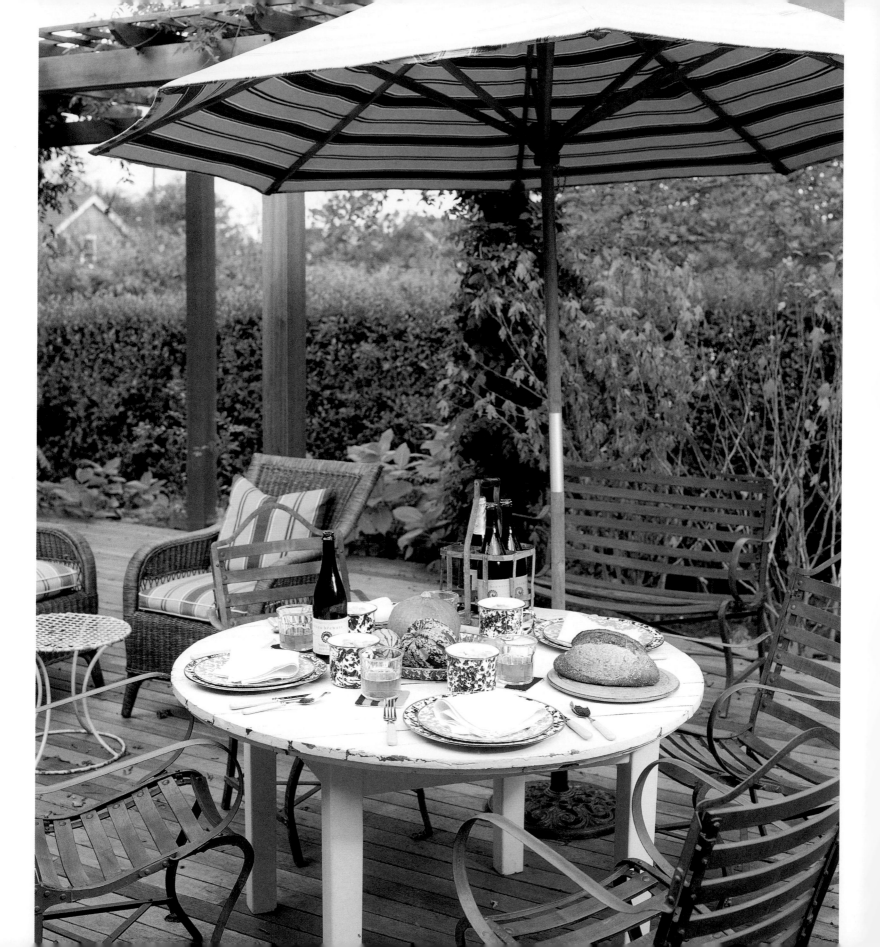

Clam Chowder

One of the great October traditions on the island is the annual Chowder Contest, sponsored by the Nantucket Restaurant Association and the Chamber of Commerce. E.J. and Robin Harvey, owners of the Seagrille since 1991, have won the local competition at least four times. According to E.J., "It's all in the clam. The type of clams that are used on Nantucket are called quahogs, which are round, thick-shelled mollusks. I never use sea clams, ocean clams, frozen or canned clams. They will impart totally different flavors to your chowder. Those flavors might be all right in the Midwest, or some other landlocked area, but they will never work in New England."

Seagrille Quahog Chowder

Note: The quahogs intended for this recipe are the size of a softball. Littleneck or cherrystone clams can be used—just adjust the quantity to end up with about 12 ounces of chopped clams.

12 quahogs

4 1/4 cups water

3 raw slices bacon, minced

11 tablespoons unsalted butter

3/4 cup Spanish white onions, diced

2 tablespoons celery, diced

1 teaspoon thyme

4 tablespoons all-purpose flour

2 cups heavy cream

2 pounds cooked russet potatoes, diced in approximately 1/2 -inch cubes

2 bay leaves

2 teaspoons Worcestershire sauce

Salt and freshly ground pepper to taste

1 tablespoon paprika

1. The first step in making quahog chowder is securing the quahogs. They can be purchased in most seafood stores. If you live on or are visiting on Nantucket, you can simply go out at low tide and rake them. If you are unable to locate quahogs, any hard-shell clam will do, but if you use cherrystones or little necks you must increase the amount, since they are half as big as a quahog or less.

2. Scrub the quahogs in cold water and place them in a soup pot with the water. Steam them open and reserve the liquid. Discard any that fail to open. Remove from shells and chop. Set aside.

3. Cook bacon down over medium heat in a large, heavy-bottomed saucepan. Add 3 tablespoons butter and melt. Add onions, celery, and thyme and sauté until vegetables are tender.

4. Stir in flour and continue to cook for a few minutes, stirring constantly. Whisk in cream and cook until smooth. Add reserved clam broth and continue to cook for about 20 minutes.

5. Stir in potatoes and chopped clams. Bring to a boil and reduce to medium heat. Add bay leaves, Worcestershire sauce, and salt and pepper and simmer on low for 15 minutes.

6. Ladle into bowls. Top each with 1 tablespoon butter and sprinkle each generously with paprika.

Serves 8

Opposite: A simple fall lunch of clam chowder, accompanied by locally produced treats—bread from Daily Breads bakery and beer from Cisco Brewers—is laid out on the back deck.

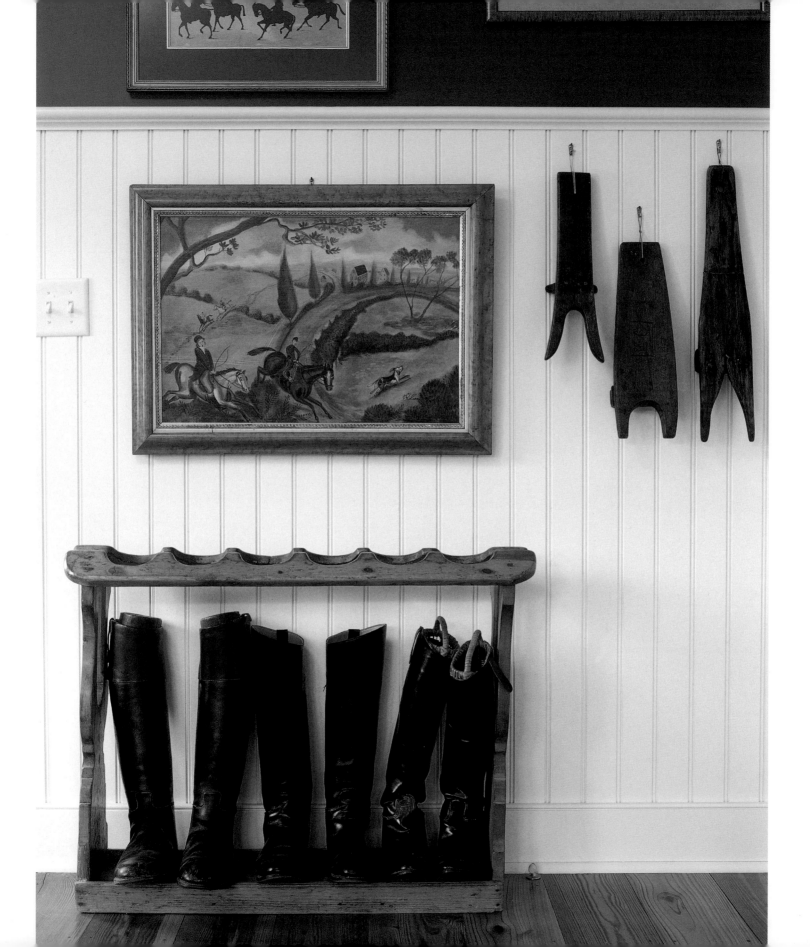

a pair of collectors

Along Madaket Road on the western part of the island, Cam and Gardiner Dutton built a home to house their myriad collections. Their property lies adjacent to the Sanford Farm—three hundred acres preserved from development by the Nantucket Conservation Foundation—so they enjoy uninterrupted views of the shrubby lowlands and, in the distance, the sea. Sitting on a low hill, the house is surrounded by a large lawn, perfect for entertaining the grandchildren. Simple hydrangea borders line the side of the house, and a walled garden has been built into the hillside in back, providing protection and privacy.

The Duttons have been married for twenty-one years, but they each began collecting long before they met. So they needed a house suitable for displaying their extensive combined collections: Gardiner loves art, and Cam's passion is antiques. They worked with the Nantucket Architecture Group and a local building company, Bruce Killen and Sons, to create their home. "The collaboration with the architect and builder was key to achieving what we wanted," says Cam. "We even hired a lighting engineer to design subtle low-voltage art lighting to highlight our numerous pieces."

Inside the front door, a double staircase draws you into the house. It leads to an upstairs gallery where paintings, antique stools, and an old marching-band drum are on display. Beyond the stairs on the ground floor is the main living room. It is large enough to accom-modate several seating areas. Black leather sofas face one another in one corner, each with its own antique quilt draped over the back. A mix of artwork hangs on the walls, lit by recessed lights. The fireplace shares a flue with another in the adjacent dining room.

The Duttons chose to give the dining room an Asian focus. Chinese junks sail across three walls in a mural painted by Pennsylvania artist Kolene Spicher. "By using the subtle lighting you can highlight certain things in the room," Cam points out. "For a dinner party, lighting can be set to highlight the table, or you can choose to give the mural more of a focus instead."

Beyond the dining room is the impressive kitchen, with a twenty-foot cathedral ceiling. This room houses several of Cam's collections. One wall is covered with antique meat cleavers, another with more than a hundred rolling pins.

Opposite: Leather riding boots are lined up in a rack. Above them, retired wooden bootjacks hang like sculpture.

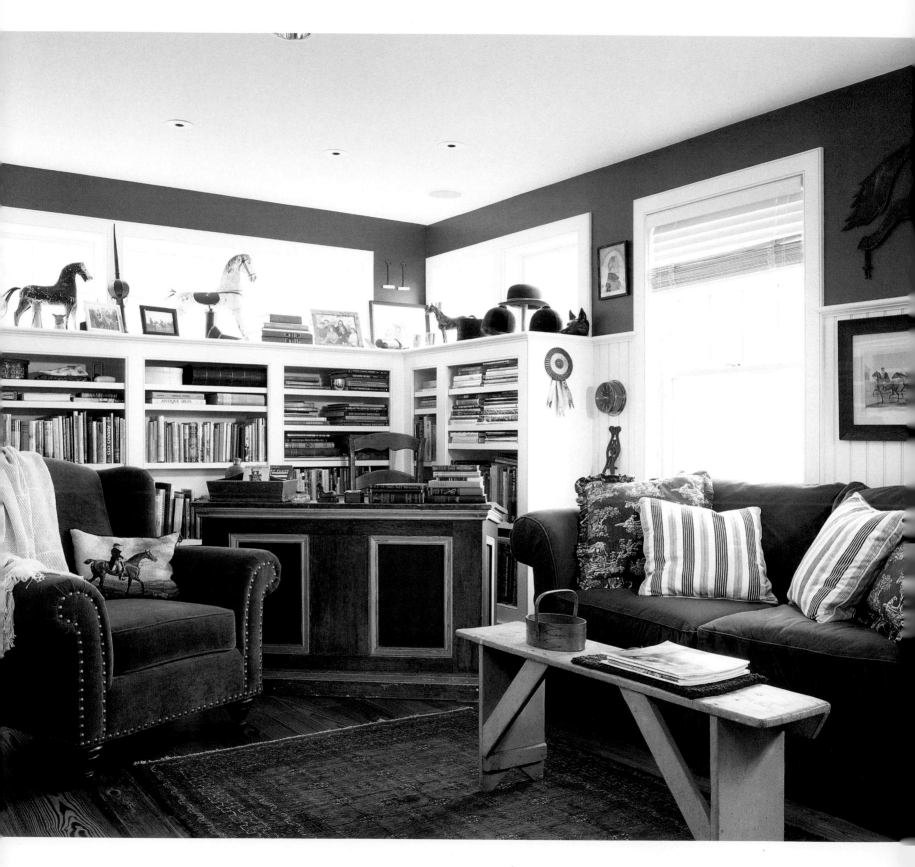

AT HOME IN NANTUCKET

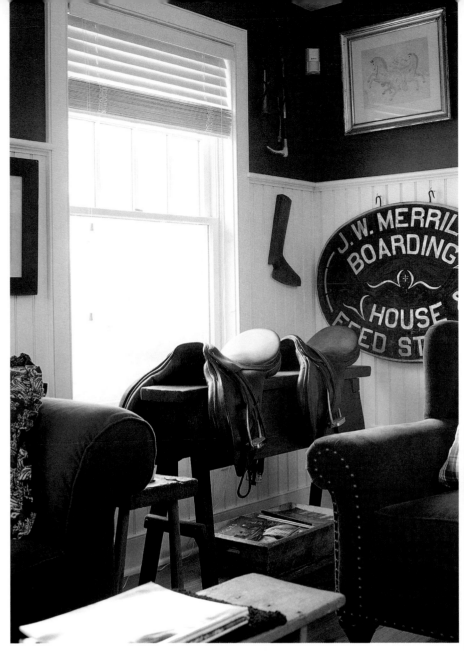

Opposite: Cam and Gardiner gave this cozy study a riding theme to remind them of earlier days spent together on horseback.

Left: In a corner of the study, saddles sit on an old sawhorse.

Below: Just inside the main entrance, two staircases ascend to the long gallery space above and the living room sprawls out in front of them. One of Cam's many antique rugs hangs over the railing.

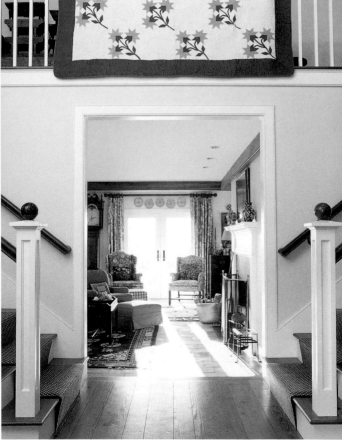

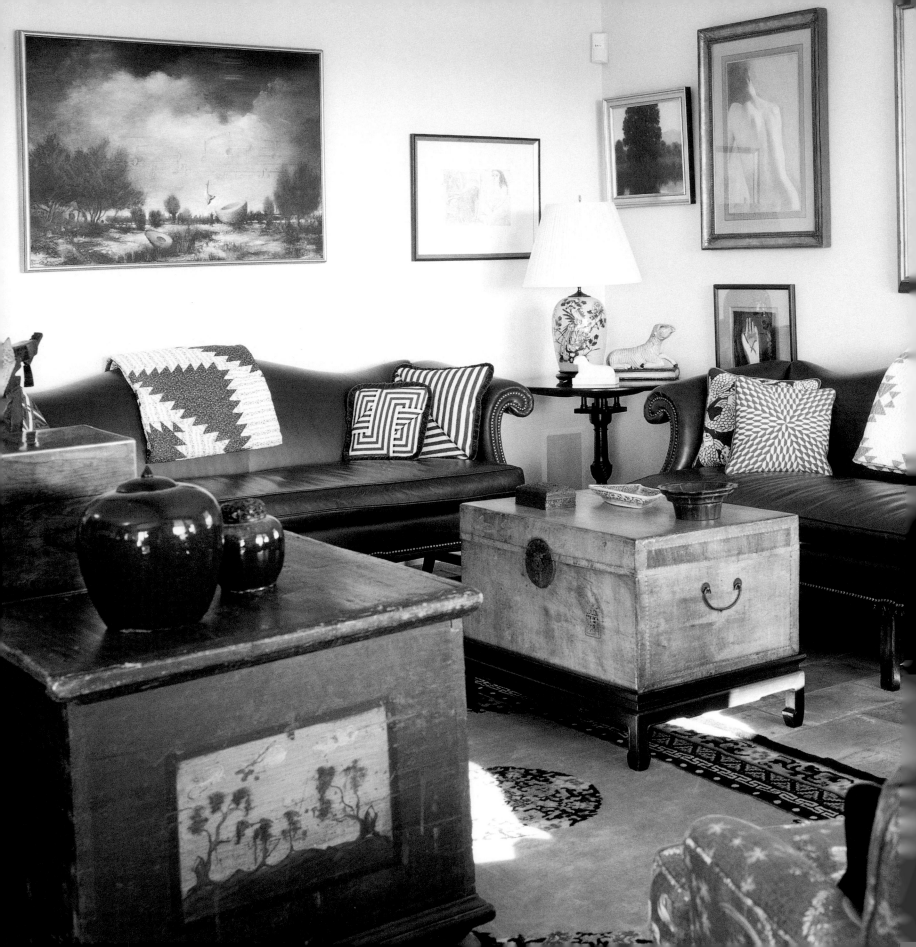

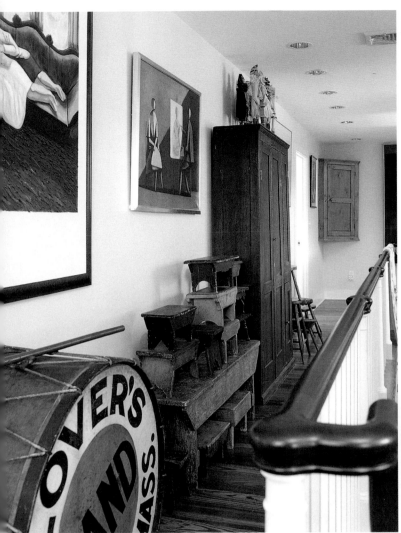

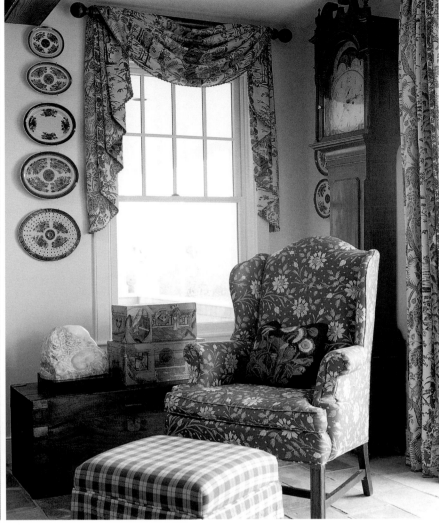

Opposite: In the main part of the living room, a pair of leather sofas sit beneath more of the Dutton's diverse art collection. In the center is a Chinese leather chest.

Above, left: In the upstairs gallery, antique stools in a variety of colors have been stacked for visual interest next to a cupboard from Maine. On top of the cupboard is a collection of old Punch and Judy dolls.

Above: One corner of the living room is filled with rich blue hues; an American grandfather clock from the early nineteenth century stands on the back wall.

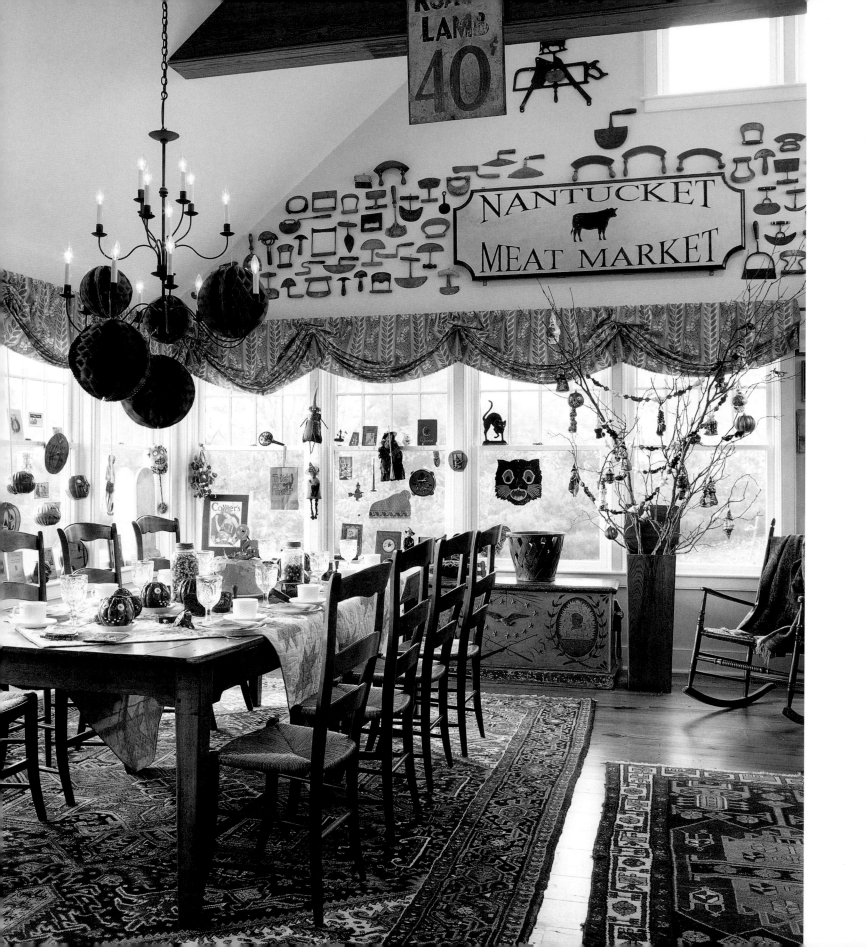

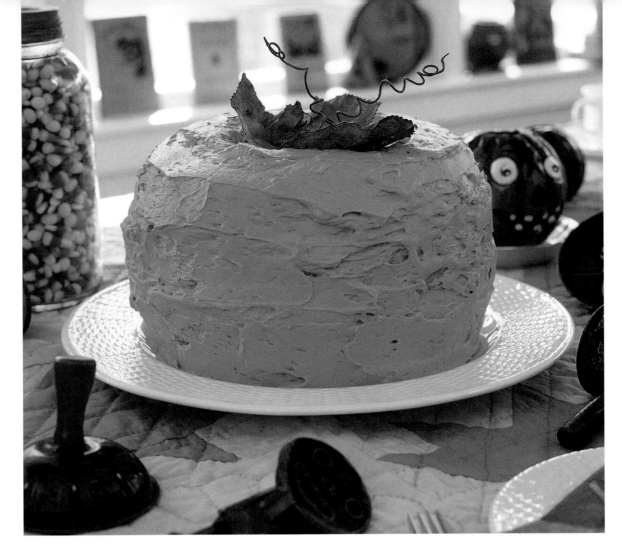

On a windowsill is a line of honey pots. Because Halloween is Cam's birthday, it has become a favorite holiday for the whole family. Needless to say, she has an extensive collection of antique Halloween ornaments, masks, trick-or-treat bags, and even books on the subject, and these are displayed in her kitchen as well.

A long hallway leads from the kitchen past the front door and into a cozy study, painted a racy red. Throughout the room, various equestrian details—bootjacks, an old saddle, riding boots—remind the Duttons of their earlier fox-hunting days.

Cam and Gardiner put most of the rooms together by themselves, though Cam did hire her decorator friend, Susan Ziscs Green, to help place artwork and furniture, choose drapery, and upholster some pieces. Cam's keen sense of arranging rooms around individual themes comes into play when she sets up displays in her store downtown, Nantucket Country. Here Cam further satisfies her love of antiques. The store is full of numerous treasures, such as antique quilts, nostalgic children's toys, and an antique book selection that is particularly amazing.

The Duttons' sense of style and avid passion for collecting can be used as a guide for any home. The power is in the visual impact of how the items are displayed.

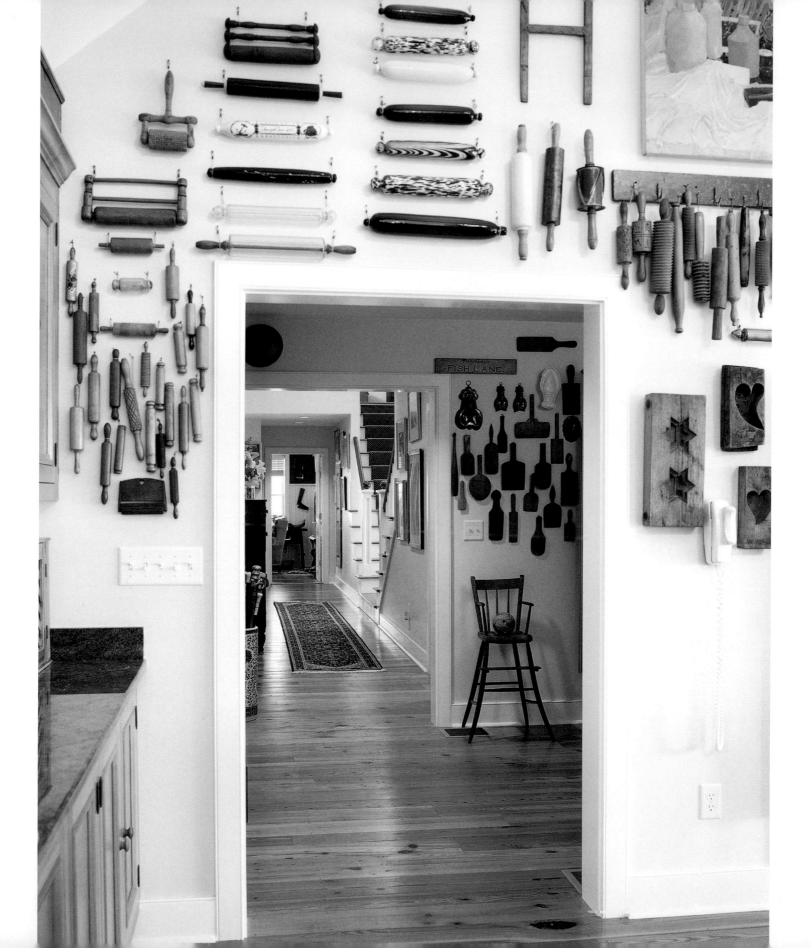

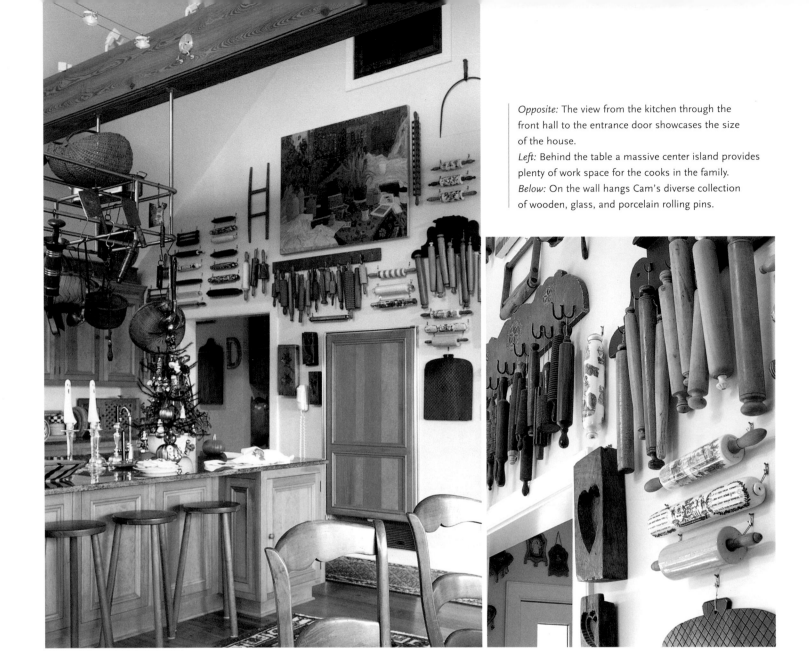

Opposite: The view from the kitchen through the front hall to the entrance door showcases the size of the house.
Left: Behind the table a massive center island provides plenty of work space for the cooks in the family.
Below: On the wall hangs Cam's diverse collection of wooden, glass, and porcelain rolling pins.

ALL HALLOWS' EVE

Nantucket is a child's paradise on October 31st. The island celebrates Halloween in typical small-town fashion, with a delightful parade of little goblins and ghosts marching on Main Street as dusk falls. Townspeople line the sidewalks, cheering them on and taking photographs. Retail stores join in and give out trick-or-treat goodies.

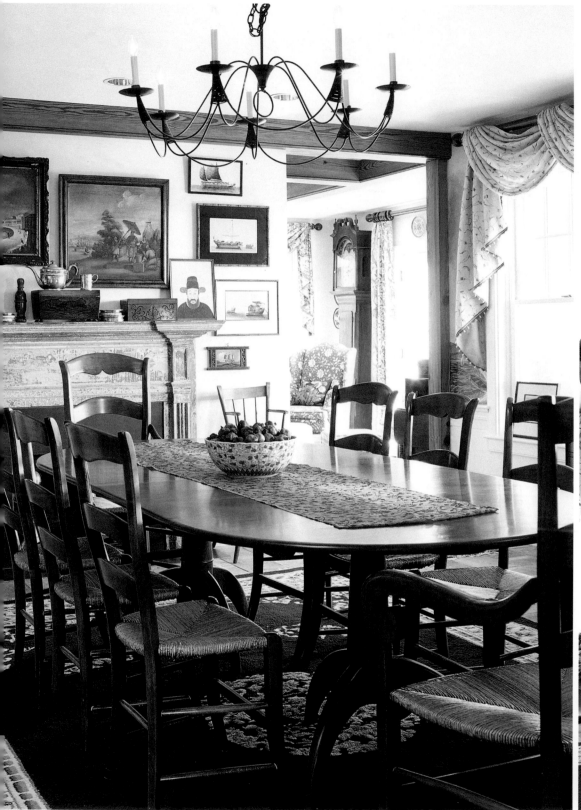

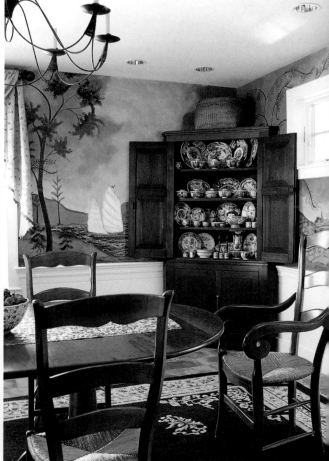

Left: The dining room, located just off the kitchen, has a colorful Asian theme.
Below: The Duttons commissioned Kolene Spicher to paint a nautical landscape on three walls of the room. The cupboard in the corner is filled with Japanese and Chinese ceramics from 1850 to the 1920s.

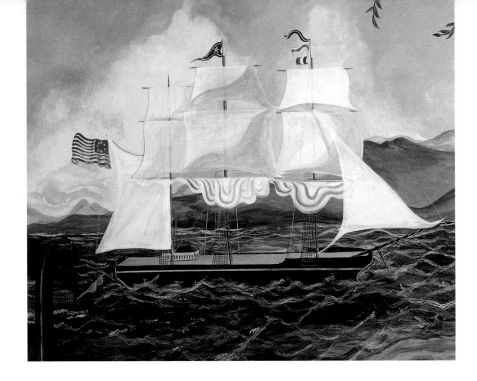

Carrot Cake

This inventive layer cake masquerades as a pumpkin. Cam and Gardiner's son and daughter-in-law, Jeffrey and Shari Dutton, who own the Daily Breads bakery in town, created this tasty treat especially for Cam's birthday.

1. Preheat oven to 350 degrees F.

2. Butter three 8-inch round cake pans and dust lightly with flour.

3. To make the cakes, sift flour, granulated sugar, baking soda, salt, and spices into a bowl.

4. In a large bowl, use an electric mixer on high speed to beat eggs for 1 minute. Add oil in a stream while beating. Fold in flour mixture and beat batter until smooth. Fold in carrots and pecans.

5. Divide batter between the prepared pans and bake on middle rack of the oven for 25 to 30 minutes, or until toothpick comes out clean.

6. Cool cakes in pans for 10 minutes. Loosen edges with knife and gently invert pans onto a wire rack. Cool cakes completely. Stack on top of each other and use a toothpick between each layer to secure in place. Gently carve away some of the edges to round out the pumpkin shape before frosting.

7. To make the frosting, beat butter and cream cheese together with an electric mixer. Add confectioner's sugar, vanilla, and 3 to 4 tablespoons milk, and mix until frosting reaches good spreading consistency. Add more milk if it's too stiff. Add orange food coloring (or mix yellow and red) for pumpkin color. Spread evenly over the "pumpkin" cake.

Serves 25–40

For the cake:

2 cups all-purpose flour

2 cups granulated sugar

2 teaspoons baking soda

1 teaspoon salt

Pinch of allspice

1 1/2 teaspoons cinnamon

4 large eggs

1 cup vegetable oil

4 cups grated raw carrots

1 cup chopped pecans

For the frosting:

1/2 cup softened butter

1/2 cup softened cream cheese

4 cups confectioners' sugar

1 1/2 teaspoons vanilla

4 to 5 tablespoons milk

Orange food coloring

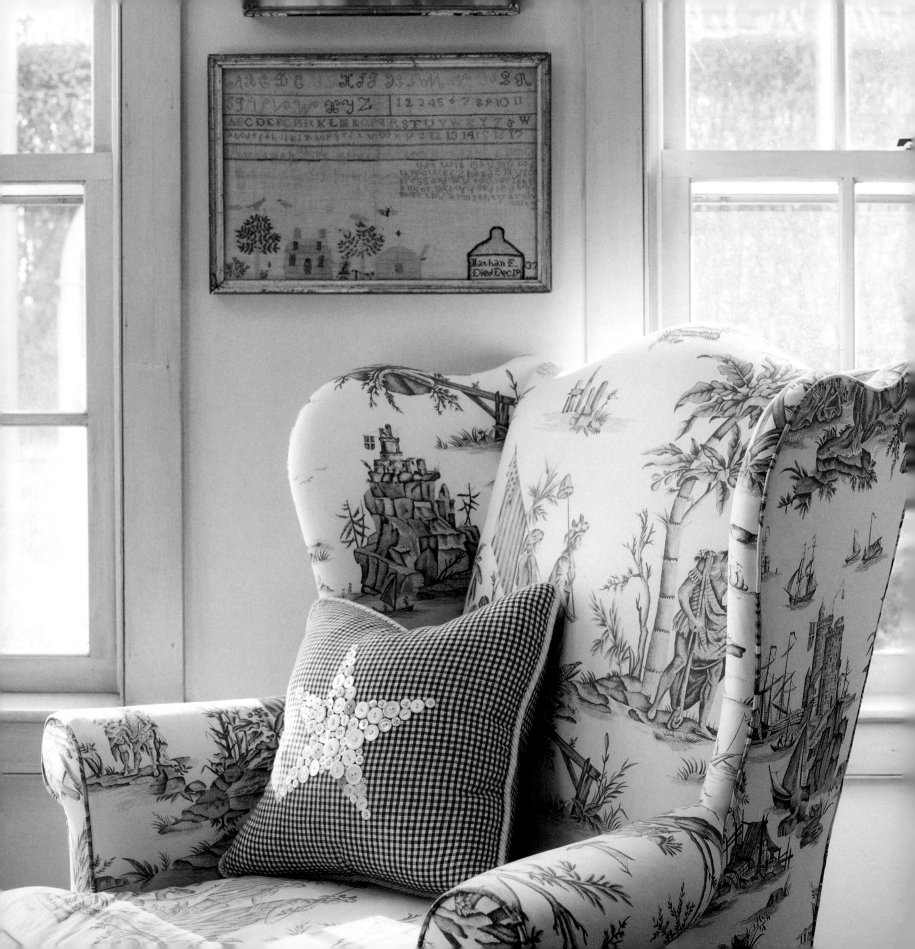

tradition restored

On July 13, 1846, a great fire swept through much of downtown Nantucket. Miraculously, it spared the house now owned by Bill and Susan Boardman, even when others just a few doors down were destroyed. The house, just up the street from the Whaling Museum, was built between 1765 and 1783 and over the years has maintained much of its original structure.

Soon after buying the house in 1989, Bill and Susan embarked on a restoration and renovation project and hired architect Chris Holland to help them complete it. In an effort to retain the house's historical integrity, they worked as closely as possible to the design of the original structure, while at the same time updating it. It had been a summerhouse since the 1920s and desperately needed winterizing. They installed a heating and central air system, restored the woodwork and flooring, designed a more convenient kitchen, and added a wine cellar in the basement. The project took almost two years to complete.

Although the house's main entrance faces out onto the street, most visitors enter through the back door, which is on a narrow lane. This entrance brings you down a short hallway right into the heart of this home: the kitchen. Susan is

frequently found here, cooking up a delicious meal or baking a new batch of bread. The kitchen is remarkably simple in design. The counters and island are surfaced in black granite. Except for the coffeemaker, none of the appliances remain out—they are all conveniently stored away in the island's rolling drawers. The woodwork is painted a soft yellow, which complements the Delft tiles inlaid along the back wall. An impeccably organized pantry is off to one side, storing everything from glasses and serving dishes to flour and homemade biscotti.

Past the kitchen island is the dining room, which has the same warm woodwork and accommodates a long dining table ideal for big family meals. A wall of windows lights up the room, and a fireplace at one end warms it in the colder months. In a corner across from the windows is a built-in bar, which is put to use for special

Opposite: A button-star pillow made by Susan sits in a toile covered wing chair. Above it on the wall is an old sampler from New Hampshire.

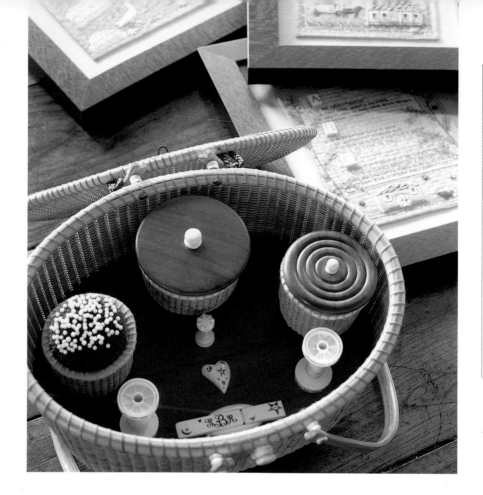

Left: Susan made this sewing basket with help from Nancy Chase, who carved the ivory fittings, and Lee Paple, who did the scrimshaw. Above the basket are three examples of Susan's work from her exhibit honoring Nantucket women: to the left is Mary E. Starbuck, in the middle, Martha Fish, and to the right Eunice Ross. *Opposite:* In the mornings, Bill sits with their dog, Rotunda, in this sunny spot to eat his toast and catch up on the morning news.

gatherings. Adjacent to the kitchen and dining room, but not a separate room, is a little seating area with two toile-covered wing chairs and a cozy sofa for watching television.

From there a long hallway leads to the front of the house and the front staircase. Because the hallway is so narrow, it was difficult to light it or hang artwork there. So the Boardmans hired Kevin Paulsen to paint a mural in the space. Kevin had painted all the woodwork throughout the house and was looking to expand his line of work. The Boardmans gave him his first commission for a residential mural. The seascape runs up the stairs from the downstairs hallway and into the second-floor hallway, and it is just what Bill and Susan had been looking for. In fact, they were so happy with it that five years later they commissioned Kevin to paint another

seascape, this one a mural for their formal living room. "We wanted a whaling scene with ports, and we let Kevin come up with the rest," Susan says. The mural beautifully complements the warm and comforting colors of the room, which has hues of purple, pink, and mauve. With its two fireplaces, Bill finds this room his favorite spot to pull a chair up and read.

Across the hall from the formal living room is a casual one, with big plush furniture, a television, and a computer. In the evenings, after Susan and Bill have fixed a delicious meal and poured some wine from Bill's extensive cellar, they sit down here to enjoy a movie over dinner.

Since Bill commutes off the island during the week, Susan spends much of her time working on her exquisite embroidered narratives. They are a fascinating combination of quilting and

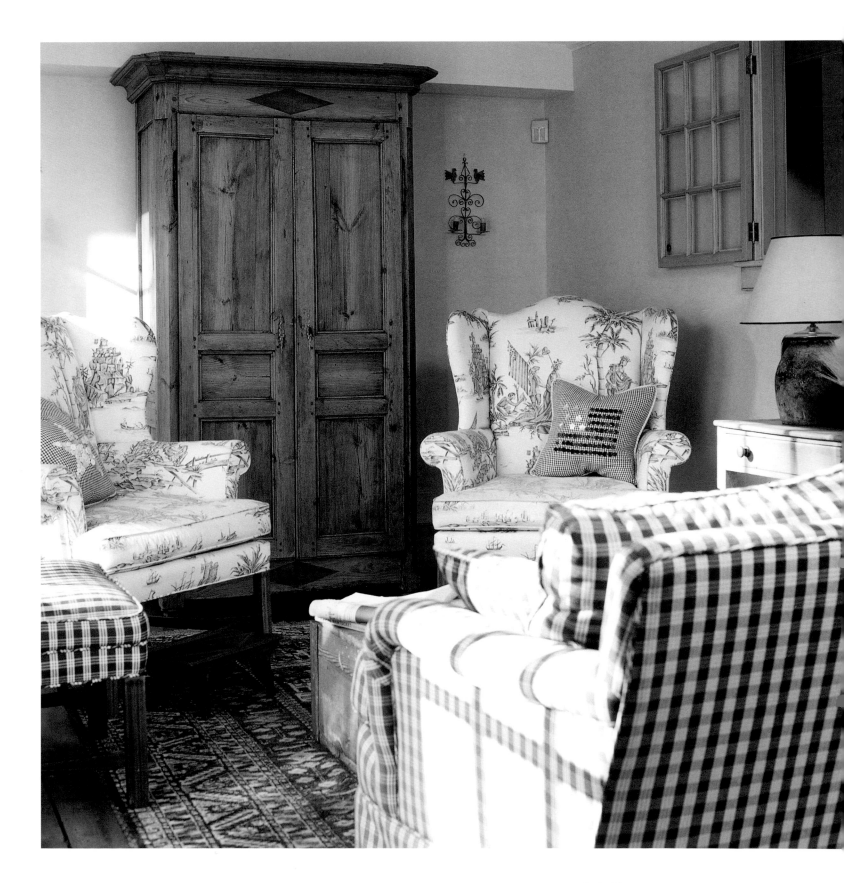

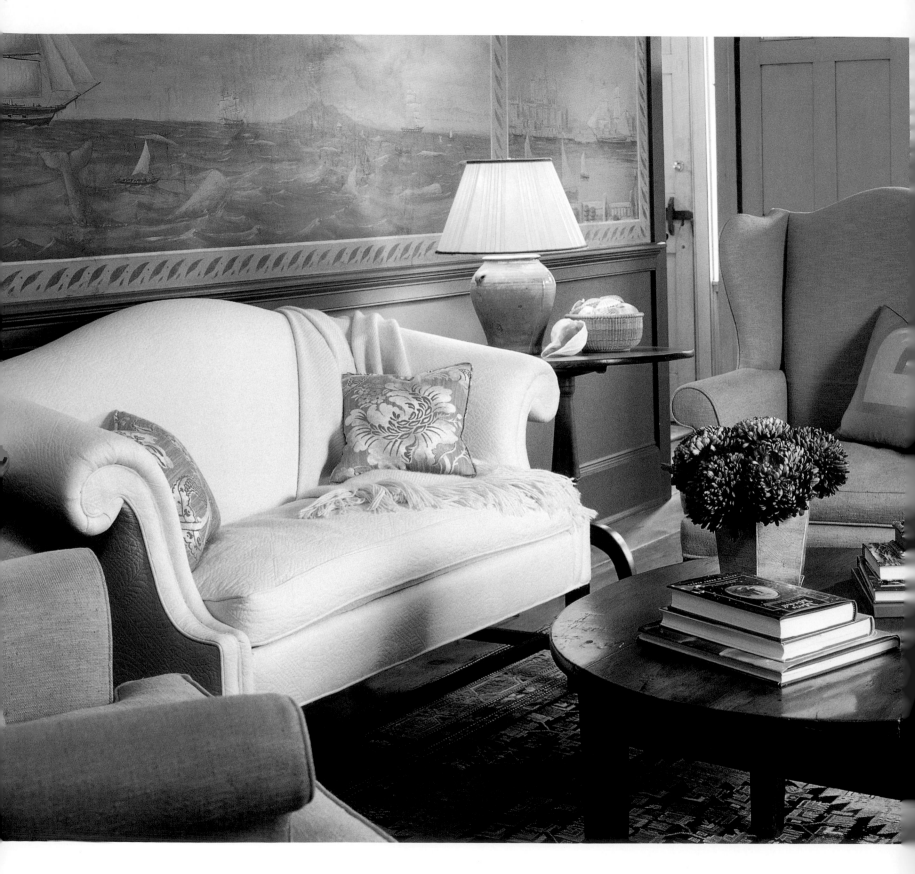

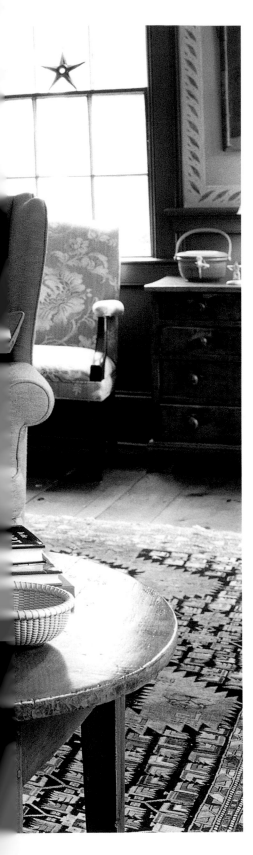

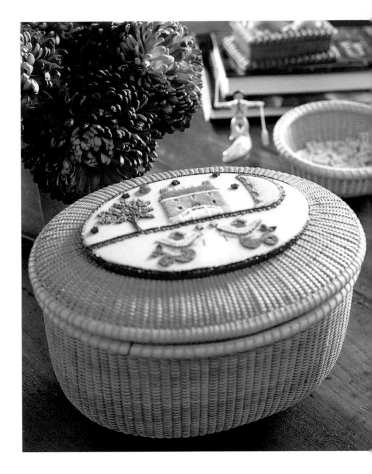

Left: Along the back wall of the formal living room, Kevin Paulsen painted a mural depicting a South Pacific whale hunt in the middle panel and a scene of London harbor in the right.

Right: The coffee table in the living room sports an ivory whirligig carved by close friend Nancy Chase. In the foreground, affixed to the lid of a Nantucket lightship basket, is an embroidered depiction of their house crafted by Susan.

embroidery, with other elements such as carvings and beading added when needed. "The island sort of embraces you," Susan says. "It's the most nurturing place; people help each other all the time." The island's embrace certainly has done wonders for her work. By chance, she discovered the illustrated journal of a namesake, Susan Veeder, in the Nantucket Historical Association's manuscript collection. Veeder kept the journal between 1846 and 1853, when she was in her early thirties aboard the ship *Nauticon*. When not out at sea, she lived at 91 Orange Street, a house located in downtown Nantucket that remained in the Veeder family until 1900.

Finding the journal catapulted Susan's attitude toward quilting as a hobby into a fascina-

tion with her new medium. In 2002, she had an exhibit on the island, showing nine pieces that celebrate important and inspirational Nantucket women, past and present.

Susan's work is evident throughout the house. In the back hallway hangs her first and favorite embroidered narrative. All the beds on the second floor are outfitted with quilts that she made, and in her office evidence of her latest project is often laid out on the table or drawn up on tracing paper.

This house resonates with the Boardmans' love of architecture and their interest in preserving tradition. Through their diligent restoration and the narratives Susan has created, it is an ode to Nantucket's dynamic whaling, social, and architectural history.

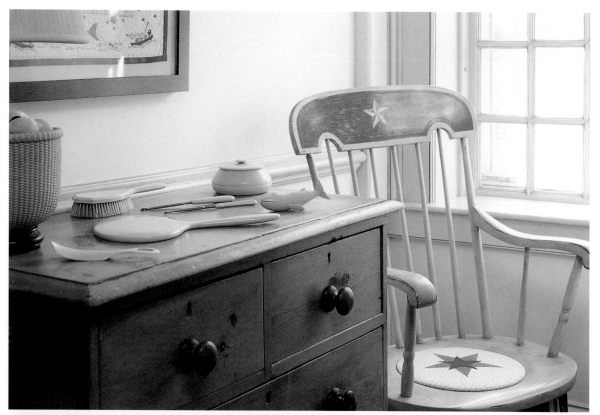

Left: In a guest room, an old Bakelite set sits on top of the dresser; above it is one of Susan's pieces. *Below:* A close look at Susan's work makes it possible to appreciate the painstaking details that go in to each piece. This piece chronicles the journal of Susan Veeder on the ship *Nauticon.* *Opposite:* Susan made the intricate quilt using a red, white, and blue theme combined with the history of America and Abigail Adams. On a shelf above the bed, which was Bill's grandfather's, are five oval baskets woven by Susan.

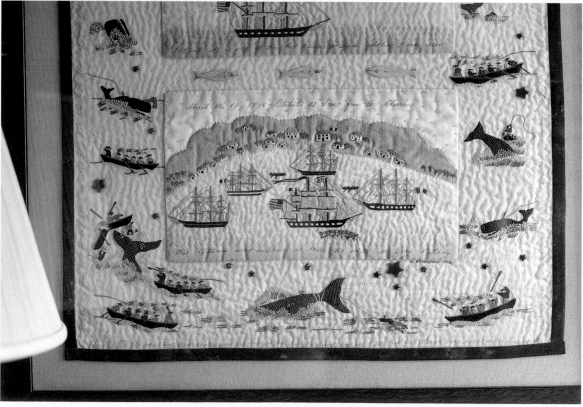

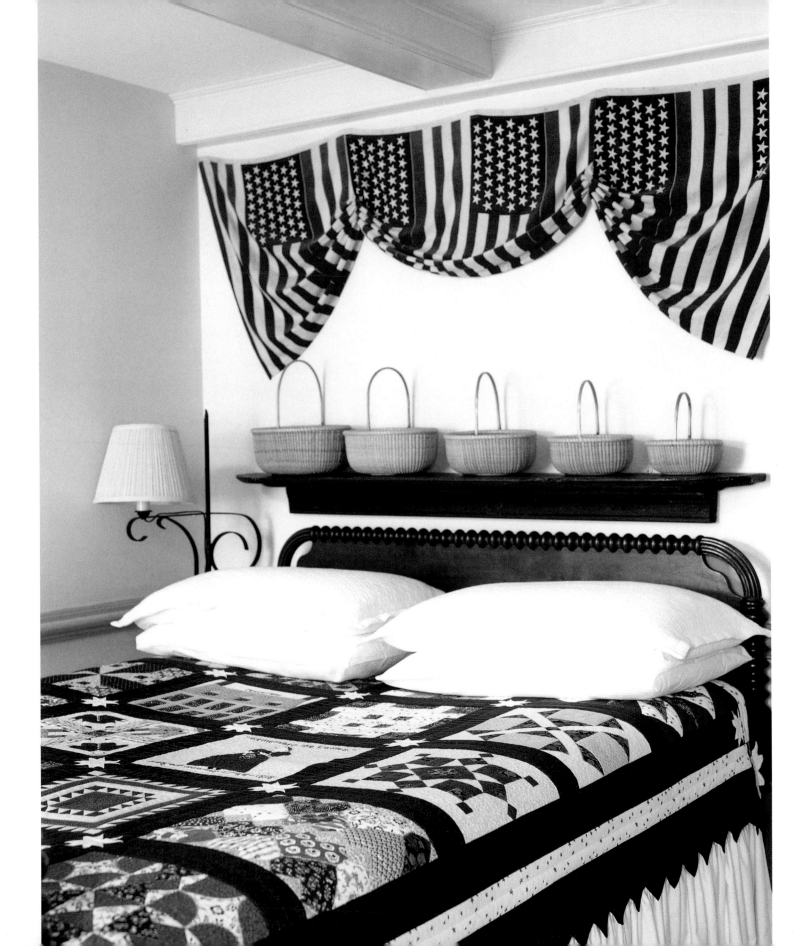

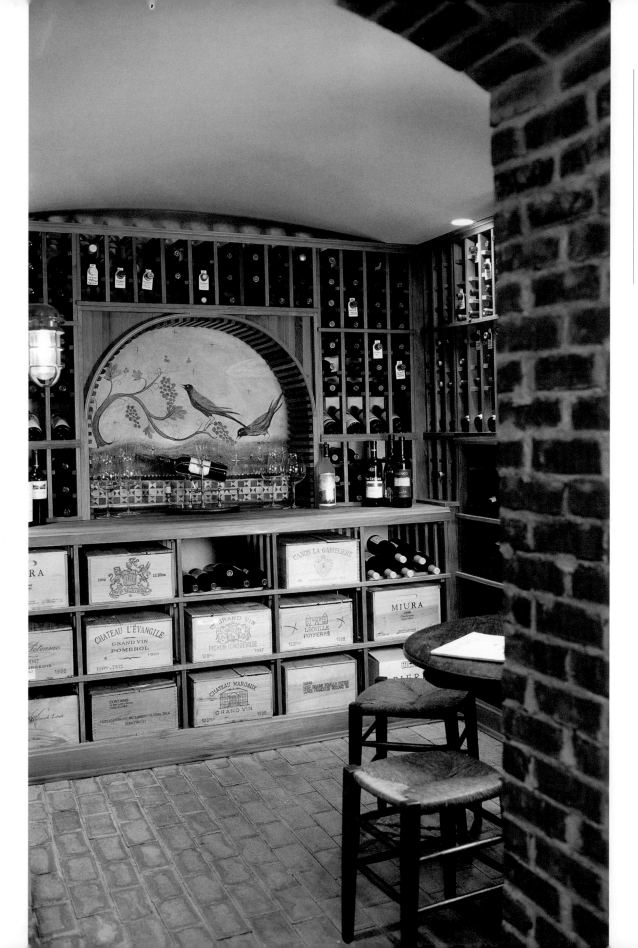

Left: The highlight of the wine cellar is the charming mural of a blackbird with grapes painted by Kevin Paulsen. *Opposite:* An English dining table from the eighteenth century provides ample room for guests. Above the fireplace is another delightful mural by Kevin Paulsen. The windows look out onto a small garden in the back.

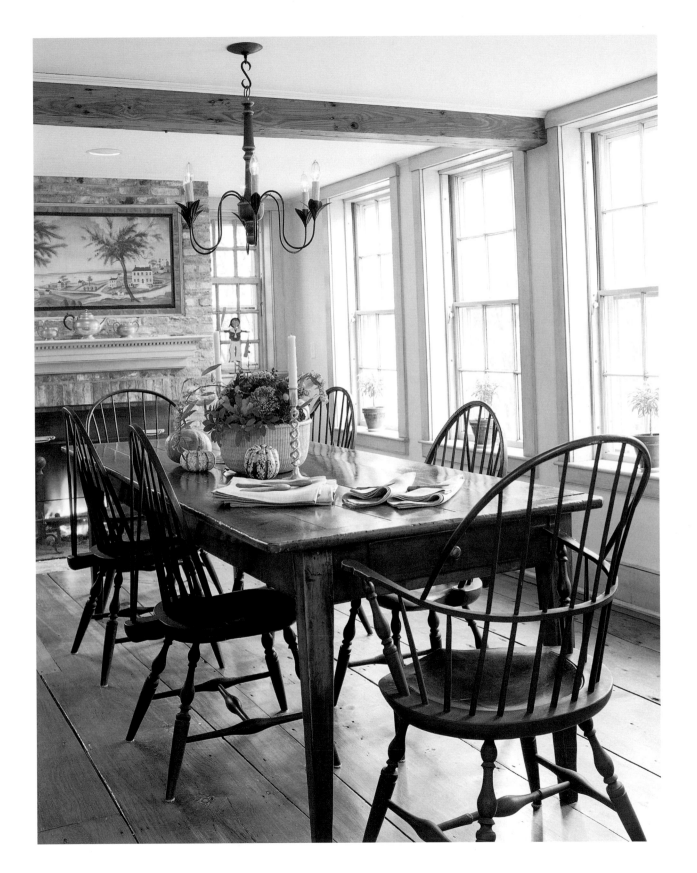

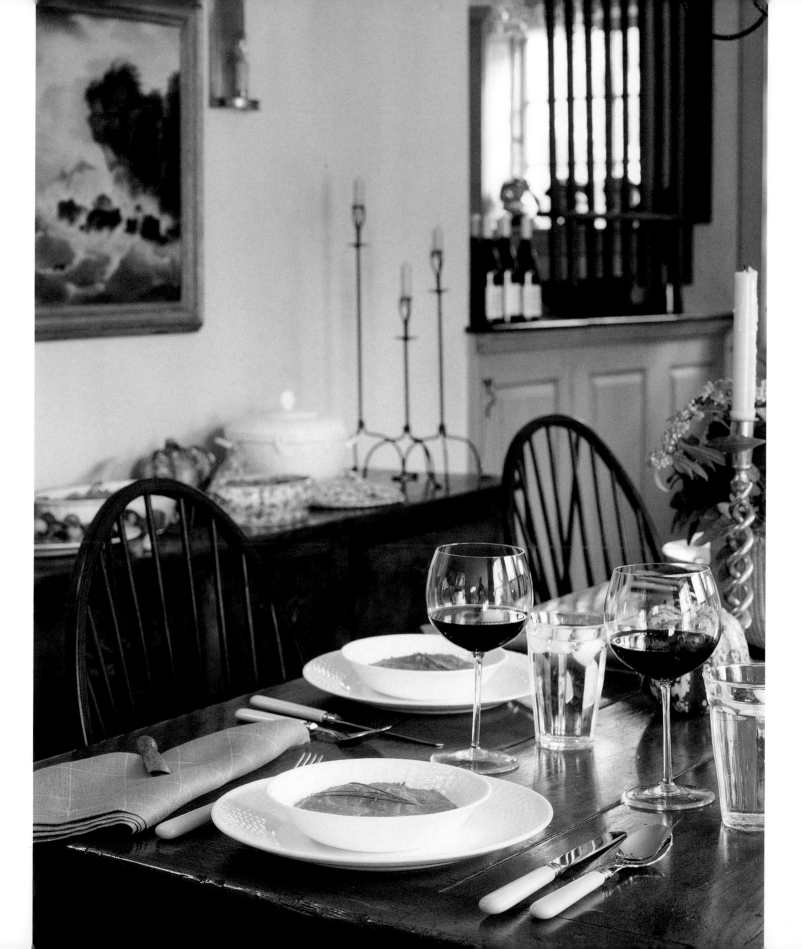

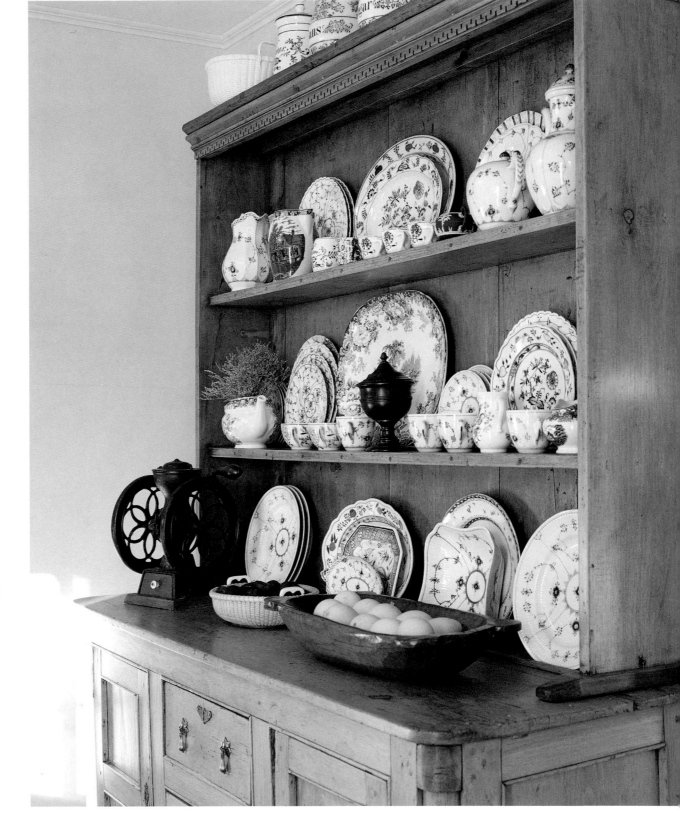

Opposite: Pumpkin soup fills bowls for the start of the Thanksgiving meal. Old Gypsy clothespins act as napkin holders.
Right: The tall cupboard is filled with a mix of blue-and-white tableware, including Royal Copenhagen plates from Bill's grandmother. On the second shelf is a wooden sugar bowl carved by Susan's great-grandfather in Scotland.

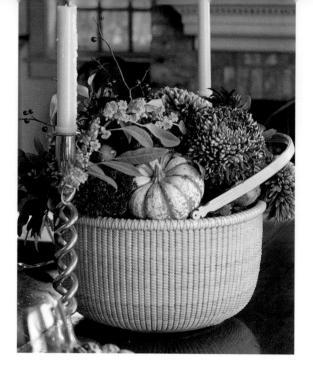

Nantucket Thanksgiving

Susan and Bill Boardman often host Thanksgiving dinner for family and friends. Bill, a wine enthusiast, enjoys pairing wines with Susan's menu of pumpkin soup, roasted vegetables, and stuffing to accompany the traditional bird. In 2002, a new annual island event was inaugurated, the Turkey Plunge. To raise money for the children's wing at the library, participants gathered pledges for a bone-chilling dip in the winter harbor. Susan bravely volunteered and survived her dip, with her enthusiastic family cheering her from the shore.

Pumpkin Soup with Potatoes and Leeks

Choose a smaller variety of pumpkin for this recipe, or use winter squash instead.

2 pounds russet potatoes, peeled and cubed (or use sweet potatoes for richer color and better taste)

2 cups water

1 teaspoon salt

1/2 cup fruity wine (preferably a Chardonnay with a subtle oak taste)

1 pumpkin (about 2 pounds), peeled and cubed, or 3 1/2 cups cooked pumpkin puree

3 large leeks, white parts only

2 tablespoons butter

2 cups vegetable broth

2 tablespoons fresh lemon juice

1/2 teaspoon sugar

White pepper

1/4 teaspoon grated nutmeg

Pinch of cinnamon

1/2 cup cream (or substitute evaporated skim milk)

Coarsely chopped chives or cilantro, for garnish

1. Place potatoes in a large soup pot with the water, salt, wine, and fresh cubed pumpkin. (If using puree, wait.) Simmer on low until vegetables are tender.

2. Trim, clean, and slice leeks, and cook in butter over medium heat. Stir often, until leeks are soft and beginning to color. Add to soup pot and continue simmering until vegetables are all very soft, about 45 minutes total cooking time.

3. Add vegetable broth and pumpkin puree (if that's what you are using), and puree the mixture in batches in a blender or food processor until perfectly smooth.

4. Return all the puree to the soup pot and season to taste with lemon juice, sugar, additional salt, and white pepper. The amount of sugar you need will depend on the variety of pumpkin or squash used; use more if you feel the soup needs a bit of sweetening. When the sweet-sour balance is correct, add nutmeg and cinnamon and stir in cream. Heat thoroughly on low and sprinkle with chives before serving.

Serves 8–10

Roasted Winter Squash and Apples

Choose the best variety of squash available in your area.

2 pounds tart apples

2 teaspoons fresh lemon juice

2 pounds winter squash, peeled,
  seeded, and cubed

1 1/2 tablespoons olive oil

1/2 teaspoon salt

1. Preheat oven to 400 degrees F.

2. Cut apples in quarters and core, then toss them with lemon juice.

3. Put squash in a large bowl, drizzle with olive oil, sprinkle with salt, and toss with your hands until all the squash is lightly and evenly coated with oil.

4. Combine squash with apples and spread on a baking sheet. Roast for about an hour, stirring the mixture every 20 minutes or so.

Serves 8–10

Fennel Stuffing

2 tablespoons olive oil

3 cups chopped fresh fennel

2 cups chopped onions

1 pound bulk country pork
  sausage, broken into
  small chunks

2 tart apples, cut into
  1/2 -inch cubes

1 cup chopped chestnuts

1 cup dried cranberries

6 cups stale bread cubes

1 teaspoon salt

1 teaspoon dried thyme

1 teaspoon crumbled dried sage

Freshly ground pepper to taste

1 cup tawny port

1 cup chicken stock

1. Heat olive oil in a large skillet over low heat. Add the fennel and onions and sauté until softened but not browned, about 10 minutes. Transfer to a large mixing bowl.

2. Add sausage to the skillet and cook, breaking up the sausage with a spoon, until it is cooked through and lightly browned, about 10 minutes. Add to the bowl with the onions.

3. Stir apples, chestnuts, and cranberries into sausage mixture. Add bread cubes and toss lightly. Sprinkle with salt, thyme, sage, and pepper. Toss lightly again. Add port and chicken stock and toss until well blended.

4. Stuffing can be cooked either inside turkey or in a casserole dish. If using a dish, bake in oven at 325 degrees F for 45 minutes once the turkey has cooked. Serve warm.

Serves 8–10

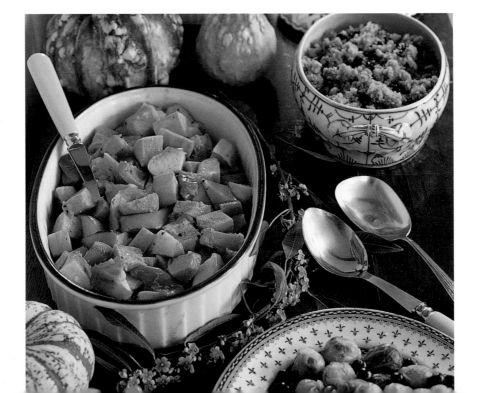

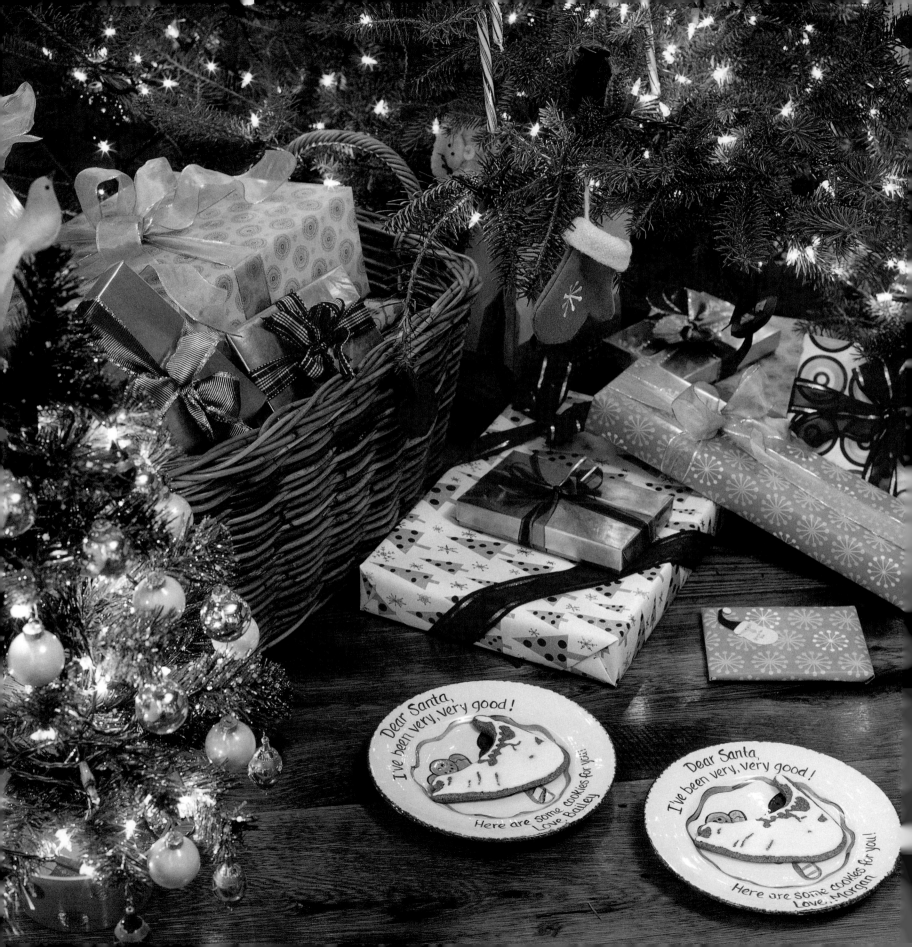

Dear Santa,
I've been very, very good!

Here are some cookies for you!
Love, Bailey

Dear Santa,
I've been very, very good!

Here are some cookies for you!
Love, Morgan

chapter four:
winter

As winter comes, only a small number of year-round residents remain to endure the cold winds that whip off the ocean. A quiet stillness settles over the island, with only a handful of restaurants open and many of the retail shops closed until spring. Thanks to an extended Christmas celebration—with Stroll Weekend usually falling on the first weekend of December and the Nantucket Noel, which runs the day after Thanksgiving until New Year's Eve (see sidebar, page 161)—a few visitors do come out to the island for weekend getaways and last-minute shopping, but from January to March, only the die-hard islanders tough it out. To survive the harsh winter months, year-round residents make sure their homes are warm and inviting.

In their updated farmhouse, Robert and Kathleen Hay are serious about Christmas. They capture the spirit of the season with a big tree laden with the many ornaments they have collected over the years. In town, Jonathan and Elizabeth Raith have designed a casual and welcoming home for their family of five. Their "gathering room," a large combined dining and living room, becomes the heart of the house during the holiday season. Out near the cranberry bogs and marshland, a timber-frame barn provides warmth and refuge from the bleak landscape for its owners. Its lofty main space provides ample room for entertaining, and its unusual collections spark much conversation. Back in town, art enthusiast Reggie Levine finds comfort during the winter months amid his treasured collection. Surrounded by favorite pieces and gifts from friends, he pays homage to his thirty-plus years as a member of Nantucket's artistic community.

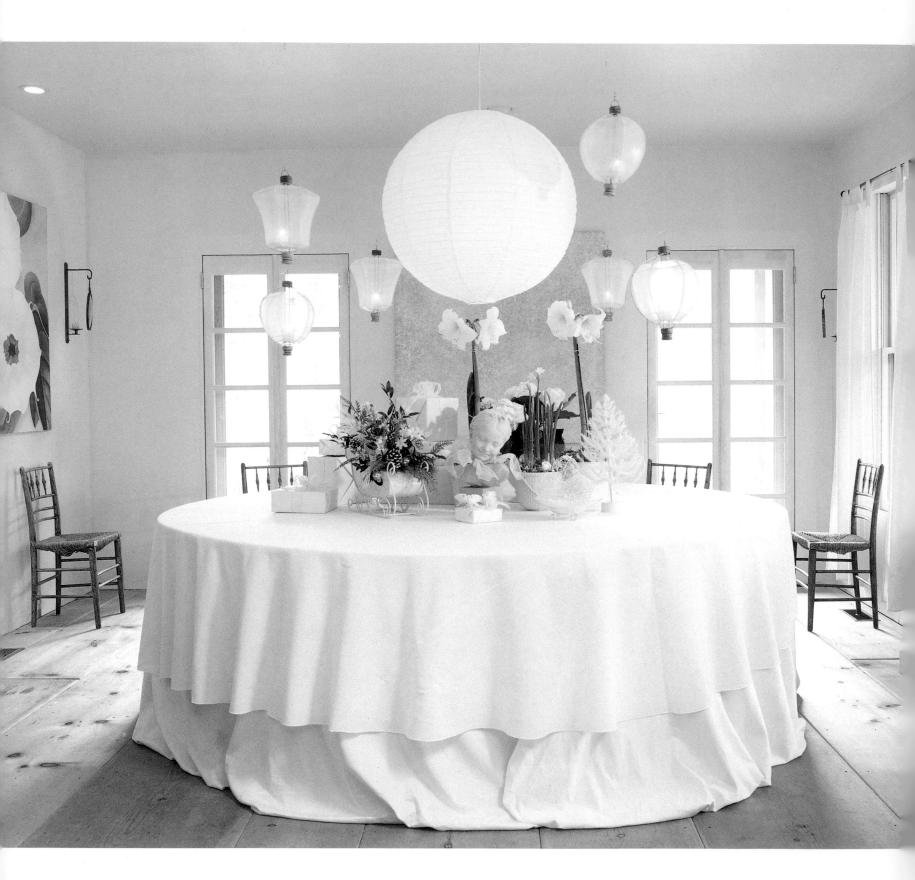

creativity abounds

Off Milestone Road, the long straightaway to Siasconset, Robert and Kathleen Hay have built their family home. Nestled among the scraggly pine trees that are common all over the island, the house is perfectly secluded from the road. Robert, a builder, and Kathleen, an interior and graphic designer, created the house together from scratch. "We designed the house with simplicity in mind," says Kathleen. "We wanted a simply constructed home, without a lot of gables and roof angles, that would have interior interest. Thus the house looks like a simple farmhouse on the exterior, with a full wraparound porch for added dimension, but on the interior it has great open spaces."

At the front of the house, a large Palladian window fulfills a longtime wish of Kathleen's. "It reminds me of a church and adds a note of formality to our country plan," she says. The window also adds great light in the entrance, which otherwise would be quite dark. The front entry floor is made of a combination of shell stone (made from crushed shells) and limestone. "We liked the shell stone because of the connection of the sea to Nantucket," Kathleen says. "Plus, I love its soft, bisque-like texture and color. I also like the organic nature of stone, bringing the outside in."

Two large, open spaces flank the front entry. One, which will ultimately be Kathleen's office, is a work in progress and contains minimal furnishings and simple wooden floorboards. Across the way is the dining room, with an ethereal feel reinforced by the large round table, draped to the floor in a white tablecloth, and the delicate fabric-covered lanterns that appear to float above it.

From the front entry, two hallways lead back to the kitchen and living room. The kitchen is quite stark and has a huge island in the center with a counter of poured concrete into which twigs, stones, shells, and other natural elements were mixed. "We designed the island to be versatile, just like the rest of the spaces in the house," says Kathleen. "It's large enough to seat ten to twelve people for dinner. We purposely didn't put appliances on the island, so it could serve a multipurpose function—table, workspace, dance platform, display area, cocktail party hub, or bar. It is most definitely the hub of our home. Daily meals are taken here, homework is done here, late-night tea is sipped here, and bills are paid here." The concrete, with its soft color and

Page 152: Nantucket Island cookies, made by Muppy, a New York business owned by Jon's sister, Kerry Raith-Dombroski, await Santa's visit. *Opposite:* Not a huge fan of red and green at Christmastime, Kathleen uses all white flowers and decorations in the dining room. Gauzy lanterns, found at Trillium, float above the table.

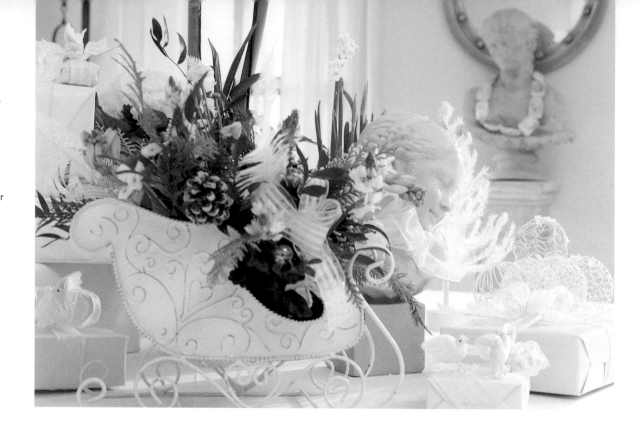

naturalistic touches, pleases Kathleen's love of organic things. The island also acts as a stage of sorts, especially during various holidays, when Kathleen hangs decorations from the ceiling above it, such as spiders and pumpkins at Halloween or silver snowflakes at Christmas.

The base color of the living room, which lies adjacent to the kitchen, is white, but with the addition of caramel, camel, and black, especially in the numerous throw pillows, it feels warmer than the other downstairs rooms. The Hays designed it to be large and open, so the family can feel a sense of freedom and space. At Christmas the tree stands between the kitchen and living rooms. Although the tree decorations never have a theme per se, Kathleen adores birds, especially at Christmas, and many of their ornaments reflect that. "I love the tree covered in winged creatures, as if they are alighting to announce the good news," she says. "I have collected many ornaments over the years, and they usually have a bird theme or something relating to our family passions—ballet, fashion, New York, or travel."

The staircase to the second floor once again evokes an organic quality, echoing Nantucket's connection to the sea. It has been designed to look like the interior of a shell, curved and smooth, wrapping around itself. "I like the curves of the staircase and the large Palladian window," Kathleen says. "They add circularity to an otherwise square house."

Upstairs there are three bedrooms, each with its own bathroom. "Bedrooms should be a getaway, a fantasy—soothing and relaxing," Kathleen comments. Each room achieves just that, designed as a quiet place to wind down and relax. The Hays's daughters, Madeleine and Isabelle, share a room at the front of the house. In the morning, sun pours in the windows through the gauzy lavender curtains and fills the room with strong Nantucket light. The twin beds have been impeccably outfitted with pale green coverlets and bed skirts, a series of crisp white pillows, and, to add to the fantasy, netting over each of the headboards.

The guest room across the hall, which overlooks the front entry and is also lit by the Palladian window, has a kind of Indian–British colonial look. Kathleen calls it "Raj on holiday." Sumptuous green velvet curtains hang at the windows and complement the walls, which are painted another shade of green. Dark pieces of furniture, such as a tall coatrack covered with Kathleen's numerous hats, add richness. Several layers of crisp white pillows decorate this bed as well, and topping them off is a group of needlepoint, velvet, and embroidered pillows. This layering of pillows on the beds, adding texture and comfort, is a signature style of Kathleen's.

That same treatment can be seen in the master suite, which takes up the rest of the second floor. Here, black and white create the overall color scheme. The four-poster iron bed has a white quilted coverlet topped by a black-and-white toile duvet. Filling the top half of the bed is a series of pillows standing upright, lying flat, and stacked on top of one another. The combination of toile, black-and-white ticking, and black wool pillows, along with the black silk bolster, gives the bed dramatic visual punch. The rest of the room and the master bath are quite serene in comparison.

Throughout the house, Kathleen has created vignettes, from a beautiful arrangement of stones and other natural objects on a tabletop to kitchen cabinets filled with an extensive collection of black-and-white English transferware. This is the direct influence of her twenty years in retail and interior-design management at Weeds,

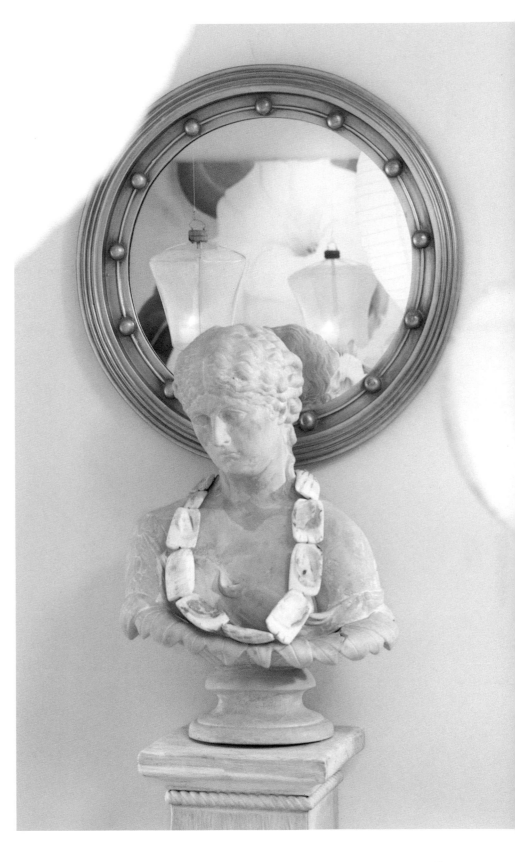

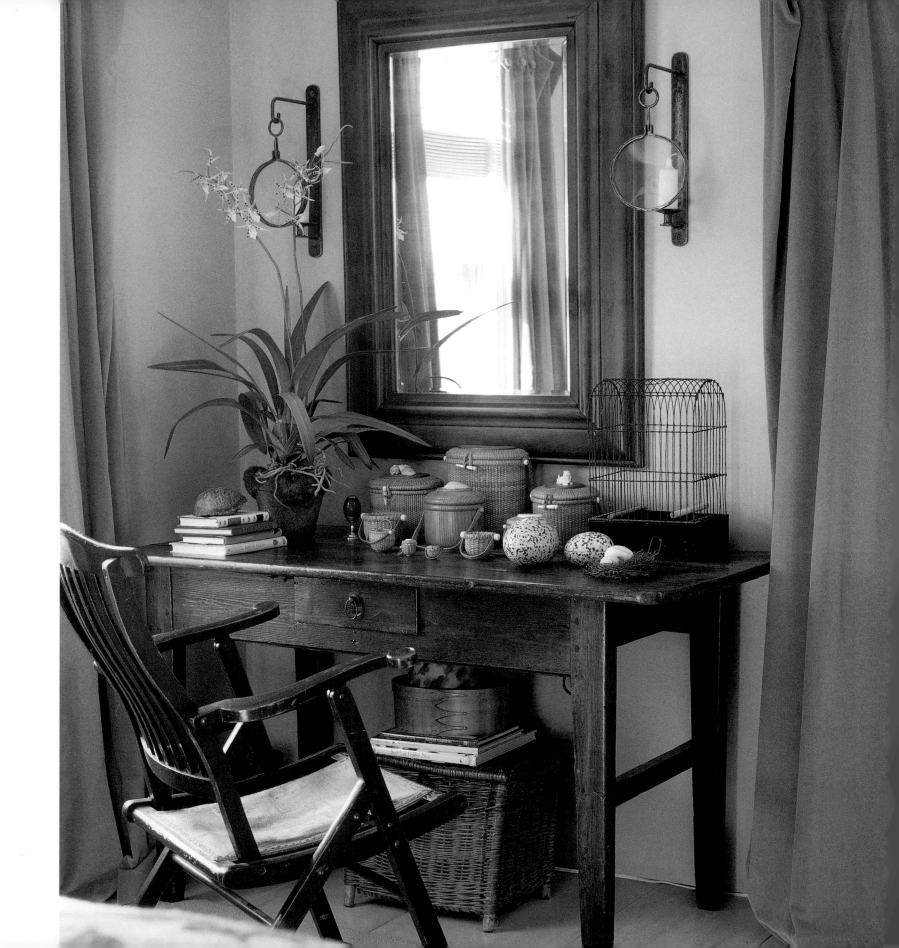

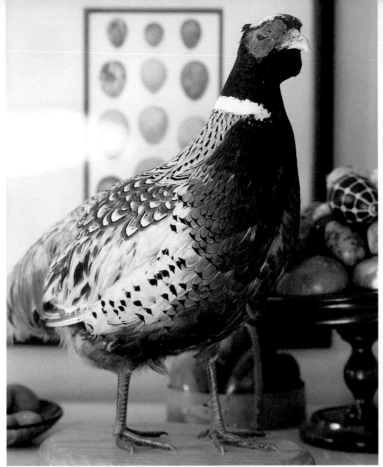

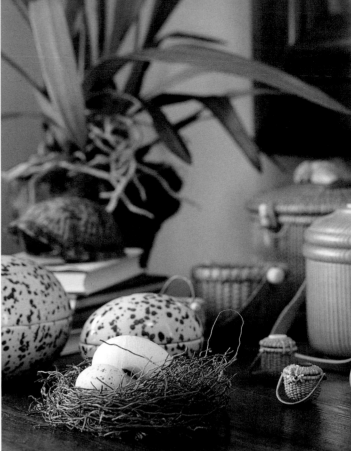

Opposite: A desk in the corner of the guest room is laden with a collection of Nantucket lightship baskets, some woven and some made of wood.

Above: Here in the guest room, a stuffed pheasant stands guard over an egg collection.

Top right: Large ceramic egg boxes sit behind a bird's nest found nearby. The two miniature baskets were made by Georgia Axt.

Right: Pillows on the guest bed add texture and color.

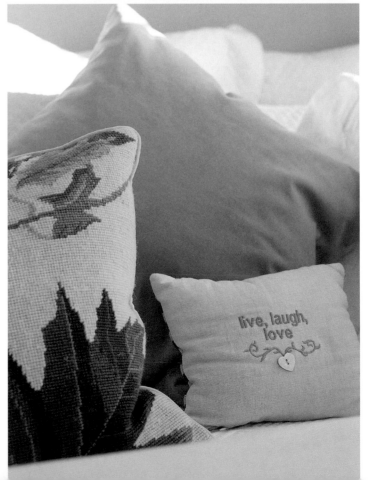

a local establishment owned by Geo Davis. She loves collections of objects and finds they create greater visual impact when grouped together.

Kathleen notes one final thing: "I like to think of my house as a stage set, ever able, ready, and willing to change. Or like a laboratory—a place where I can experiment with color, pattern, and floor plans. Each room has a feel of its own, and yet the house flows together."

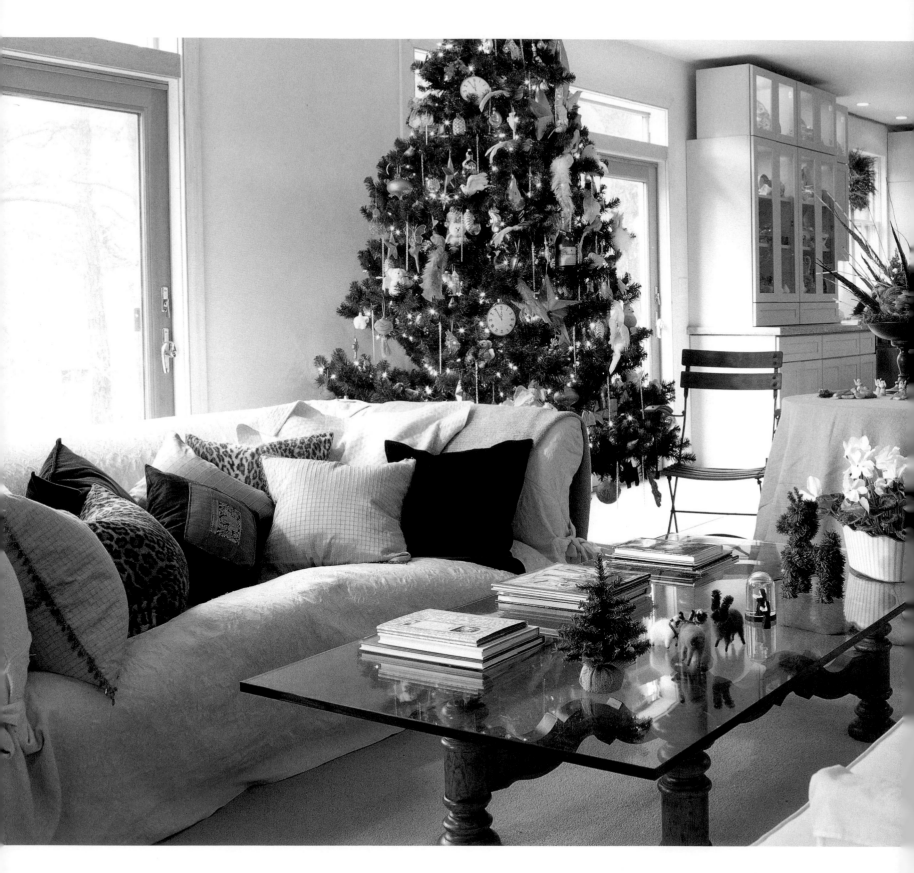

AT HOME IN NANTUCKET

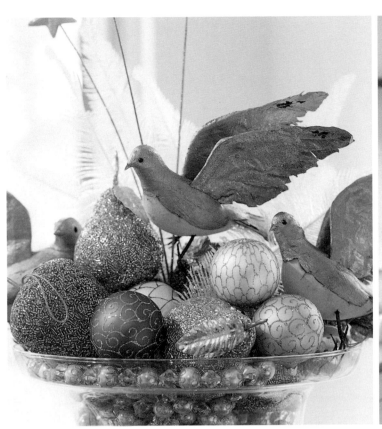
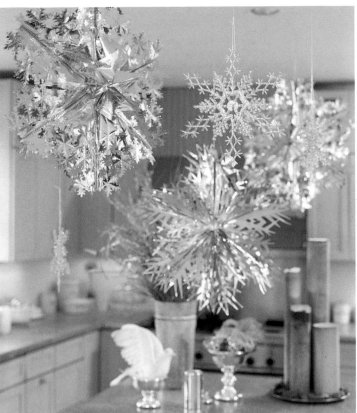

THE CHRISTMAS STROLL

Back in 1974, Nantucket retailers were looking for a way to encourage locals to do their Christmas shopping on the island instead of going to Cape Cod. So the Chamber of Commerce, along with other island business organizations, launched the Christmas Stroll for one long weekend of shopping. Surprisingly, when news of the stroll reached the mainland, visitors flocked to the island to shop as well. Soon the whole Christmas season was extended to include the Nantucket Noel, which runs from the day after Thanksgiving until New Year's Eve. The Nantucket Noel kicks off with the lighting of the tree at the top of Main Street. Additional trees line both sides of Main Street, and the major shopping streets are decorated by local schoolchildren and retailers. Because of the increase in holiday activities, Nantucket has become a popular destination even in December, and sales in restaurants and stores are comparable to those during the summer months, if not better. People stop over from the mainland for a night or two, or just pop over for lunch and a day of shopping. For more information about the Nantucket Noel and Christmas Stroll, contact the Nantucket Chamber of Commerce at (508) 228-1700.

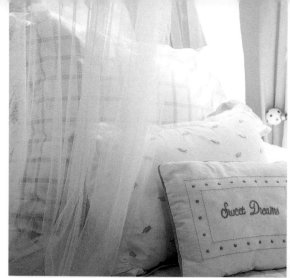

Previous spread, left: The view from the living room toward the kitchen. The tree is covered with colorful ornaments, including many birds, a personal favorite of Kathleen's.

Previous spread, middle and right: Birds play an important theme throughout the house. Here, gold doves alight on a vase filled with ornaments, and a white dove alights on the kitchen counter under big metallic snowflakes.

Above: Layers of pillows sit under mosquito netting on the girls' beds.

Right: Building your own house is an ongoing work in progress, so to speed up completion of the master bath, Kathleen made a make-shift counter out of an insulation panel.

Opposite: Daughters Madeleine and Isabelle share this delightfully feminine bedroom.

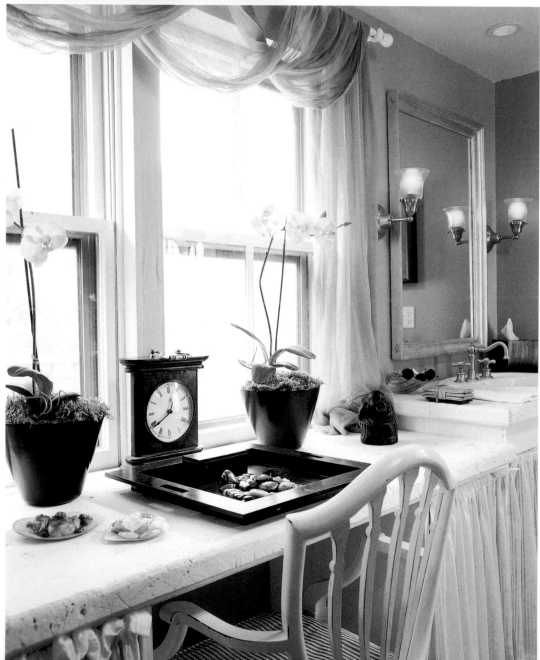

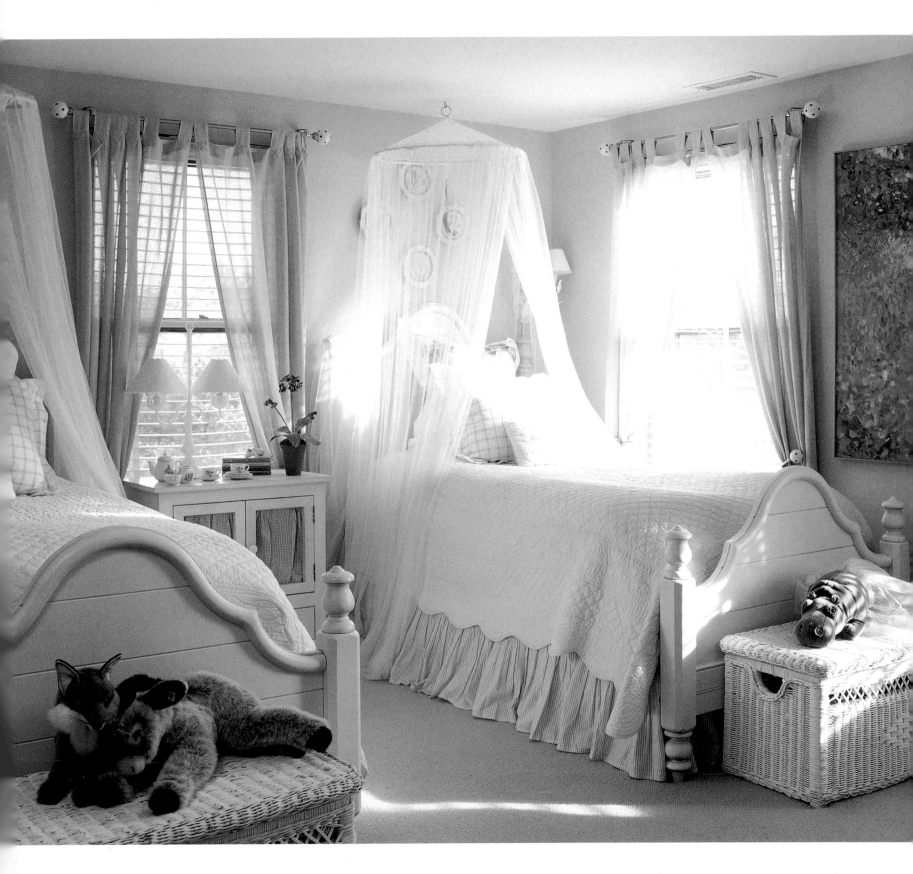

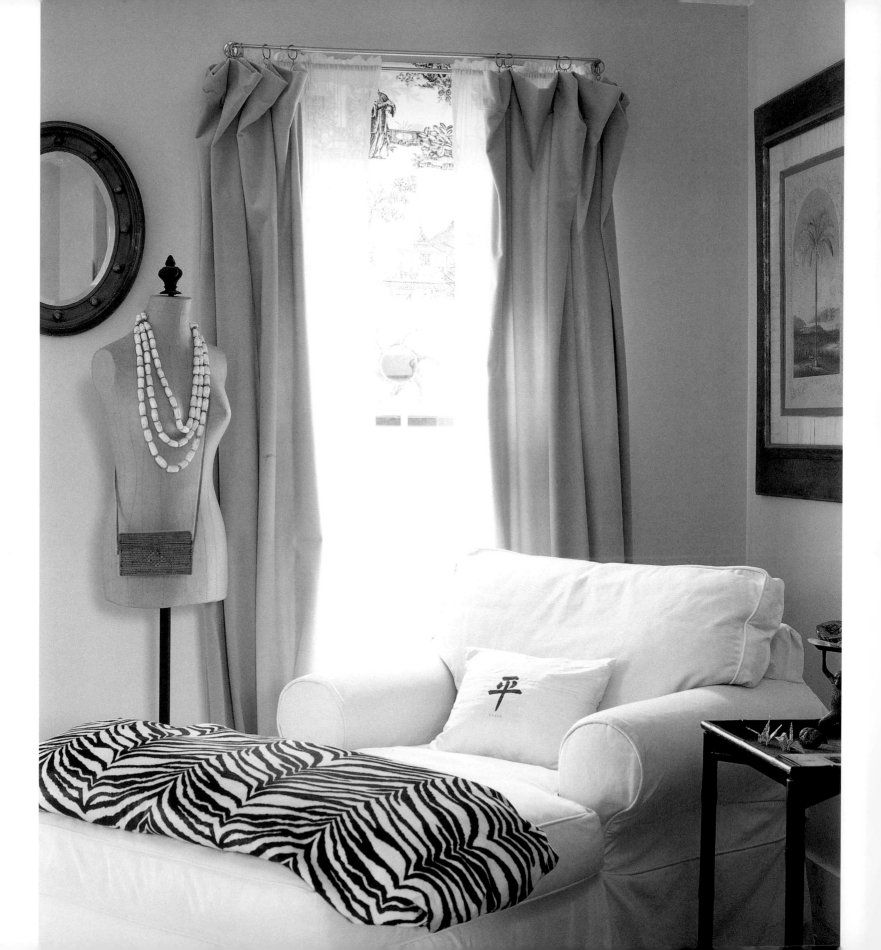

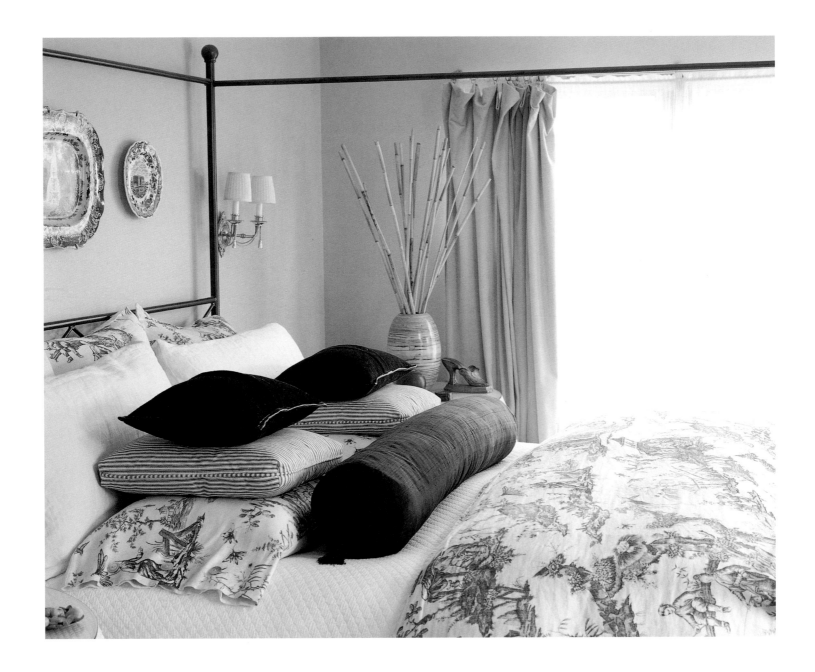

Opposite: A corner of the master suite offers a tranquil spot to relax. *Above:* On the bed in the master suite, Kathleen stacked layers of pillows, her signature style; a platter and two plates hang above the headboard.

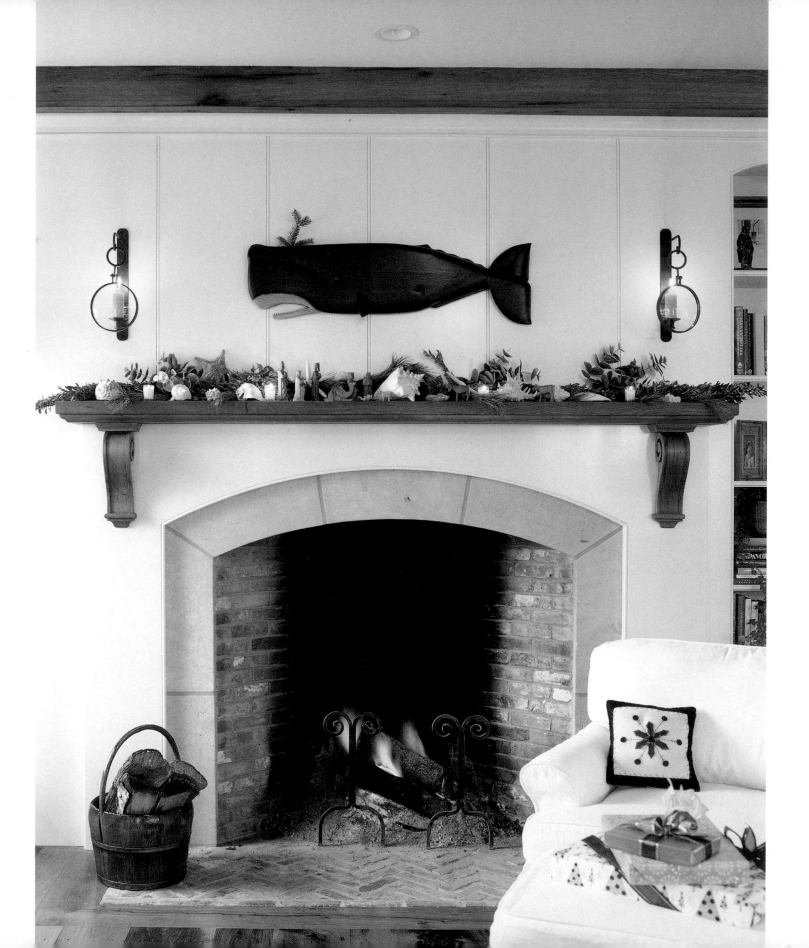

family haven

Up a quiet lane on the way out of town, Jonathan and Elizabeth Raith have created a soothing haven for their family of five. "We designed the house together. We gathered ideas from historic Nantucket details and other period houses and incorporated elements we observed while traveling in southern Italy and Tuscany," says Elizabeth. The house was built in 1992 by Jon's company, which specializes in historic restoration and reproduction houses.

The house suits the Raiths' lifestyle well. Elizabeth notes, "With three children ages nine to seven months, we live casually with the beach, coming in and out like the tide, but we also appreciate good design and antiques."

The entry hall is furnished simply. Multiple pairs of shoes are lined up under a green bench, and an antique pine porridge table has been placed against the far wall. Above it is a wrought-iron mirror flanked by two white botanical prints found in a local store.

From there you enter the "gathering room," a combination living and dining room, which opens into the spacious kitchen. None of these three spaces is truly divided from the others in a casual layout that still enhances intimacy. If you are in the kitchen, it is easy to carry on a conversation with someone in the living room and keep an eye out for children running around. This is ideal for the Raiths, who often invite family and friends over for a meal.

Elizabeth, who runs her own interior design business, chose a pale palette for these rooms, with sunny yellow walls and white or off-white upholstery and slipcovers, but she added just enough red in the sofa and window treatments to give it a bit of a lift. "We wanted a Tuscan farmhouse feel in the kitchen with plenty of room for several cooks," she says. Using a lot of reclaimed oak in the island and in cabinetry details, the Raiths designed a kitchen both inviting and easy to work in. A tiled recess behind the stove is perfect for holding cooking oils and spices. Refrigerator drawers and bins for vegetables are hidden in the island. From the big farmhouse sink, it's easy to see who is at the front door.

Opposite: In the "gathering room," a fireplace provides the focal point. Jon's company built the mantle, and the whale suspended above was carved by Carter Melton.

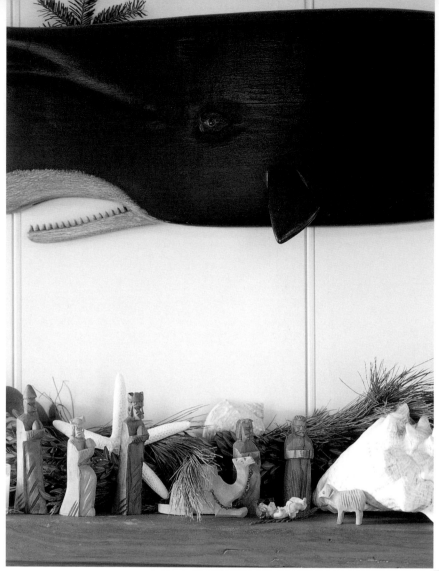

The Raiths also have included whaling details in the house, which is appropriate on more than one level. Above the fireplace there is a beautiful wooden whale carved by local artist Carter Melton, and on another wall hangs an etching of Elizabeth's great-grandfather's ship. Elizabeth notes, "Nantucket was the whaling capital of the world in the mid-nineteenth century, but I have an interesting family connection as well. My middle name, Walker, is from my great-grandfather David Walker, the captain of the whale ship *John and Elizabeth*." It seems it was written in the stars for Jonathan and Elizabeth to meet and together create this nurturing environment for family and friends.

Above: Wooden crèche figurines found in Jerusalem mix with seashells for a true Nantucket Christmas.

Right: On an English side table found locally at The Lion's Paw, paper white narcissus fill a ceramic lightship basket and a "Whaler" guitar, made by Elizabeth's brother for her son, sits on a reproduction fan-back armchair.

Opposite: The floor in the "gathering room" is made of reclaimed antique oak. The "Pick Your Own Apples" sign was purchased at a Nantucket crafts fair to remind them of the apple-picking trips they take to Vermont every fall.

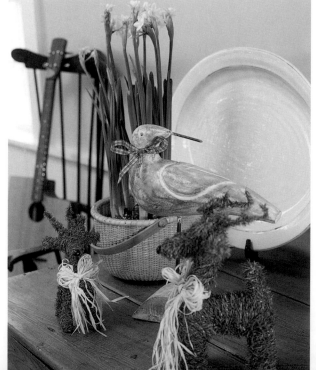

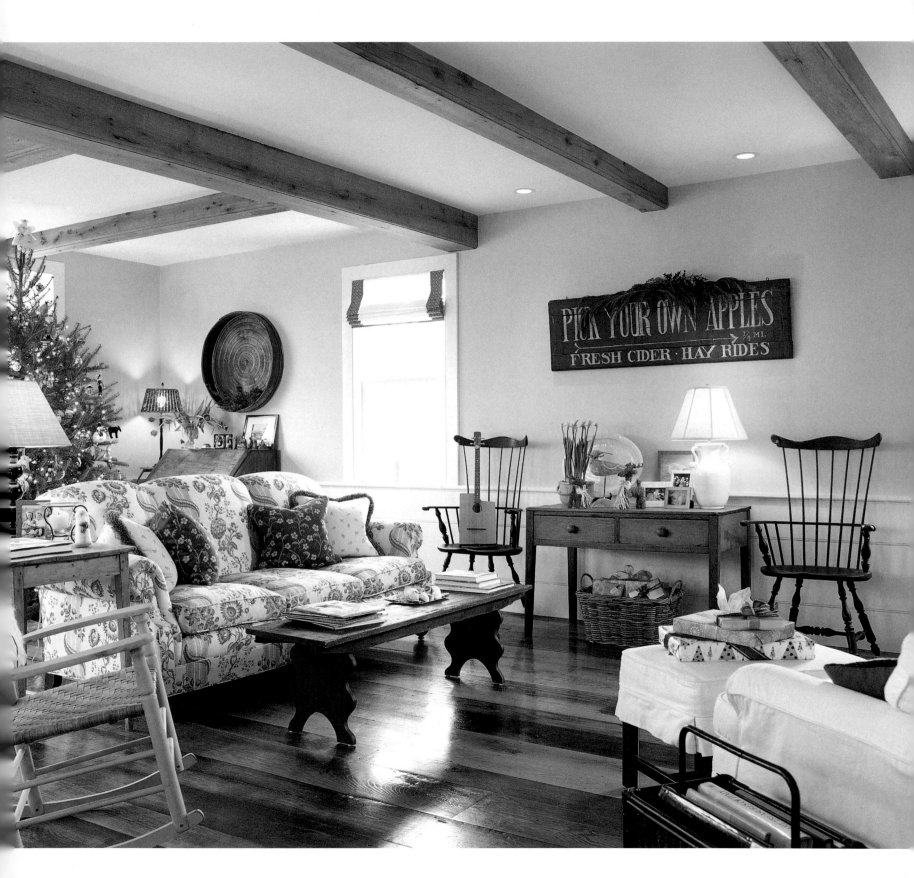

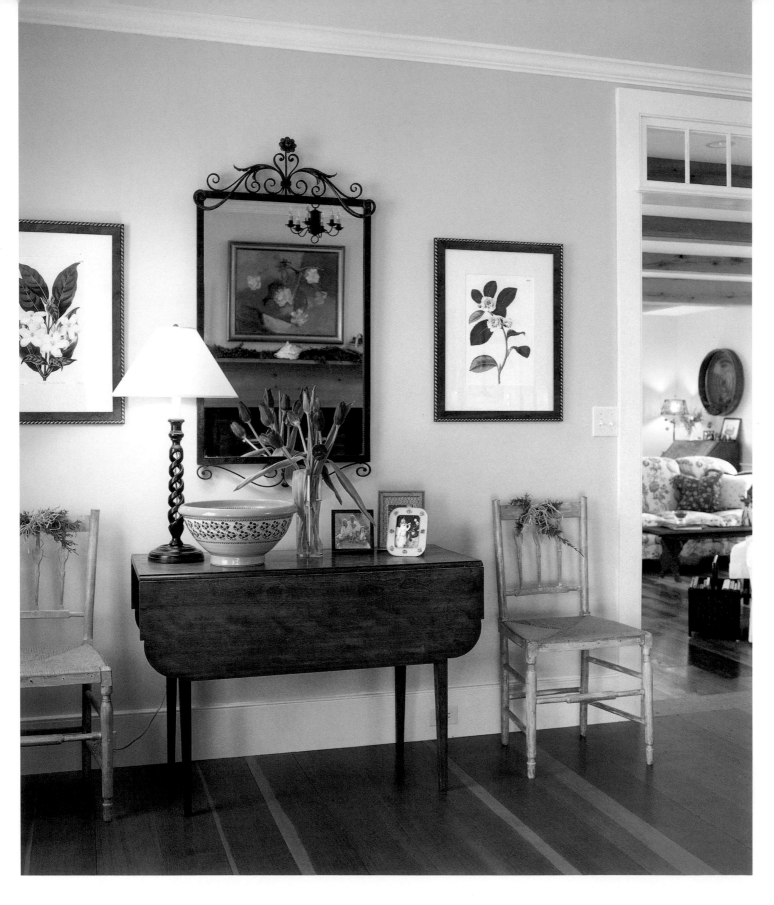

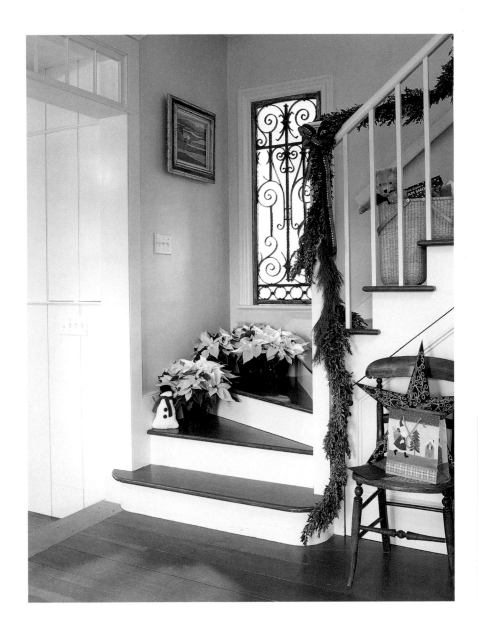

Opposite: In the entry hall, an antique pine porridge table holds a favorite bowl from Nicholas Mosse pottery. *Left:* On the stairs, white poinsettias and a plain garland keep the decorations simple. A lightship basket, made specifically for stairs, holds an antique teddy bear.

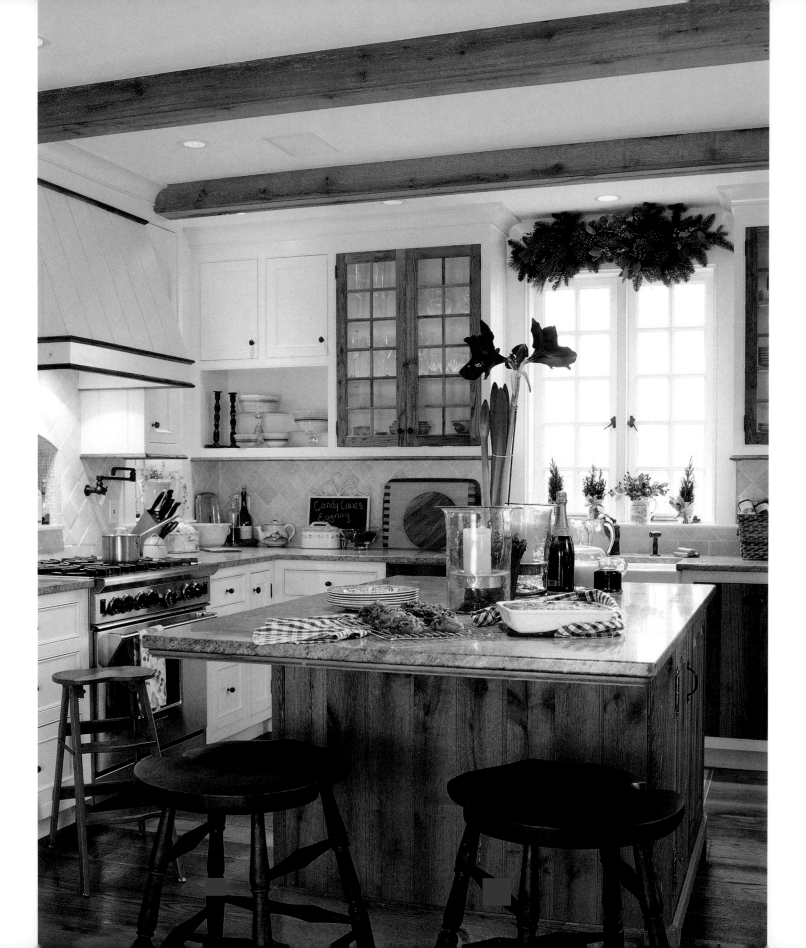

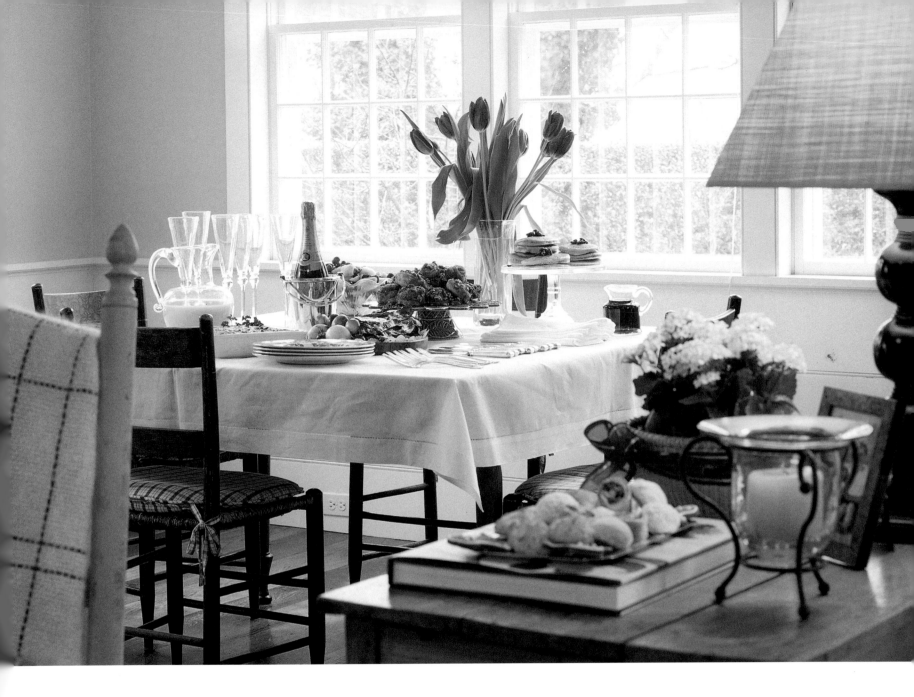

Opposite: The spacious kitchen has been given a Tuscan feel. The island is made from reclaimed oak and discreetly hides an icemaker, two Sub-Zero refrigerator drawers, and bins for vegetables. The Windsor-style stools came from Bryce M. Ritter & Son in Pennsylvania.

Above: A Christmas brunch made by friend and caterer Kendra Lockley starts with champagne mimosas in glasses from Simon Pearce, leading into a decadent repast of pancakes, bacon, frittata, and sticky buns hot from the oven.

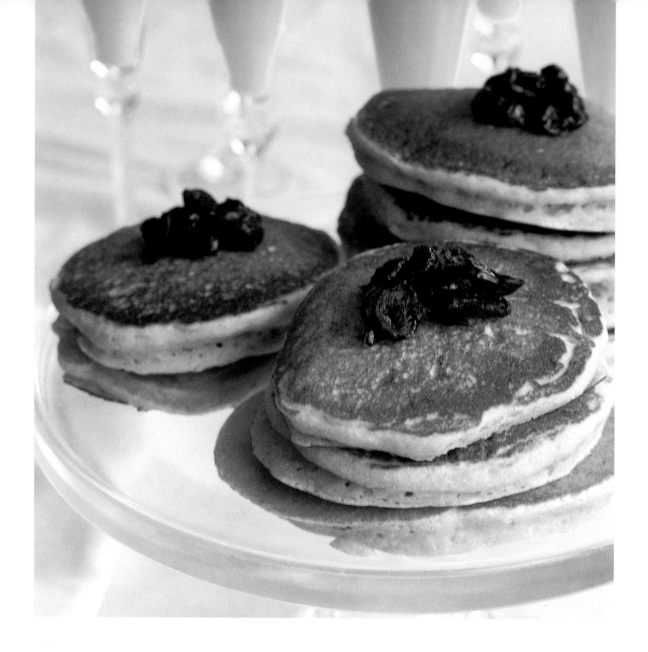

Christmas Morning

Like the rest of the year, Elizabeth and Jon often have a household full of family and friends around Christmastime. To start off the day, Elizabeth's good friend Kendra Lockley, a local caterer who owns her own business called Simply with Style, recommends a buffet breakfast when the house is full of guests, because it's easier on the cook and on the diners. In addition to big plates of bacon, stacks of pancakes, and an ample supply of mimosas, Kendra suggests making sticky buns and a frittata or two to satisfy everyone's appetites.

Frittata

1 large yellow onion

1 red bell pepper

1 yellow bell pepper

2 plum tomatoes

2 Yukon gold potatoes

4 mushrooms

4 tablespoons olive oil

Kosher salt and pepper

10 eggs, lightly beaten

1/4 cup heavy cream

1/4 cup grated Parmesan

1/4 cup grated mozzarella

1/2 cup fresh basil, chopped

1. Preheat oven to 400 degrees F.

2. Coarsely chop vegetables and place in a bowl. Add olive oil and salt and pepper to taste and toss until vegetables are well mixed and evenly coated with oil. Put in a large baking pan and roast for 12 minutes, or until they are somewhat crispy. Set aside.

3. In a large bowl, combine eggs, cream, Parmesan, mozzarella, basil, 2 teaspoons salt, and a pinch of pepper. When thoroughly mixed, fold in roasted vegetables.

4. Pour mixture into a well-buttered casserole dish and bake for 35 minutes, or until center is soft. Remove from oven. The frittata will continue to cook after leaving the oven. Let it cool for 10 minutes before serving.

5. Serve warm.

Serves 10

Sticky Buns

For the dough
(make the day before):

1 1/2 cups warm water

2 tablespoons yeast

3 tablespoons granulated sugar

1 tablespoon salt

5 cups unbleached all-purpose flour

1 cup (2 sticks) sweet butter, softened

For the topping
(make the day of):

1 cup butter

2 cups brown sugar

1/4 cup light corn syrup

2 cups pecan pieces

1/4 cup granulated sugar mixed with 1 teaspoon cinnamon

1. To make the dough, put water, yeast, and sugar in the bowl of a heavy-duty stand mixer fitted with the dough hook. Mix lightly with a fork and let stand 5 minutes. Add salt and flour and mix until very smooth, 8 to 10 minutes.

2. Let dough rest for 10 minutes, then turn out onto a floured work surface. Roll out into a rectangle about 1/2 inch thick.

3. Spread butter over the rectangle to within 1/4 inch from edge. Flour and fold dough into thirds, roll out again, flour and fold into thirds, then pat into a thick rectangle. Wrap in plastic wrap and refrigerate overnight.

4. To make the topping, place butter, brown sugar, and corn syrup in a saucepan and bring to a boil over medium heat. Be careful not to burn. Add pecans and remove from heat.

5. Spread mixture over the bottom of a 13-by-18-inch baking pan. Set aside.

6. Remove dough from refrigerator. Place on a floured work surface and roll into a very thin rectangle (the thinner the better).

7. Sprinkle cinnamon sugar over the rectangle. Starting at one end, roll dough up in a tight cylinder. Cut into 1-inch slices and place slices on top of the carmelized nuts in the pan. Set aside for about an hour to let rolls rise.

8. Place pan on a baking sheet (sugar will melt and smoke if it hits the bottom of the oven) and bake at 350 degrees F for 25 to 30 minutes, or until the tops of the buns are medium brown.

9. Remove from oven and let rest for about 5 minutes. Cover the buns with another pan or baking sheet and invert carefully. Serve warm.

Serves 10

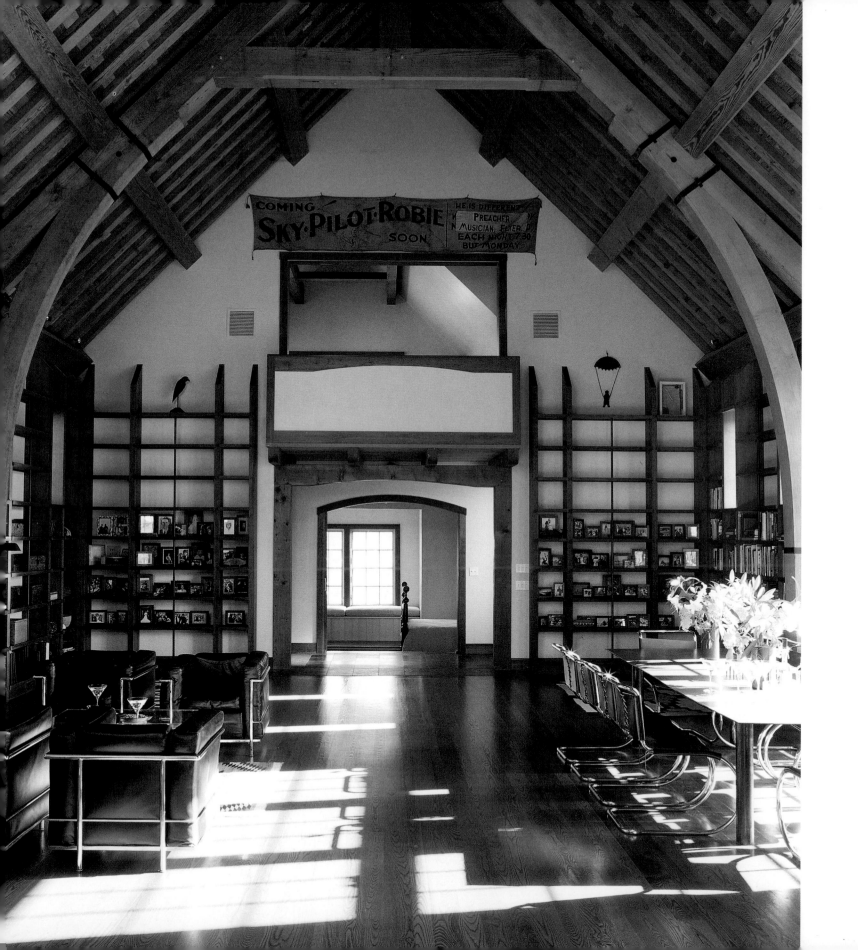

minimalist barn

In a glade down a sandy lane from the main house sits a majestic, timber-frame barn. Its owners, who are avid bird-watchers and nature lovers, bought the property because of its secluded locale—and in deference to their wishes for privacy, they will remain anonymous. But the barn certainly speaks for itself. In the midst of four thousand acres of conservation land known as the Middle Moors, the barn faces toward Sankaty Lighthouse, out in Siasconset. Nearby lie cranberry bogs and the mysterious Hidden Forest, where gnarled, ancient hardwood trees grow so close together that they intertwine with one another.

From the outside, the barn is simple and unadorned. An expansive lawn surrounds it, running right up to the foundation. Inside, the vaulted ceiling, with its beautifully carved timbers, is awe inspiring. It has the look of a chapel, with its simplicity of design and beautiful proportions. Built in the early 1990s by Tedd Bensen Woodworking, the structure replicates the proportions of an English barn constructed by Cistercian monks in the thirteenth century. The timbers have an interesting history: they are recycled from a lumber mill built in 1928 in Washington state and were brought to Nantucket specifically for this building.

The structure itself is composed of one main room. A series of shelves fills each corner, to accommodate books, family photographs, and various collections such as lidded boxes and pottery fragments. The homeowners use the barn primarily as a guest house, although they often choose to have dinner with friends here instead of in the main house because of its dramatic space. Minimalist furniture by such noted designers at Le Corbusier and Mies van der Rohe complements the space perfectly, side-stepping the distortion of heavy, overly "busy" furnishings. The homeowners bought the furniture in the 1960s, when it was new and cutting edge. They've held on to it for thirty-five years, and now it has seen a resurgence in popularity, which only enhances the timelessness of the barn's interior.

At one end of the barn, a kitchen has been discreetly incorporated into the space, and big glass doors lead out to a patio. At the opposite end, near the front door, a sunken bedroom looks out onto the bogs. Sliding cherry doors can be closed for privacy. The long window seat

Opposite: Pictured here showing the view toward the downstairs bedroom, the capacious main room features a huge metal table accompanied by Mies van der Rohe chairs made of leather and chrome.

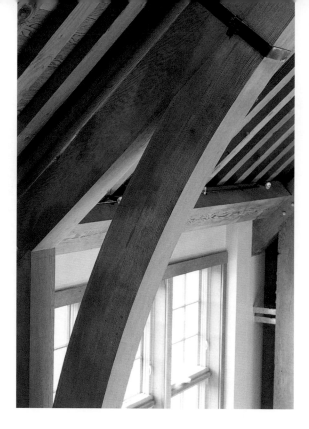

Left: A detail of the carved timbers show their massive size and the skill of the hands that made them. *Opposite:* Shelves are filled with myriad collections. On the bottom shelf, lead birds from an old shooting gallery have been massed together for greater visual impact. Above them are woven basket fragments from Africa. On the next shelf, pre-Columbian Mayan pottery fragments stand on miniature pedestals.

is a nice spot in the evening, when the distant light from Sankaty Lighthouse flashes into the room. Down the hall, a sleek, modern bathroom is situated at the bottom of the stairs. Its frosted-glass counter and shower walls are complemented by pale blue mosaic tiles. A chrome basin sink sits on the counter, and simple cabinetry above stores basic necessities.

Upstairs is a second bedroom, really a loft, with several beds and a balcony that overlooks the huge main room below. From this perspective it is much easier to appreciate the stunning craftsmanship that went into building the barn. Even the color of the wood takes on a rich, warm glow.

The barn reflects the homeowners' philosophy that simpler is better. It is a cozy, welcoming space for guests and entertaining or for solitary reflecting. It gives great pleasure when you unexpectedly come upon it in the clearing, and it leaves you with the sense that simply by entering it, you will feel inspired.

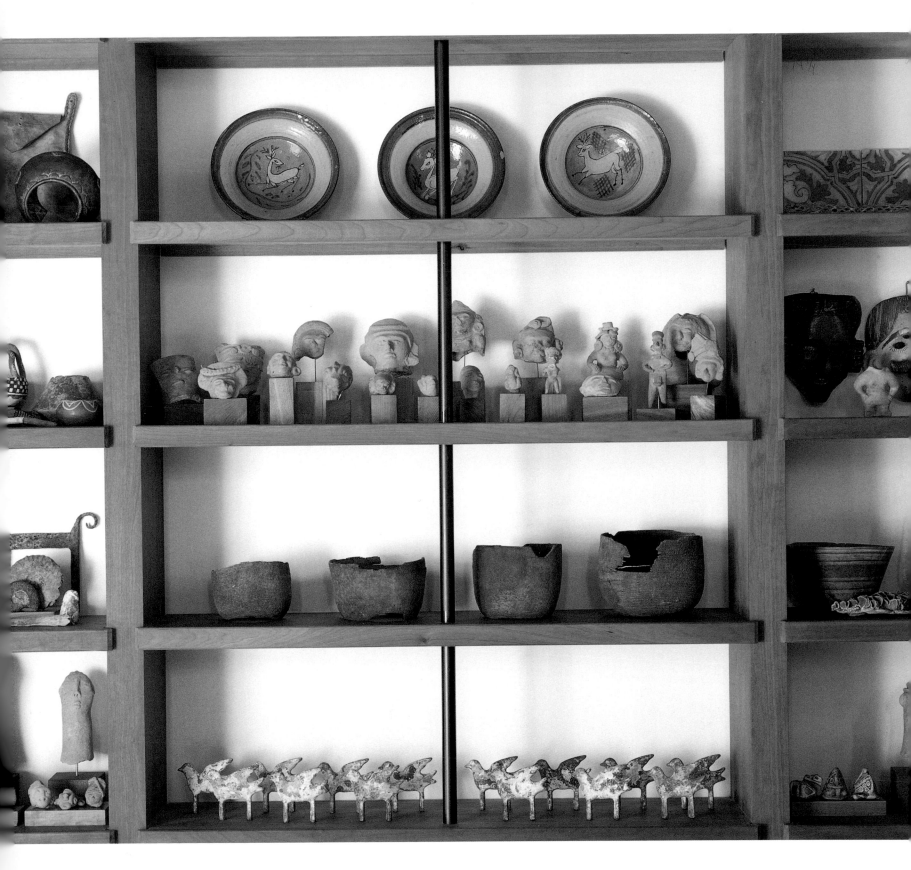

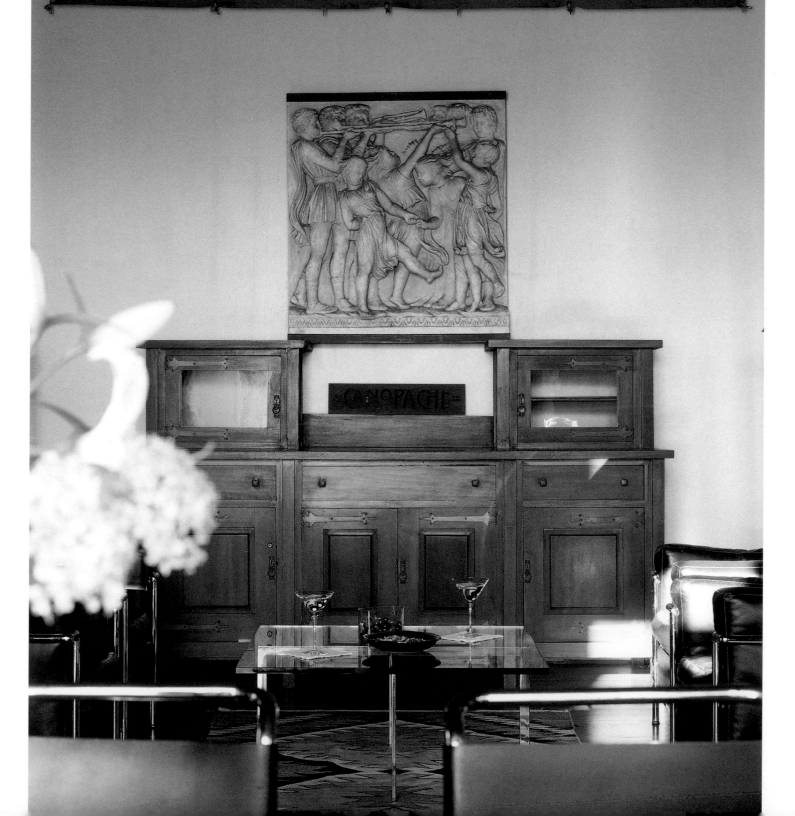

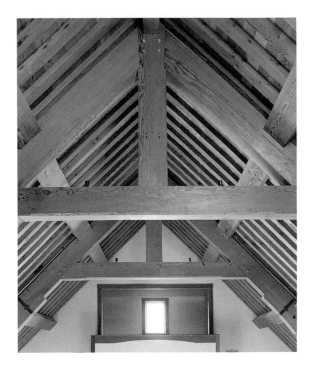

Opposite: A seating area located below an old Victorian frieze comprises four Le Corbusier leather chairs clustered around a Mies van der Rohe glass coffee table.

Above: The soaring vaulted ceilings give life to the interior.

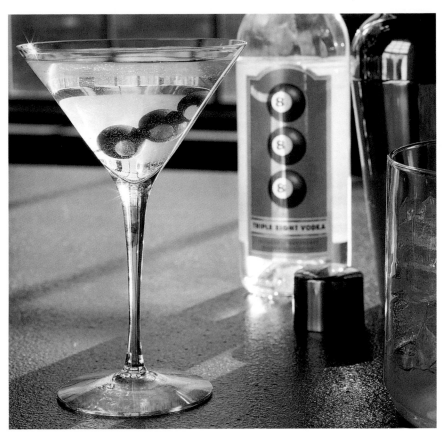

Holiday Cocktails

Adam Sabin, the "mixologist" at Triple Eight Distillery, created the Triple Eight Martini for holiday entertaining. Triple Eight Distillery is part of the conglomerate of beverage makers on the island that also includes Cisco Brewers and Nantucket Vineyard.

Triple Eight Martini

Shake 5 $^{1}/_{2}$ ounces of Triple Eight Vodka for eight seconds in a martini shaker. Strain into a martini glass and garnish with 3 black olives filled with goat cheese.

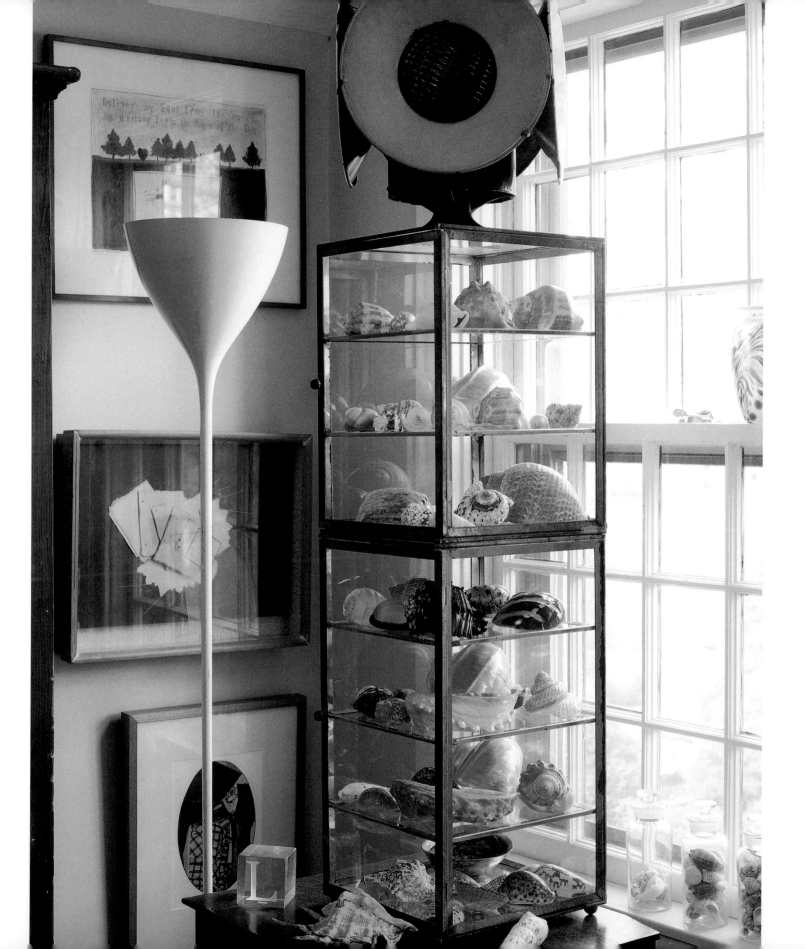

private museum

At a busy intersection just at the edge of the town of Nantucket there sits a little cottage that has been transformed into a veritable private museum. Its owner is Reggie Levine, and it reflects Reggie's deep involvement in the Nantucket artistic community for more than thirty years. Reggie owned the Main Street Gallery for most of that time, representing many local and some national artists. When he closed his business in 1999, Reggie became an art consultant, advising his clients on what to buy and how to hang it.

Built in the 1950s, the cottage was originally his parents' home. When Reggie moved in, some forty years later, he needed to make some renovations to accommodate his ever growing art collection. Most importantly, he raised the ceilings to allow for more light and to create more space for hanging artwork.

The house has a small kitchen just inside the front door to the right, and a small dining room to the left. The dining room is just the right size to sit four for dinner, and its sloped ceiling allows light to enter from a high window. The dining room leads into the living room, where cathedral ceilings add tremendously to the space. Lanterns hang from the ceiling at either end, and a large mirror is mounted over the fireplace to give the room added depth. Every space has been filled with a piece of artwork. "I don't really have a favorite medium or style or period of time," says Reggie. He just knows what he likes.

On the coffee tables sitting in front of the two sofas, various objects are carefully set out on display. Side tables, cupboards, glass cabinets, and even windowsills are laden with personal treasures, and paintings hang on all four walls. A cabinet in one corner houses Reggie's beloved collection of shells, which he has been adding to since childhood. On a coffee table is a handmade checker set, and stained-glass windows on either side of the fireplace send colorful flashes of light into the room.

From the living room, the house stretches back in warrenlike fashion. Reggie's bedroom is to the right; down a hall to the left is another small room; then comes the library. The bedroom is impeccably tidy and, despite the many objects on display, quite simple and modest. The other room houses such collections as red Bohemian glassware and Treenware from England and the United States. The library is tiny but has enough room for a sofa and a desk. Dark and cozy, it is the perfect place to settle down with a book on a wintry day.

Opposite: A railroad lamp from the 1920s sits on top of a glass cabinet that houses a seashell collection Reggie started as a child.

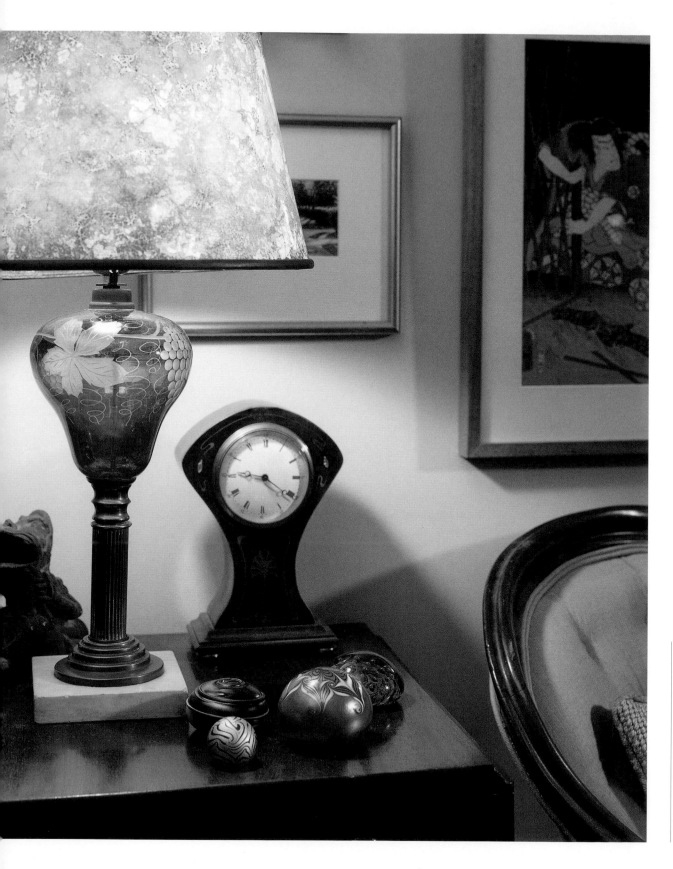

Left: The red-glass lamp was originally fueled by kerosene. The odd-looking red troll is a French toy that you use by tossing coins into its mouth. *Opposite:* A quick glance at the living room gives an immediate sense of the scope of Reggie's collections. Above the Victorian sofa hangs a painting by Keith McDaniel.

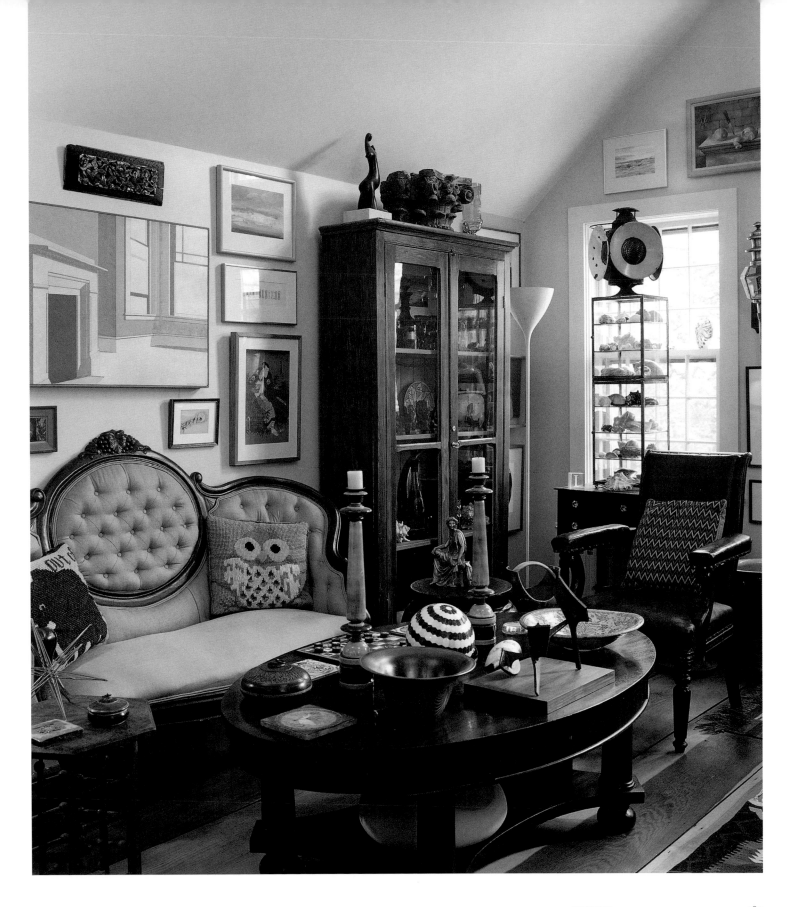

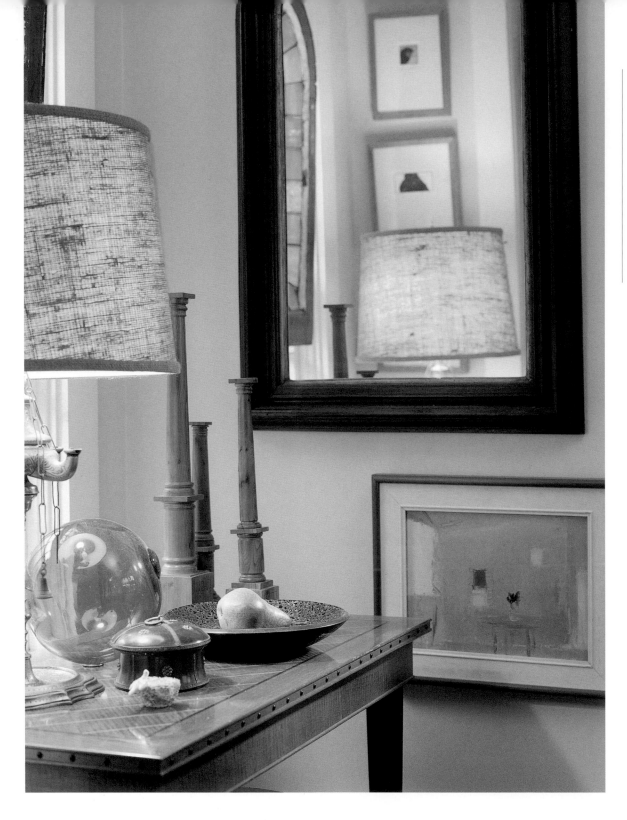

Left: A Turkish lamp seen here was originally a water pipe. Below the mirror is a painting by Nantucket artist Charlotte Kimbel.

Opposite: In this view of the living room, the dining room is visible in the background. An American stained-glass piece hangs in the window. In front of the fireplace is a Turkish prayer rug from the mid-nineteenth century.

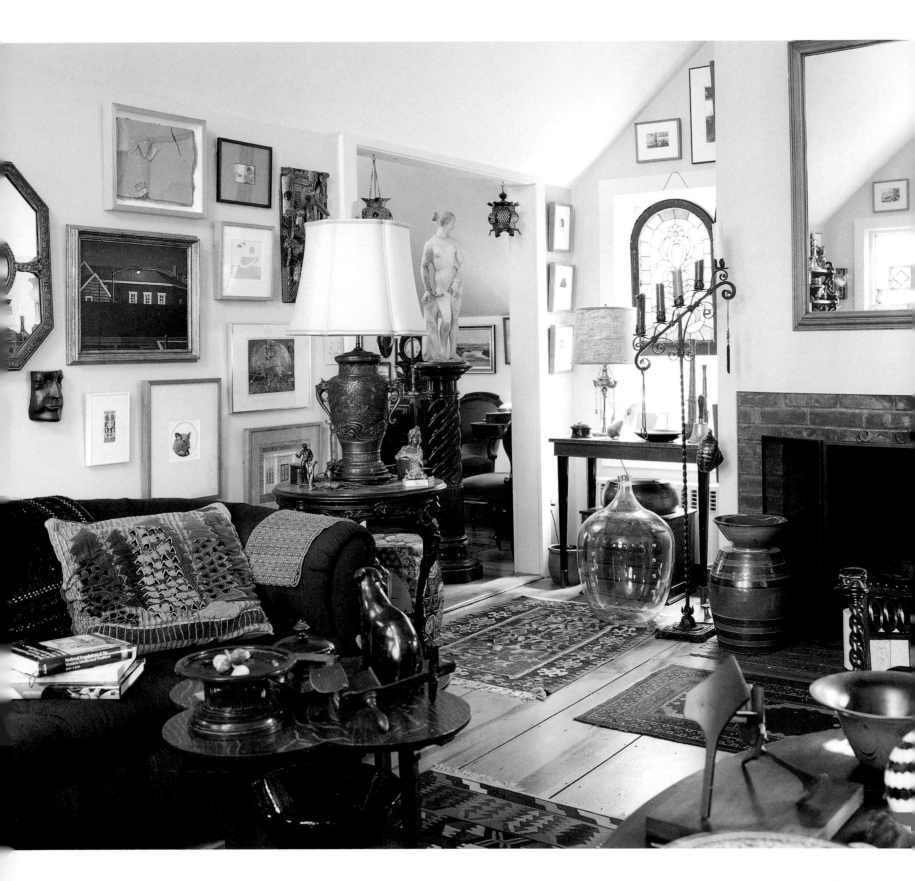

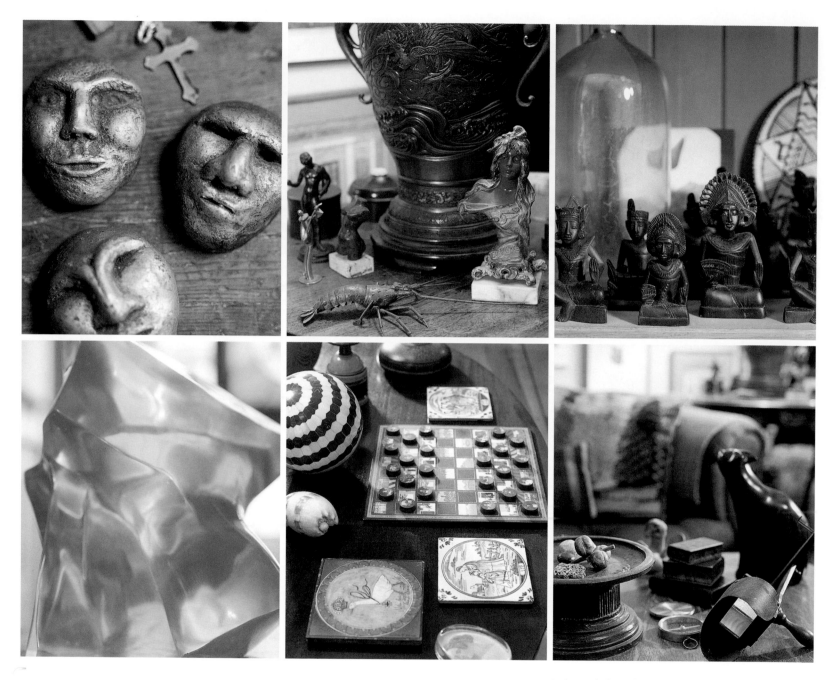

Above (clockwise from top left): Intriguing conversation pieces include contemporary masks by Will Adair, a Chinese bronze lamp towering over an assortment of miniature sculptures, wooden figures from Indonesia, and an abstract resin sculpture. On the coffee table sits a delightful hand-painted checkerboard, and a goose tile from Siena, Italy; and on another a favorite sculpture of a cat. *Opposite: The Greek Slave*, a sculpture by Hiram Powers, stands between the living room and dining room.

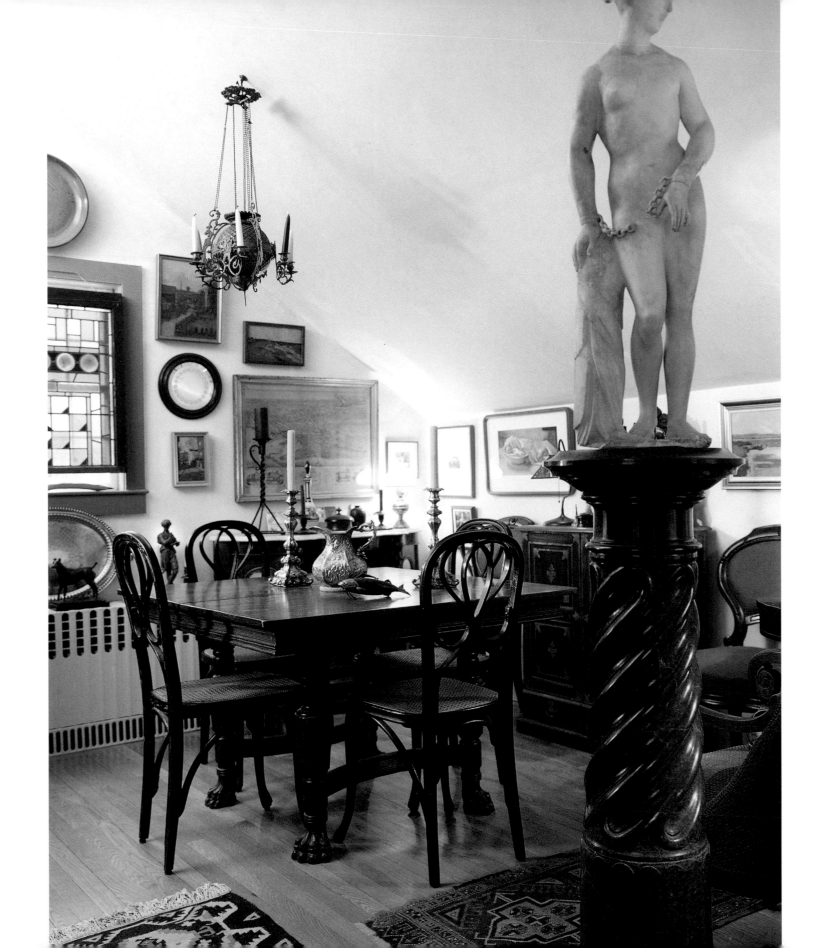

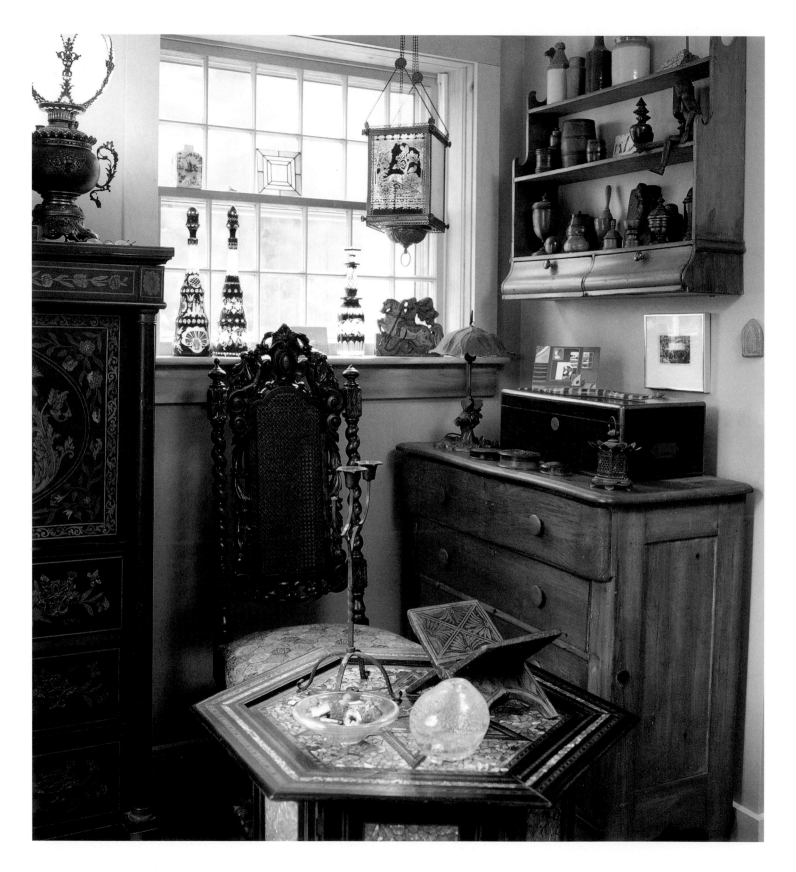

AT HOME IN NANTUCKET

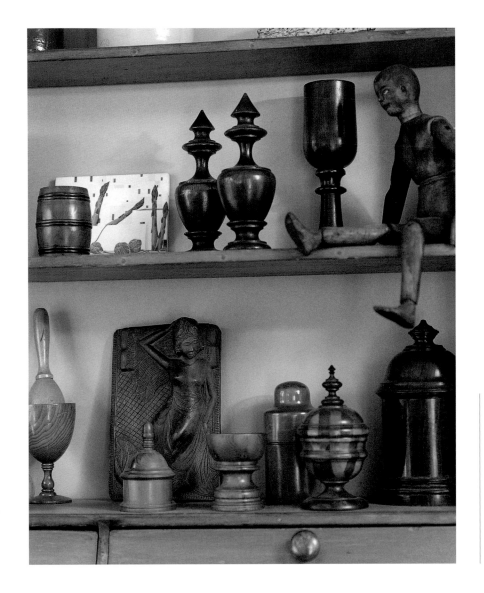

Opposite: A Middle Eastern table inlaid with mother-of-pearl stands in the center of a small room, just outside the library. On the windowsill are Bohemian glass decanters.

Left: Reggie's collection of Treenware is a combination of functional and collectible pieces.

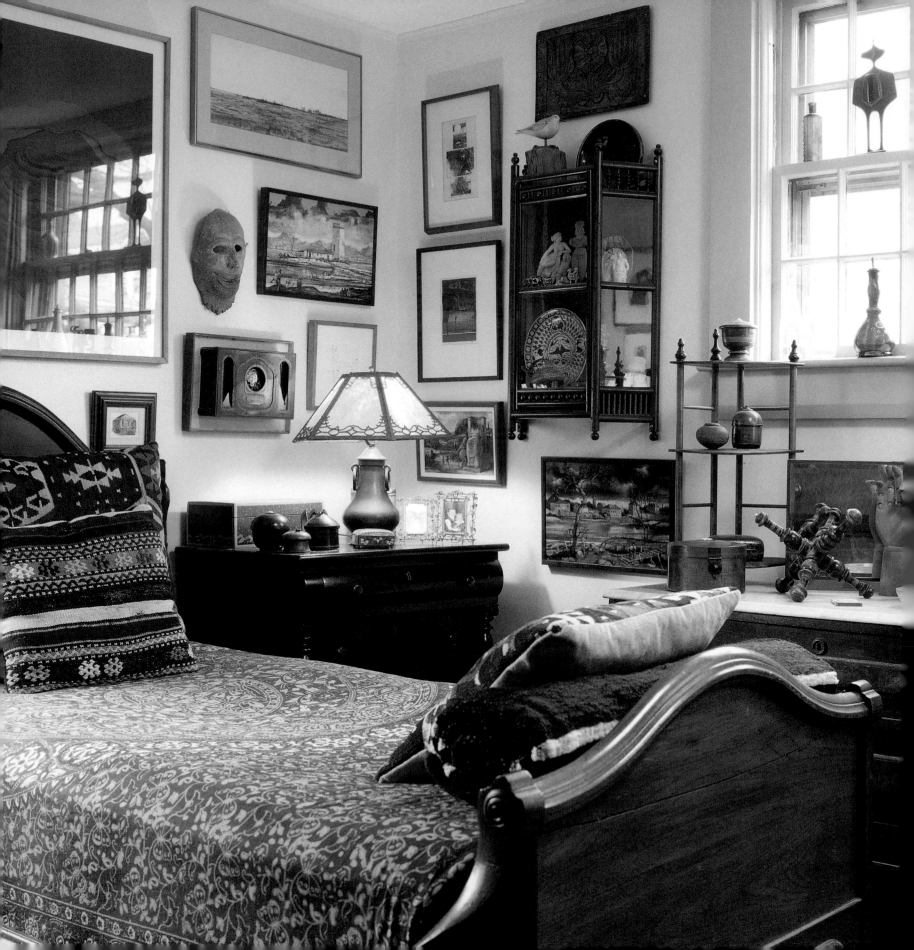

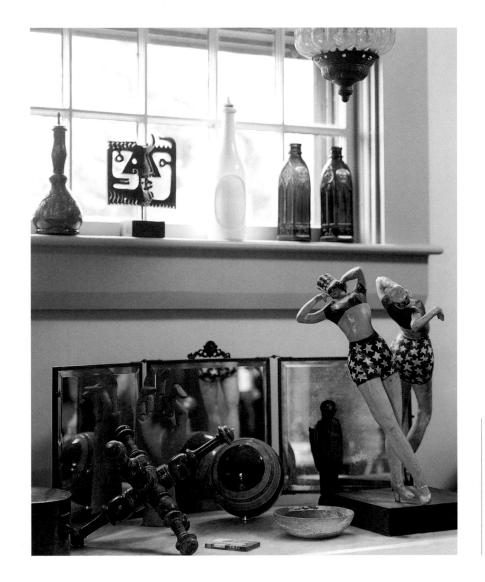

Opposite: In Reggie's bedroom, a simple Victorian bed has been accented with kilim pillows.
Left: On a bureau, a wooden jacklike Indian tray stand keeps company with a third-century Greek glass bowl.

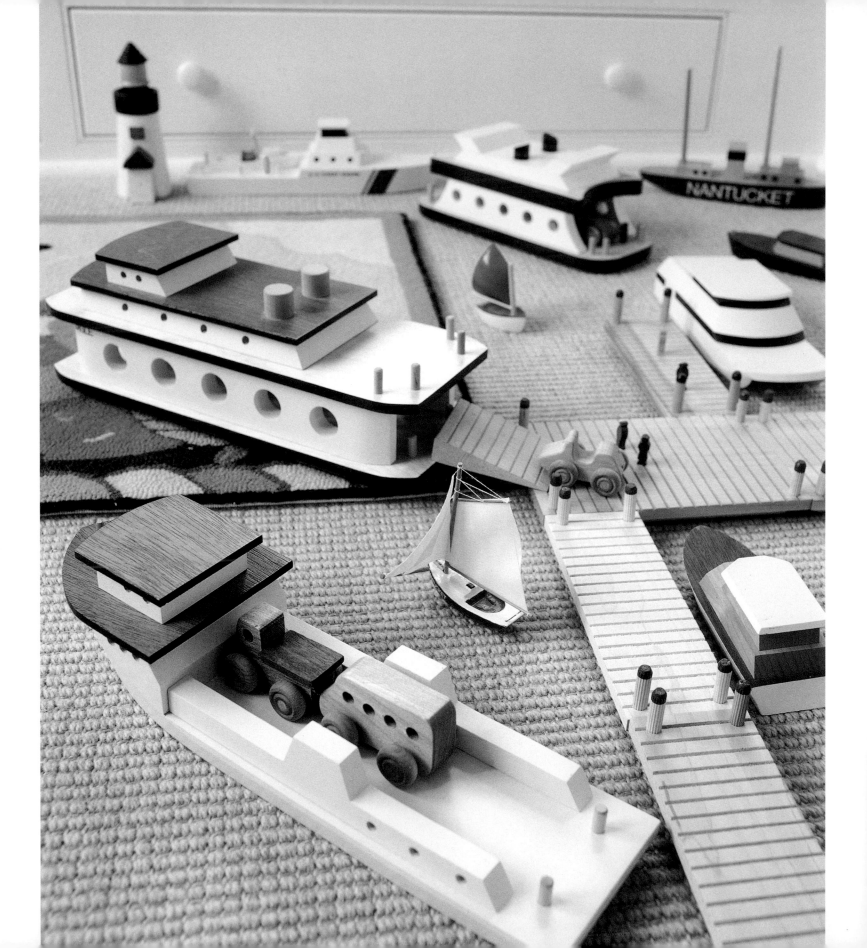

visitor's guide

Nantucket's rich whaling history, world-class restaurants, diverse retail stores, and plethora of opportunities for outdoor activities make it an ideal vacation spot. Toward the end of the nineteenth century, the whaling industry went into decline; the year-round population became quite small and all business slowed. But by the 1920s, summer tourism had picked up, and soon it became Nantucket's new industry. Today, the peak season is still in the summer, but each year visitors stay longer or come earlier to enjoy the idyllic Nantucket lifestyle.

Although you can take a quick flight from Hyannis or Boston, part of the allure of going to Nantucket is taking the ferry. The trip is as short as an hour from Hyannis, and it adds to the adventure of arriving on the island. Nantucket slowly comes into view on the horizon, and as you approach the harbor, church steeples and the beautiful homes that line Cliff Road rise up. Once off the ferry, you are a quick walk from the main part of town or an easy cab ride to your accommodations.

If you want to visit during the summer, plan well in advance. Accommodations are limited, and bringing a car onto the island requires a reservation on the car ferry sometimes as much as a year before hand. But there are plenty of places to rent a car when you get there. To help you plan your visit, here are some services and recommendations.

getting there

Since Nantucket lies thirty miles out to sea, the only way to get there is by boat or plane. Flights and ferries leave daily from Hyannis. Direct flights also depart from several regional cities, such as Boston, Providence, and New York.

Cape Air/Nantucket Air
(800) 352-0714
www.flycapeair.com
Departs from Boston, Hyannis, and Providence.

Island Airlines
(800) 698-1109
www.nantucket.net/trans/islandair
Departs from Hyannis only.

US Airways
(800) 428-4322
www.usairways.com
Departs from Boston, New York, and Providence.

Steamship Authority
(508) 228-3274
www.islandferry.com
The only company that offers a car ferry.

Hy-line Cruises
(508) 778-2600
www.hy-linecruises.com
Ferry for passengers only.

accommodations

Nantucket has many kinds of accommodation, from small inns to bed-and-breakfasts to rental homes. Although it gets pricey during peak season, with some advance planning you should be able to find something to suit your budget. If you have children, keep in mind that many places do not accommodate kids under twelve; make sure you inquire when you call.

Nantucket Accommodations
(508) 228-9559
Give them a price range and dates, and they'll do the searching for you. Incredibly efficient and pleasant.

Nantucket Visitor's Service
25 Federal Street
(508) 228-2925
(508) 228-3866
www.nantucketlodging.com

Union Street Inn
7 Union Street
(508) 228-9222
www.unioninn.com

A beautifully decorated traditional bed-and-breakfast located just one block off Main Street. Don't miss the delicious country breakfasts and delightful staff.

Vanessa Noel Hotel
5 Chestnut Street
(508) 228-0400
www.vanno.com

A chic boutique hotel created by the couture shoe designer. It has just eight luxurious rooms with all the right amenities, including plasma televisions.

The Wauwinet
An Inn by the Sea
120 Wauwinet Road
(508) 228-0145
www.wauwinet.com

Located eight miles from Nantucket
Town in an unspoiled corner of the island,
this inn has a restaurant on the grounds
and a sweeping lawn down to its own
private beach.

museums

There are a variety of museums to explore
in Nantucket. Call ahead for hours. Most
museums close during the off-season.
Those open year-round are noted below.

Maria Mitchell Birthplace
1 Vestal Street
(508) 228-2896

Observatory
3 Vestal Street
(508) 228-9273
Open year-round.

Aquarium
59 Milk Street Extension
(508) 228-8690
www.mmo.org

Nantucket Atheneum (public library)
1 India Street
(508) 228-1110
www.nantucketatheneum.org
Open year-round

Nantucket Life-Saving Museum
158 Polpis Road at Folger's Marsh
(508) 228-1885

A great way to visit this museum is to
pack a lunch and ride a bicycle out along
the Polpis bike path.

Nantucket Lightship Basket Museum
49 Union Street
(508) 228-1177

Nantucket Historical Association
15 Broad Street
(508) 228-1894
www.nha.org

Properties include:
Quaker Meeting House, 7 Fair Street
Old Gaol (old jail), 15 Vestal Street
Old Mill, 50 Prospect Street
Oldest House (the oldest house
   on Nantucket), 16 Sunset Hill

Whaling Museum
15 Broad Street
(508) 228-1736
Open year-round, limited hours

activities

The activities available to visitors are numerous:
sailing, fishing, biking, surfing, golfing, and
more. To check out a calendar of current
events, go to www.yesterdayisland.com. For a
listing of stores and restaurants along with
activities, check out www.nantucketonline.com
or www.nantucketchamber.org. You may also
want to stop by the Chamber of Commerce in
person to pick up a schedule of island activities.

Nantucket Chamber of Commerce
48 Main Street
(508) 228-1700

contributors

Many thanks to the restaurant staffs and numerous companies and stores that created recipes and loaned accessories and products to feature in the homes in this book. Here is a listing of those that contributed, along with other resources mentioned in the text. Where appropriate, page numbers have been listed to correspond with specific products. Unless otherwise noted, the mailing address is Nantucket, MA 02554.

Stores and Galleries

The Complete Kitchen
25 Centre Street
(508) 228-2665
Serving bowl, page 72

The Lion's Paw
0 Main Street
(508) 228-3837
Martini glasses pages 180, 181
Platter, page 40

Nantucket Country
38 Centre Street
(508) 228-8868
Collectibles, page 24
Bears, Child's rocker, page 25
Pail and shovel, page 26

Nantucket Looms
16 Main Street
(508) 228-1908
Throws, pages 22, 25, 28
Various items pages 52–63

The Toy Boat
Straight Wharf
(508) 228-4552
Toy boats, page 27

Weeds
14 Centre Street
(508) 228-5200
www.weeds-nantucket.com
Pitcher, page 24
Rabbit tureen, page 28

Food and Beverages

American Seasons
80 Centre Street
(508) 228-7111

Bartlett's Ocean View Farm
33 Bartlett Farm Road
(508) 228-9403

Cisco Brewers
5 Bartlett Farm Road
(508) 325-5929
Beers, page 124

Daily Breads
147 Lower Orange Street
(508) 228-8961
Pumpkin cake, page 133
Bread, page 124

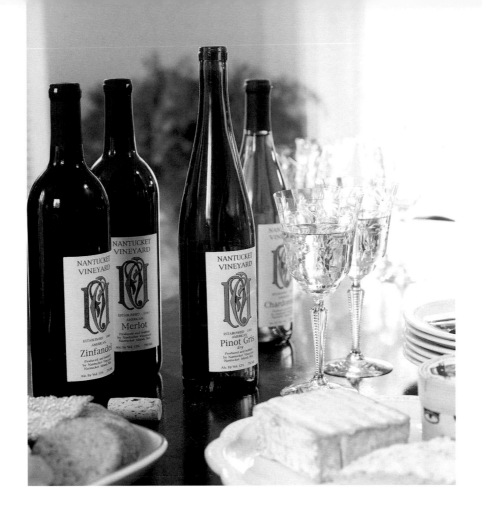

Fahey and Fromagerie
49-A Pleasant Street
(508) 325-5644
Indoor picnic foods, page 80

Nantucket Vineyard
3 Bartlett Farm Road
(508) 228-9235
Wines, page 40

Simply with Style Catering
63 Somerset Road
(508) 228-6248
www.simplywithstyle.com
Brunch, page 173

Triple Eight Distillery
5 Bartlett Farm Road
(508) 325-5929
Vodka and martini recipe, page 181

West Creek Café
11 West Creek Road
(508) 228-4943

Florists

Flowers on Chestnut
1 Chestnut Street
(508) 228-6007
Flowers, pages 76, 77

Trillium
17 Centre Street
(508) 228-4450
Flower arrangements, page 59

Architects, Artists, Contractors, and Interior Designers

Anne Becker Design
12 Ipswich Street
(508) 257-4023

Kathleen A.S. Hay
Design and decoration
Box 801
(508) 228-1219

Robert Hay
Carpentry and property
   management
Box 801
(508) 228-1219

Chris Holland
Architect
8 Williams Lane
(508) 228-6968

Hugh Newell Jacobsen
Architect
2529 P Street, NW
Washington D.C. 20007
(202) 337-5200

Christopher L. Maury
Design and construction
3 Windy Way
(508) 228-6599

Gary McBournie
Interior design
33-A North Main Street
Sherborn, MA 01770
(508) 655-3887

Lyman Perry
Architect
78 Polpis Road
(508) 228-3340

Kevin Paulsen
Painter, muralist
Box 3432
Kingston, NY 12402
(845) 338-8046

Elizabeth Raith Interiors
5 Kite Hill Lane
(508) 325-8698

Audrey Sterk
Brown & Sterk, Decorative Artists
Box 3251
(508) 325-7050
www.nantucketmurals.com

Jonathan Raith Company
Building design and custom millwork
25 Nobadeer Farm Road
(508) 228-7627
www.jonathanraith.com

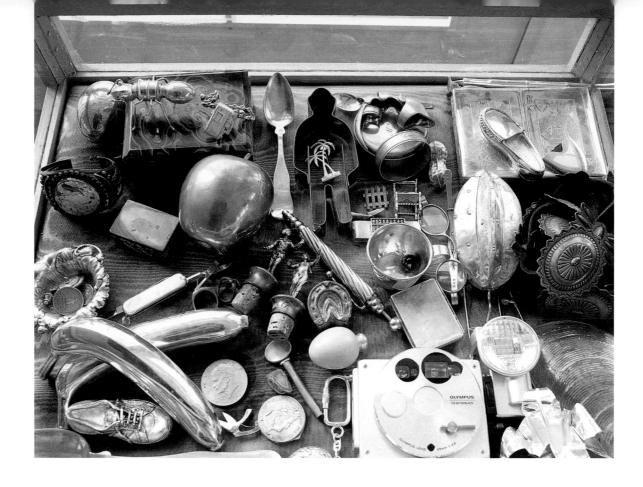

Wholesale Manufacturers

Catstudio
232 Liberty Street
Petaluma, CA 94952
(707) 778-1100
Pillow, page 15

Greenhorn Trading
30 Arbor Street
Hartford, CT 06106
(860) 236-3859
Napkins, pages 12, 124, 148

Golden Rabbit II
Box 188
Arlington, VA 22210
(888) 841-7780
www.spattermatter.com
Enamelware, page 70

Mariposa
The Barn
5 Elm Street
Manchester, MA 01944
(800) 788-1304
www.mariposa-gift.com
*Ceramic and aluminum accessories,
  glassware, pages 12, 31, 124*

Vietri
(800) 277-5933
www.vietri.com
Serving pieces, page 30

Waverly
(800) 423-5881
www.waverly.com
*Blue-and-white ticking from
  Williamsburg collection, page 70*

index

A

accommodations, 195, 196–97
activities, 197
Adair, Will, 188
Adams, Abigail, 144
American Seasons, 29, 71
Apples, Roasted Winter Squash and, 151
Axt, Georgia, 159

B

Bacle, Mike, 54
barns, 65–69, 101–11, 177–81
Bartlett's Ocean View Farm, 63
Becker, Anne, 21, 23
Bensen, Tedd, 177
Berry Tart, Flag, 73
beverages
    Captain Pentecost's Iced-Tea Punch, 63
    Triple Eight Martini, 181
Boardman, Bill and Susan, 99, 139–40,
    143, 144, 149–51
Boston, 195
breakfast, 174–75
Buns, Sticky, 175

C

Cake, Carrot, 137
Captain Pentecost's Iced-Tea Punch, 63
Caramelized-Onion Potato Salad with
    Pommery Vinaigrette, 71
carriage house, converted, 75–83
Carrot Cake, 137
Chamber of Commerce, 125, 161, 197
Chase, Nancy, 140, 143
Chase, William, 65, 71
cheese
    Frittata, 175
    Kalamata Black Olive and Vermont
        Goat Cheese Potato Pave, 29
chowder
    Chowder Contest, 125
    Seagrille Quahog Chowder, 125
Christmas, 153, 156, 168, 173, 174–75
Christmas Stroll, 153, 161

Cisco Brewers, 125, 181
clams
    Seagrille Quahog Chowder, 125
    types of, 125
Classic Summer Lobster Salad, 71
climate, 8
Coatue, 14
collections, 48
    antiques, 127, 133
    art, 131, 183
    books, 43, 78
    flag-based, 65
    Haviland Limoges, 90
    lightship baskets, 53, 57, 159
    Quimper ceramics, 110, 113
    seashells, 183
    silver objects, 86
    Staffordshire figurines, 43, 44
    toy soldiers, 43, 44, 45, 48–49
Corbusier, Le, 177, 181

D

Daffodil Weekend, 11
Daily Breads, 125, 137
Davis, Geo, 51, 85–86, 90, 93, 94, 159
de Musset, Alfred, 37
desserts
    Carrot Cake, 137
    Flag Berry Tart, 73
Dilts, Bruce, 90
Dutton, Cam and Gardiner, 99, 127, 129,
    131, 133, 135–37
Dutton, Jeffrey and Shari, 137

E

Easter, 29–31
eggs
    Frittata, 175

F

ferries, 195, 196
Ferris, Ken, 68
Finney, Franck, 63
Fish, Martha, 140
fishing charters, 18
Flag Berry Tart, 73
flights, 196
Fowler, Frank, 102
Franco, Richard and Kim, 11, 21, 23, 24
Frisée, Seared Bay Scallops with, 112
Frittata, 175

G

Geary, Rob, 99, 115–16
Getter, Michael, 71
Green, Susan Zises, 133

H

Halloween, 99, 133, 135, 156
Harlow, John, 116
Hartman, Cedric, 78
Harvey, E.J. and Robin, 125
Hay, Robert and Kathleen, 153, 155–57, 162, 165
Hidden Forest, 177
history, 195
Holland, Chris, 139
Hurley, Jaime, 112
Hyannis, 195

J

Jacobsen, Hugh Newell, 75, 77, 78, 81
Jetties Beach, 94
July Fourth, 65, 71, 73

K

Kagan, Illya, 121
Kalamata Black Olive and Vermont Goat Cheese Potato Pave, 29
Killen, Bruce, 127
Kimbel, Charlotte, 186

L

Lamb, Pesto Crusted Rack of, 31
La Scola, Michael, 29
Leeks, Pumpkin Soup with Potatoes and, 150
Levine, Reggie, 153, 183–84, 191, 193
The Lion's Paw, 168
Lobster Salad, Classic Summer, 71
Lockley, Kendra, 173, 174

M

Magee, Doc, 53
Main Street Gallery, 183
Martinet, 115, 119
McBournie, Gary, 99, 115–16, 119, 121, 122
McDaniel, Keith, 184
McLaughlin, Diana, 11, 43
McNair, Mark, 58
Melange of Truffled Petite Spring Vegetables, 30
Melton, Carter, 167, 168
Memorial Day weekend, 18
Mencini, Anne, 11, 33–34, 37, 40
Middle Moors, 177
Mies van der Rohe, Ludwig, 177, 181
Miller, Bruce, 71
Mills, W. Roy, 44
minimalism, 75, 177
Mitchell, Maria, 197
Mosse, Nicholas, 171
Mulberry, Sterling, 54
Munthe, Axel, 33
Muppy, 155
museums
    private, 183–93
    public, 197

N

Nantucket Architecture Group, 127
Nantucket Conservation Foundation, 127
Nantucket Country, 133
Nantucket Historical Association, 143, 197
Nantucket Looms, 53, 54
Nantucket Noel, 153, 161
Nantucket Restaurant Association, 125
Nantucket Vineyard, 181
Nantucket Visitor's Service, 18, 196
Napoleon, 77

O

Olive, Kalamata Black, and Vermont Goat Cheese Potato Pave, 29

P

Paple, Lee, 140
Paulsen, Kevin, 121, 140, 143, 146
Pearce, Simon, 173
Pesto Crusted Rack of Lamb, 31
potatoes
   Caramelized-Onion Potato Salad with
      Pommery Vinaigrette, 71
   Kalamata Black Olive and Vermont
      Goat Cheese Potato Pave, 29
   Pumpkin Soup with Potatoes and Leeks, 150
   Seagrille Quahog Chowder, 125
Powers, Hiram, 188
Prisby, Bush, 68
produce, 63
Pumpkin Soup with Potatoes and Leeks, 150
Punch, Captain Pentecost's Iced-Tea, 63

Q

quilts, 37, 140, 143, 144

R

Rainbow Fleet, 14, 18, 19
Raith, Jonathan and Elizabeth, 153, 167–68, 174
Raith-Dombroski, Kerry, 155
Rapp, Steven and Daisy, 51, 53, 65–66, 71
Ritter, Bryce M., 173
Roasted Winter Squash and Apples, 151
Ross, Eunice, 140

S

Sabin, Adam, 181
sailing, 18
salads
   Caramelized-Onion Potato Salad
      with Pommery Vinaigrette, 71
   Classic Summer Lobster Salad, 71
   Seared Bay Scallops with Frisée, 112
Sandcastle and Sculpture Day, 94
Sanford Farm, 127
Sankaty Lighthouse, 177, 178
Scallops, Seared Bay, with Frisée, 112
Seagrille Quahog Chowder, 125
Siasconset, 11, 21, 155, 177
Simply with Style, 174
Smith, Van and Ann, 11, 13–14
soups
   Pumpkin Soup with Potatoes and Leeks, 150
   Seagrille Quahog Chowder, 125
Spicher, Kolene, 127, 136

Squash, Roasted Winter, and Apples, 151
Starbuck, Mary E., 140
Starck, Philippe, 81
Sterk, Audrey, 21
Sticky Buns, 175
still lifes, 37, 58, 97
Stuffing, 151
Swift, Stephen, 63

T

Tart, Flag Berry, 73
Thanksgiving, 149, 150–51
tourism, 195
The Toy Boat, 27
transportation, 195, 196
Trillium, 58
Triple Eight Distillery, 181
Triple Eight Martini, 181
Turkey Plunge, 150

U

Umberger, Connie, 99, 101–2, 107, 108, 110

V

Veeder, Susan, 143
vegetables
   Frittata, 175
   Melange of Truffled Petite Spring Vegetables, 30
Villa San Michele, 33
visitor's guide, 195–97
Vorhees, Eugenie, 51, 75

W

Walker, David, 168
Wampanoag tribe, 21
weather, 8
Web sites, 196–97
Weeds, 85, 157
West Creek Café, 112
whaling, 167–68, 195
Whaling Museum, 139, 197
whirligigs, 65, 71
Wiggins, David, 121
Wine Festival, 40
Winship, Todd and Liz, 51, 53–54, 57, 58